Heidegger's Poetics

MERIDIAN

Crossing Aesthetics

Werner Hamacher
& David E. Wellbery
Editors

Translated by
Jan Plug

Stanford
University
Press

Stanford
California
1998

THAT IS TO SAY

Heidegger's Poetics

Marc Froment-Meurice

That Is to Say: Heidegger's Poetics
was originally published in French
in 1996 under the title
C'est à dire: Poétique de Heidegger
© 1996 by Editions Galilée

A version of Chapter 8 was previously published in
L'Esprit créateur 35 (Autumn 1995, pp. 3–17),
in the issue titled *Beyond Aesthetics?*
and edited by Rodolphe Gasché.

Assistance for the translation was provided by the
French Ministry of Culture.

Stanford University Press
Stanford, California

© 1998 by the Board of Trustees of the
Leland Stanford Junior University

Printed in the United States of America

CIP data appear at the end of the book

Contents

Abbreviations, with a
Note on the Translation — ix

Before Saying: A Foreword — 1

§ 1 Hermes' Gift — 22

§ 2 The Eye of the Word — 43

§ 3 The Path to Language — 60

§ 4 The Essence of Poetry — 80

§ 5 The Witness of Being (*Andenken*) — 102

§ 6 In (the) Place of Being, Antigone
(The *Retrait* of the Polis) — 121

§ 7 On the Origin (of Art) — 149

§ 8 Step (Not) Beyond — 178

§ 9 The Different Step: From
     Heidegger to Derrida   195

     Farewell   222

     Notes   237
     Works Cited   255

Abbreviations, with a Note on the Translation

The following abbreviated titles are used throughout the book to refer to Heidegger's works. If a reference is given with two page numbers, the first number refers to an existing English translation and the second to the relevant German text. As necessary, I have modified existing English translations (so as to remain consistent with the French translations given by the author, for example, and with his commentaries). When no English translation is cited, the reference is to Heidegger's German.—Trans.

The following books by Heidegger are all cited from the *Gesamtausgabe* (Klostermann):

GA4	*Erläuterungen zu Hölderlins Dichtung* (1981)
GA12	*Unterwegs zur Sprache* (1984)
GA13	*Aus der Erfahrung des Denkens* (1983)
GA39	*Hölderlins Hymnen "Germanien" und "Der Rhein"* (1980)
GA52	*Hölderlins Hymne "Andenken"* (1982)
GA53	*Hölderlins Hymne "Der Ister"* (1984)
GA54	*Parmenides* (1982)

GA55	*Heraklit* (1979)
GA65	*Beiträge zur Philosophie* (1989)

The following German editions of additional works by Heidegger are also cited:

EM	*Einführung in die Metaphysik* (Max Niemeyer, 1966)
Identity	*Identität und Differenz* (Neske, 1977)
Satz	*Der Satz vom Grund* (Neske, 1957)
Schelling	*Schellings Abhandlung über das Wesen des Menschlichen Freiheit* (Max Niemeyer, 1971)
BT	*Sein und Zeit*, 11th ed. (Max Niemeyer, 1967)
Sojourns	*Séjours*, bilingual edition, edited and translated by F. Vezin (Le Rocher, 1992)
UZS	*Unterwegs zur Sprache* (Neske, 1959)
Thinking	*Was heisst Denken?* (Max Niemeyer, 1984)
What	*Was ist das—die Philosophie?* (Neske, 1956)
ZSD	*Zur Sache des Denkens* (Neske, 1969)
Question	*Zur Seinsfrage* (Klostermann, 1956)

Citations are also drawn from the following English-language editions of Heidegger's works:

BT	*Being and Time*. Trans. John Macquarrie and Edward Robinson. New York: HarperCollins, 1962.
Nietzsche	*Nietzsche*. Vol. I. Trans. David Ferrell Krell. New York: Routledge, 1961.
Questions IV	*Questions*. Vol. IV. Trans. J. Beaufret et al. Paris: Gallimard, 1976.
Way	*On the Way to Language*. Trans. Peter D. Hertz. New York: HarperCollins, 1982.

Parm.	*Parmenides.* Trans. A. Schuwer and R. Rocjcewicz. Bloomington, Ind.: Indiana University Press, 1992.
Poetry	*Poetry, Language, Thought.* Trans. Albert Hofstadter. New York: HarperCollins, 1971.

THAT IS TO SAY

Heidegger's Poetics

Before Saying: A Foreword

How are we to understand this fore-word? Be-*fore* saying? But before saying, the word *before*, and even the word *saying*, will always have been said. There is no before to saying, if in that before we hear and understand an original silence (if that can be heard), something like God's original thought before creating the world.... The world has no before nor, *a fortiori*, does it have a fore-word, a before-saying.

I take this somewhat precious (fore)word from Mallarmé's Foreword to the *Treatise of the Verb*. In this Foreword, it is already a question of nothing other than saying, and even of Saying, capitalized, of Saying *before everything*: "Saying, before everything, dreams and sings, is found again in the poet...." Before everything, Saying will have been there (to be said), and that, even if the first word of this Foreword is *everything*: "Everything throughout this notebook ... is organized with a view in mind, the true one, that of the title...." (Mallarmé 858). If we in turn must proceed in view of this view, we must begin with the beginning, that is to say, the title: *C'est à dire* (*That Is to Say*). How are we to understand this title, as a question? But is it in fact a question? Since there are no hyphens,[1] we can also understand it as an affirmation: yes, that (what is at issue, the thing itself, so to speak) is to be said. It is to be said, just as it is to come, to be done, to be seen.... But, to start with, about what do we say that it is (about) to be said? About to do or to say what? About to start with what? Nothing, perhaps, but simply about to start, about to begin. We will have to return, here, to another Foreword, that of *La chose même*,[2] if I might be permitted to return to myself, to cite myself: "Yes, how to say it, how, to begin with, to say it. . . . " Thus ended the Foreword, upon the injunction to say (it) [*(le) dire*], that is, beginning with . . . Saying. Here, "*le dire*" is understood just as much as a noun (Saying [*le Dire*], to begin with) as it is as a verb (to begin, to say [*le dire*]). Which comes first, the noun or the verb? And what is saying? It is there, perhaps, that what will not be a Treatise of the Verb (nor of the Noun) begins, what will simply be the demand to begin to say (it). This is an almost impossible point of departure. The verb remains in the infinitive [*dire*], and the noun refers to an indeterminate "it" ([*le dire*—"to say it"], the thing itself), that is perhaps without name. A simple neutral pro-noun, before the noun, but announcing it, promising it, without, however, giving it. For the name is not the terminus of the voyage; on the contrary, it is but a place to be passed through, transitory and, above all, transitive (I was about to say transitional). In all of the above, the "that is to say" is neither said nor given. Everything remains to be said, even in saying "everything." It is a white stone marked by the memory of a dawn to come, of the whiteness of the hesitating early morning: it is . . . to be said, and in the ellipses we notice another title conceived of by Mallarmé—*It is* [*C'est*], "the title of an interminable study and series of notes that I have in my hands and that reigns in the depths of my spirit."[3] The study is interminable, because who could think of having finished with Being and, even more, with the impossible task of saying it? But is saying "it is" the same thing as saying "Being"? Is Being to be said? Is it not rather to be thought? There is a world of difference there: even if thinking does not go without saying, the inverse has taken place only too often. Thus, we say, "I said it without thinking," and, in all rigor, this manner of speaking describes our habitual way of talking. If we had to think about every word, soon we would no longer be able to utter a single one, or only one—the Word, the final word.

Foreword

Being, thinking. Immediately, the name of the man who asked, "What Is Called Thinking?" springs up. What calls us there, if not the "it is," that is to say, Being? Yes, the name Heidegger weighs heavily in this question, whether we like it or not. And it is thus that we can say that "contemporary thought never stops being explained through Heidegger. It can think with or against him, but rarely without him" (Zarader 13). But has it not been thus with all great thinkers? Thinking is always thinking *with* (or *against*), and even thinking *with*out is still thinking with.

But is Being a question? *Is* it even? And is "Is Being a question" a question? Does putting a question mark at the end of a sentence suffice to make a question? Or is not the questioning of which Heidegger (up to a certain point) made the supreme gesture of thought but a manner of saying? By way of an answer, I come to René Char's *Aromates chasseurs*: "The interrogative response is the response of Being. The response to a questionnaire is but a fascination of thought" (Char 516). In this division, and that also means hierarchization, between a good and a bad response, I am sure of neither the order of precedence nor even the pertinence of the distinction. To be sure, Being is not a questionnaire to which we respond with a Yes or a No, a True or a False. How, then, can we speak of "Being's response"? How would Being respond? This is exactly like the story of the two lunatics: "Are you going fishing? No, I'm going fishing! Oh, good, I thought you were going fishing. . . ."

Fishing after Being, we in fact risk being taken in, or mystified, at any rate, we who thought we would reel it in. The question always presupposes its own meaning, the meaning of Being, and, first of all, the meaning of being a question. It is like asking a stone for directions, even if, like Hermes' stone,[4] it points out the right path. In order to question, we must already know what a question is and must dispose of the means to *say it*. I see quite clearly what Char means: the response to the questionnaire puts a term to questioning, whereas the "interrogative response" revives questioning, sharpens it, makes it more pointed, more thinking, more "pious" (*fromm*). Most of the time this response [*réponse*] is but a replication [*répons*], an echo that has been sent back and that is interrogative only in coming afterwards. But if there is a question of Being, it cannot come after Being; it can only precede Being. But nothing can precede Being (if not Being). We might well say that these two "but's" cancel each other out. And even if, late in the game, Heidegger renounces questioning in preference to "simple" listening, the same procedure is carried out there. Can Being be heard (to speak)? Do we not always lend it speech? From that point on, what is the difference between the response and the question? The two lunatics pronounce their soliloquies along the banks of the water. They are the same in having been but the invention of an author, himself perhaps no less crazy. But since he will not give his name, he saves face.

No one has really posed the question—of Being. We have indeed asked its name, its identity, where it was going, from where it was coming, in short, all the questions one normally puts to a stranger. But we have forgotten to ask it its meaning. True enough, this is a loaded question—these are not things one talks about. The question probably makes no sense, at least not if we are waiting for a clear answer. What do you want Being to answer? You yourself, in its place . . . you would be hard put to answer, wouldn't you? "Meaning," you see, would be its "interrogative," or simply its rogative, response. (In the past, the rogations named a prayer procession instituted on Saint Mark's Day and the three days preceding Ascension. But prayer, *supplication*, is not a tormented plight [*supplice*], which rhymes with delight [*délices*] in a poem by Nerval that I cannot put my finger on at the moment.) Indeed, that is the whole question. . . . "Meaning" is not simply a question of orientation, even though we must orient ourselves in thought. First, we must discover the meaning of the question (of meaning). . . . Would this be something like a final word that, short of responding, stops us upon the slippery path of the *that is to say?* But the final word, if it comes, will always be the word of the end, of the end of everything, including the word. Yet, to begin with, how can the word still be to be said? This cannot be: even Being (or its meaning, or the forgetting of its meaning) will never be the final word. Even the word *word* is a word, one among others, calling all the others and thus having lost any privilege over them. What would not *be* a simple word? Perhaps this is the question that guided Heidegger. But toward [*vers*] what? Not a word, but the thing itself, unsaid, but to be said, to be thought. Perhaps he was not led toward a "what" but toward the *toward* itself, the "to" of the to-be-said.[5] This is *something else* altogether, says Mallarmé, another beginning toward which a thought without name advances: "The metamorphosis [of thought] takes place as a migration in which one place is left for another. . . . The first place is Metaphysics. And the other? I leave it without name" (*Way* 42, 138). *Metamorphosis* is perhaps not the right word either. Is there, in fact, a name for this displacement? The other (place) must be left without name. This strategy is perfect, since all names come from the first, abandoned place. As we will see in connection with Hölderlin, to the extent that this operation rests upon the force of the name (*Nennkraft*), this other place, for lack of a name, will never take place or will remain the other of the thought of the Same. All thought is the thought of the Same, in that it *is* thought. Parmenides foresaw this about thought, and nothing will break this alliance, this nuptial ring wedding Being to thought, not even a thinking of the other that, if it wants to be thought, must be the other of the Same. Thus, "the" thought (of Being) will be able to reach this "other place" only in renouncing it*self*, which is to reach a constitutive limit. Arrived there, it would cease to be (thought, and the thought of the Same). At the *same* time, this place is thought's proper, but inaccessible (except metaphorically), place. What, then, is the "metamorphosis" if not that poetic voyage that advances toward . . . let's say, what withdraws every arrival and every shore? It is *Abschied* . . . that is to say? Death? True enough, "poetic" (or metaphorical) death is not "real" death, which is all the more difficult to name thus. But in this gap, this difference between one death and *the other*, a space (as white as a stone) is marked that digs into thought to the point of opening it up to its other, its other *verse*-ion. In his poetics, which is the ultimate or first gesture of a thought driven to find the name of the other that, however, is without name, Heidegger introduced thought into the other place, but not necessarily the place thought had in mind, not the place of Being, finally delivered from its metaphysical shadow, but only the place of metaphor. Or rather, Being [*l'être*] has indeed reached us, but in the (poetic) mail [*la boîte à lettres*]. . . .

Letters in *place* of Being? With this postal forwarding, what can we hope for, that Being return to us with an acknowledgement of receipt we are to sign in order to certify that it is indeed Being? But would not the "thinker of Being" (assuming that he named himself thus) turn in his grave upon hearing me play in this way? A nice metaphor. . . . If by "Heidegger" we do not only understand mortal remains but a *corpus*, for example that of the *Gesamtausgabe*, the definitive edition that is to be completed posthumously—as though torn from his hands—then "Heidegger," both name and locality, might well come out completely turned over by this plough, overturned into a verse (versus) or a poetics. Is this so illicit? We will have done nothing but read the other side (verso) of the page, and how are we to read it if not by turning it over? (RSVP: Is that to return or to respond?) That Heidegger's clerk held onto the page with both hands so as to let us read nothing of it is only fair (play): perhaps he knew that there is nothing, nothing but a blank space, on the other side. But this grip must be loosened the day that it becomes the grip of a dead man—or the grip of a text, which, as Heidegger's handy-*work* (of art), it will have been from the beginning. Handy-work, an allegorical hand, this is the hand taking the place of Being, one more hand taking Heidegger's place. Offering a hand to Being, this turn of phrase figures how, here and there, the thinker effaces himself in order to take the dictation of Being literally, gives way or plays dead, takes Being's place, even though without him the game cannot be played. He acts as if (he were no longer anything at all): his is a metaphorical, displaced death, and that makes all the difference.

Let me be sure that I am making myself understood here. (This injunction would itself demand that it be understood.) We might be surprised by the fact that Heidegger made the experience of death *as* death (that is to say, as what?) the pivotal question of *Da-*

sein, to the extent that *Dasein* is never defined in relation to "life." In the horizon of Being-there, "dying" is not simply ceasing to live; it is always some-thing else. Or rather, it is not a thing, not even dying, but Being *toward* death, just as saying is not simply saying, but Being toward saying. This is even the secret of the "it is," its coffin (*Schrein*) inasmuch as it contains precisely no secrets. In a letter, Mallarmé confides his secret as a man of letters: "Everyone has a Secret in him. Many die without having found it and will never find it because, dead, neither it nor they exist any longer. I died and was brought back to life with the key to the precious stones of my final spiritual casket." The conjunction of these two sentences explodes the transition from one death to the other. We (everyone, or many of us, at any rate) can die without having found the Secret—death proper. Inversely, only he who is already dead can, not die, but be *toward* death. In Mallarmé, there is an echo of the dialectic or of the fable of the turtle and the hare; the turtle always finishes first because it has doubled itself—its other, its imperceptible (better) half, is already positioned at the finish line. This is to say that the secret is always like Punchinello's secret. . . . How can one *say*, "I am dead"? Therein lies the whole secret: perhaps (let us weigh our words carefully) we can only *say* it, and not be it. When we *are* dead, we can neither say so nor die. Is this what Heidegger "wanted" to say when he said, "When death comes, it disappears. Mortals die death in life. In death, mortals become *im*-mortal"?[6]

Everything is thus played out in the difference between one death and another. The first is what we common mortals call death in order to see it at work in others: parents, friends, strangers, it makes no difference; the "fact" of death remains just as banal and unthinkable. Death happens—to others, never to oneself. This is how Heidegger described the "improper" relation to death in *Being and Time*, the "one dies." The other death is mine, the one no one can take from me, my inalienable property (even if I die for something else), even more so than my liberty or my life, which is as much as saying, my Being. But my death is secret, since far from being mine, I belong to it, am toward it without knowing it most of the time. The trick is believing that in the name of the secret (a name that is common to the core of its very being-mine) I become immortal. This is salvation through the work (as death, death is not mine, but I must "be dead," efface myself as myself in order to give birth to it), which has always been literature's secret. Since Homer, the only immortality is fictive. It is the immortality of fiction itself, of the proper name. I am dead in that I have become the other who can say so. By the same token, the death that comes there only ever comes fictively, in the sense that coming is in the first place (to begin with) coming to speech. That the death that comes there (to speech) be allegorical removes nothing of its power; on the contrary, it increases it in this doubling. It testifies to a limit, and it is in this relation to the limit that what Heidegger calls appropriation (*Ereignis*) is shown. The secret to appropriation resides in its other side, de-propriation (*Ent-eignis*) which alone promises the coming of the Proper, but *only* as a promise. Being toward death, the mortal loses and thus finds his own identity, the ek-sistence that resides precisely in nothing, has no consistency, does not even belong to itself.[7] Still, we must keep our heads, if only to be able to *say* this death. To act as if I were dead, and thus to sing the "songs of the Departed" (*Trakl*), I must keep one foot on the ground, if I can say so, the other being already in the grave. Thus, the voyage to death can only be a return to that place from which no one is supposed to return, at least not in their right mind—the "madness" of an inflamed spirit is never "simple" alienation. Just as a dead person can never say that he or she *is* dead, a madman will not say he is mad. Or if he does, then this is another madness.

René Char says somewhere that there is but one death, the good one, if it can be put thus, the one from which we do not recover. How is one to recall a "self" to what will no longer be able to say that it is or that it is nothing, unless by imagining it as returning—from the dead? Is it in this return, this future anterior (or the conditional, as when we say, "I wish I were dead") that the secret of saying, but also the difference that maintains the letter [*la lettre*] and Being [*l'être*] separate *and* united, are maintained? Both the letter and Being name the Same: Being is the fiction of the letter, since the letter carries the signature of the very hand of Being. But the difference between them inscribes itself, passes into, the Same: Being has neither a hand to sign with nor a mouth or voice with which to speak (not even to say that it *cannot speak*). Being always needs an other: mortals, human beings (you, me), whose properness, like that of the letter, is to have nothing proper to them. The difference between the two deaths is an effect of this strange property, a turn in the thought that creates fictions: spiritual death is the only one that is thinkable, no matter what takes place, but it is precisely the death that never takes place, or that only takes place fictively, which does not diminish it, but situates its proper place in meta-phor, in poetic metamorphosis. To conclude, we can never arrive at what Bataille called "the impossible bottom of things," since the thing itself, as such, refuses to be grasped other than metaphorically, in the image, for example, of the "thing itself." This is another way of saying that the other side of the page (the "other place") will remain cryptic. It does not forbid but rather calls for deciphering, on the condition that we know that the hidden letter will always be missing, or that this letter will always have to be (re)invented.

There is no thought except at the limit of what forbids thought. There is no thought except as the experience of aporia, the passage through what blocks passage. Death is one name for this impossibility and as such it must always be thought as such an impossibility, even though it cannot present itself as such. But that also means that we must think the "as such" differently, must think it in the experience of its impossibility, which makes possible all identification with the self, for example, death as death (and not simply as the end of existence), that is, as simultaneously impossible in the horizon of Being and presence *and* making this very horizon possible. At once impossible and making (the) possible, death opens up another experience of both finitude and simultaneity, of the "at the same time" that is always doubled by its other time. To elaborate a concept that would not only be transcendental (in the Kantian sense of the conditions of possibility of experience, which are at the same time the conditions of possibility of the experience of objects) but also lead to an aporia (since the conditions of impossibility of experience also make it possible), to elaborate such a concept in the end amounts to experiencing the limits of the very concept of experience. Put differently, it amounts to making a concept of the experiencing of the aporia of the concept of concept. Every concept is always hollowed out from the inside not only by its other, its double (represented metaphysically as its negative trace, its shadow, which always inscribes itself *in* the integrity of the concept "proper"), but by that infinite and yet in-existent interval that inhibits the concept from sticking to itself and closing its identity upon "itself," including upon the concept of identity, which always presupposes a difference that cannot be expressed *as such*.

How, then, are we to think the title *Heidegger's Poetics*? What does that title have to say or to say again? But first, we should recite the title, that is to say, cut it up, put it between quotation marks, and thus put it into question as well: "Poetics"? "Heidegger's Poetics"? Who would have known Heidegger was a great poet? A philosopher, perhaps, although some doubt even that; but a poet, no! We find something like poems in his oeuvre, brief texts, but these are only exceptions, hors d'oeuvres (outside the oeuvre), we might say, compared to the main dish—an austere thought, rigorously philosophical through and through, even (or especially) if it refuses this description and evokes the "end of philosophy." But perhaps "poetics" signifies a theory of poetry, like Aristotle's poetics. Heidegger in fact wrote a great deal about poetry, or rather (the restriction is considerable) about the *essence* of poetry. It is with the essence that he began, in his lecture on "Hölderlin and the Essence of Poetry." But it is also with the question of the essence that he remained. Does that mean that beyond Hölderlin there is no recognition of any poet, to the point that for Heidegger Hölderlin represented the only poet worthy of the name (or rather of that even more worthy name of *Dichter*)? Heidegger also wrote on Trakl and Rilke,[8] and I would be the last to ignore that. But whatever the greatness of these poets, they never achieve Hölderlin's stature. They are expressly not the "poet of the poet." We must therefore ask if Hölderlin is not but a pseudonym, and must ask how it happens that he represents the sole example of a genre without precedent (nor successor, for that matter), in short, without exemplarity, a true *hapax* in history. He represents a genre outside genre. Such a genre would situate *Dichtung* less as a literary genre than outside of any recognized site, outside literature and the law of genres. The simple thought of *this* poetry, then, would have nothing to do with a "poetics" in the traditional sense, even though Hölderlin himself speaks explicitly of regaining the technical level of the Ancients. . . .

Perhaps it makes no sense to want to explain a privilege. A privilege cannot be justified, is not even an exception tolerated by the rule, because it puts itself forward, purely, as being in itself the law, divine law. This is what seems to have taken place: we cannot even say that Heidegger interpreted Hölderlin. No, he encountered him as his Law, his destiny, and we argue neither with destiny nor with God. We listen to their Word, transcribe it. We might concede, perhaps, that for the others who have not yet experienced the Revelation, enlightenment is necessary. I caricature, but barely. I have already spoken of a cannibalism of interpretation, but I must revise my terms, for it is not a matter of devouring the other but of appropriating the same; and moreover, it is not the living body that serves as food but the bones: names, or the part belonging to the dead. In a sense, to speak of "Heidegger's Poetics" is to build the tomb of poetics. Let us be clear about this: all interpretation is violence, unless it is but a paraphrastic rephrasing. And yet, even in this case there is violence, the worst kind of violence, that violence that believes it makes the other speak of and from himself, believes it lets what he carried in himself without knowing it be born "naturally." This is something of the Socratic method, but also of the naïveté of a Heidegger who, while putting in other words what the poet could *only* have said poetically, at the end of this interminable explication pretends to "efface himself before the pure presence" of the poem, as though he lacked nothing but speech (as we say of certain animals). I would not linger over this strange method (that refuses this name and prefers the name of "path," which is in all respects more poetic) if it only arose from bad faith or from "philosophic" superiority. What is decisive is always the relation to the other *as such*. In the past, philosophy sought to reduce the other to its mercy through nothing other than the force of universalizing discourse, of which the philosopher held himself to be the sole representative, the only one empowered to speak, or, in another version of the discourse of the master, in making the other a simple moment of the One, not yet and nonetheless already beforehand passed over and appropriated. We could say that Heidegger escapes this shortcoming (though not always) in positing the other as the irreducibly other under the name of *Dichten*. This obliges him to posit the One with which the other is in relation as other than it was in "metaphysical" (let's say, to move quickly) relations. It is thus that he will speak of *Denken* and even of an "other thought," instead of philosophy, reason, discourse, etcetera. This is an audacious and virtuous approach, but if it does not come down to the same (thing), it leads back to the philosophical attitude in relation to its (here, "poetic") other by presupposing that there is a common element between them, and that this element is *one*: here, *saying*. The presiding unity in the relation is always the one (the first), which will say what the other is, *even if it is in the name of the other*. Thus it is the one and it alone that will master alterity, precisely in positing it as such, in the element of Being, of the one, of meaning.

Let us read, for example, these sentences taken from *The Experience of Thought*:

> The poetic character of thought is still veiled.
>
> Where it discloses itself, it usually resembles the utopia of a half-poetic understanding.
>
> But a thinking Poetics (*denkende Dichten*) is in truth the topology of Being. It assigns to Being the place of its essence [GA13 84].

Heidegger first accords to the "poetic" a power that the philosophical tradition has refused it since the exclusion of the poets from the (ideal) City by Plato. But to defend himself against the philosophic accusation that would not fail being addressed to him (the accusation of irrationalism, of "half poetic" ramblings . . . was not lacking, in fact), Heidegger raises the stakes in a sense by making "thinking Poetics" a "topology of Being," as though Being were necessarily the first and last poetic word, the word of poetics in its "essence." In this way, it is assigned to the poet to become the founder (*Stifter*) of Being, no more, no less! But what if Being has nothing to do with the matter, the "thing itself" of poetry? That is impossible, since Being always goes hand in hand with saying, just as eternity is the sea in harmony with the sun.[9] It is this going-with, this harmony, perhaps, in which it is a question of the status of poetry, of poetry's place, its *topos*, that we will have occasion to put into question once again. Who assigns that status?

"What remains, the poets found." Hölderlin's statement (from *Andenken*) recurs often in Heidegger's writing as a sort of ordering principle, a guiding word (*Leitwort*). And yet, it puts thought in a critical position: what are thinkers good for if they always come *after* the poetic word? How are they to reach the level of this inaugural founding, by interpreting it? Does interpretation not always come second in relation to the gift of speech? But speech must be received, heard. Would an unheard speech remain? Would it not be lost? And does not the addressee therefore become more essential than the sender, especially if we realize that the sender creates nothing, does not fabricate this given speech, but contents himself with transmitting it, more or less faithfully, like a simple copyist to whom one dictates a message that he does not necessarily have to understand? But who is this "one" who dictates? No one, and this is why this situation applies to all speech to the extent that it is not we who speak, in the first place, but speech . . . or language (*Sprache*—we will have to return to this word). We content ourselves with hearing it speak, and our speaking is but a resaying of the first Saying, which Heidegger will name *die Sage*, though this too might very well be a resaying. But there is hearing and there is hearing.[10] There is acoustic hearing and there is hearing in the sense of grasping meaning. For the latter, a poet is not sufficient.

Even if, according to an ancient tradition, poets are the messengers of the gods, yet another person is necessary to hear (understand) this divine speech, especially if, in the meantime, the gods have withdrawn, without this withdrawal meaning nothing. Perhaps it is even this withdrawal that calls for the poet through its "distress" (*Not*), just as the withdrawal or the forgetting of Being is what properly makes *sense* for the thinker. Not only is this forgetting not nothing; it "is" the only trace of a liberation of Being—for what destines it. In a text entitled "The Lack of Sacred Names," we read:

> Upon first view, the "forgetting of Being" names a lack, an omission. In truth, the name is a name for the destiny of the clearing of Being inasmuch as Being as presence cannot but become manifest and determine every being, when / if the clearing of Being retains in itself and preserves for thought what came to pass at the beginning of occidental thought and what ever since characterizes the epochs of the history of Being up until the current age of technology, without knowing anything of this forgetting of Being as its principle [GA13 234].

The forgetting of Being is Heidegger's only "thesis," even though this is not a thesis *about* Being. Being came as presence: this is Heidegger's first thesis, the thesis marking his point of departure. But it is also the departure from any thesis on Being, from any philosophical position, from any epoch of the history of Being. This thesis concerning Being, its coming into presence as presence, is also the forgetting of Being, the forgetting of what sends Being. Being forgets itself in presence, and when this presence in turn withdraws, we are free to think the sending of Being. Forgetting is thus not a lack so much as an open possibility, in this end of epochs (the epochs of presence), to return to the source of the destination of Being as presence, a source that nonetheless is itself never present (otherwise it would be but a figure of Being) and thus *is* not, without, however, simply being absent.

To common understanding, the meaning of Being (its "truth") makes no sense, is nothing but a hallucination. Let's not talk about it any more and move on to something else, as Hegel says about death. But what could we move on to if there is nothing outside of Being, or if there is nothing but the beings who, deprived of the light of Being, flounder in the shadow of their insignificance? In order to certify a death, there must be a body. But if Being "is" indeed dead, has gone missing, we can say nothing more about it. Nor can we file it away: it threatens to return, deviously, one of these days. And we know even less about its mode of disappearance, which could well be a supreme form of Being, what I will call Being-in-disappearing [*disparêtre*]. Once again, this is not a privileged path, not a path at all, but a sending. It is that sending that determines the very aporia known by the name of "Being." It is from within the experience of this aporia that we will read Heidegger's gesture [*le geste*]—and his saga [or *Sage* (*la geste*)]. The question (of Being) is not [*pas*] asked, and it is even in that—not [*pas*] being asked—that it is a question—of taking an other step [*pas*]. This is what cannot be understood immediately, what is not understandable in itself but always through the other, which "properly" makes sense. It makes sense in that it makes a sign. There is no sense or meaning residing *in itself*. Put differently, sense can only ek-sist, that is to say, inexist. From the very name of the Occident, *nightfall* [*tombée*], but perhaps tomb [*tombe*] as well, we know that Being got lost along the way without properly being able to know this. In its very disorientation, this name calls for another orientation, an other orientation, not the same one, and thus not that of a lost, legendary Orient. We can say nothing about a source or a mythic origin, even a pre-Socratic one, nothing that would not already be fiction, a projection into the future of an invented past in order to mask the lack of a present that is nonetheless our only present, and our only chance. It is here that I part with Heidegger. And yet this separation is not simple, does not simply lead back to a return (to the things themselves, to take one example of the return). Return to whom? To sender? But he has left, one might say, without a forwarding address, or leaving only the address that always comes back to us, that is, reading. But what is reading? "Reading properly speaking is the gathering together upon what, without our knowing, has already reclaimed our Being so that we might wish to respond or conceal ourselves before this demand" (GA13 111). This demand (*Anspruch*) is a promise that is addressed so that we can answer to and for the demand, that is, give it free course (liberate it, co-respond to it: *ent-sprechen*) or on the contrary refuse to let it speak (*ver-sagen*). We will always *already* be exceeded by a demand that gets us into debt, makes us indebted to a response, makes us fail to keep our word. This excess marks the irresistible overdraft of sense, which will always have a large advance. Before even being present, if it ever is, *there is* sense, and it is this structure that I call "pre-sense." But this "there is" never makes sense (at least not immediately), nor simply non-sense, this latter being but the opposite of what it negates. To read, then, is to leave the demand, the *Anspruch*, suspended, suspended by this "step" [*pas*] that, before being, *passes sense* in every sense of the word: surpasses sense and passes it on, like a password that will never be given except in being passed from hand to hand. I give this "step" a name that itself can barely be heard (understood), that suspends all reduction to a *one-way meaning*: *passance*.[11] If *only* the poem *dwells*, it dwells in this suspension, almost in levitation in a space it does not create but that it nonetheless makes *come*, that it calls to come. There is nothing to say about this call, nothing that is either sensible or senseless, insane. The poem is made, woven from this coalescence of virtualities of sense that are immediately de-posited, and there will be no other way to understand the poem except in undoing this veil. But this *deposition* will always also be an *exposition*. To finish, we will never arrive at a pure nudity which is not itself but a supplementary veil. There is no transparency for sense, not that it is like a mirage, always farther away; on the contrary, the closer it is the more it burns. Even as clearly as it incessantly enlightens, this flame still delivers no final text behind it. It burns in order to burn, no more and no less, and thus it always conceals itself. Perhaps we should even call it the *Concealed*. But how do we know if it "is" concealed? Must there not have been a day, distant but that we can remember, when it was given, delivered into the proper hands? Must we situate this moment in a language of the origin? Will there finally be a moment when we find the access to it again, finally separated from its forgetting (as religious asceticism was in another era)? And would this poetry be "the future life inside requalified man"?[12] But poetry does not save anyone, Georg Trakl will say, and especially not someone who is *re*qualified. If the Occident has indeed come (or is welcomed) to the light of day like that "deleterious" nostalgia (Rimbaud) of an Orient or of a lost origin, what must be confronted at present is this "loss" of sense, this loss that is singular for being the loss of *nothing*, and that therefore is not truly a loss. What qualifies poetics is precisely that it disqualifies all appropriation in terms of gains and losses, but also disqualifies any definition of a capital one would possess, of an "essence" or goods it would represent. One cannot have it, only be it. But this is a being that does not have itself, does not belong to itself. Concealed thus, it remains all the more (still) *to* be in that it refuses to *belong to itself*, and even therein lies its manner of being—differing / deferring all self-presence. Its place of being is this step that defers the coming into presence, into the proper, to which it does not come except in coming as event [*é-venant*].[13] There is no place for an understanding of a place proper in the word *place*; rather, this dying-indwelling [*de-meure*] always differs / defers presence in deferring to its event-uality or, if you prefer, its happening.

"Poetry happens where, against all expectation, language gives up. . . . Poetry is the spasm or the syncope of language" (Lacoue-Labarthe 74). We can never properly say what poetry is, and thus no more so could we say that it is the unspeakable or the "spasm of language": with what language would we say this, since language ceases, de-ceases when poetry comes or gains access? However, this improper language will still be the most just, witnessing the deposition of common language, the only language to implement poetic speech—if the very name of "poetry" is not already a mark of this infrangible impropriety. We cannot say what poetry is, what its *essence* is, for it exceeds the category of essence. But if this is so, this is not to say that poetry is sublime or sacred, the reign of the beyond-language. We cannot say what poetry is because it and it alone *says that*, but says it in being it and not in saying it. Poetry says this like the blow of suspended language (always taking our breath away), of language cut off and thus coming—not to itself, not to language, but to its event. The poetic event is not what happens but rather that it so happens that something happens in no language and thus cuts language (off), cutting out its mark there, its trace. The meaning of the trace is never in itself, nor is it elsewhere (in some transcendent realm). The meaning of the trace is to be on the trace of meaning, if I can put it thus. The poem springs forth from the call to speak what demands *and* refuses a language, demands it as "pure" language, and refuses it as "simple" language. The poem is thus doomed to be missing from its word. But even in that, it is doomed to keep its word, like a promise.

A promise announces. But poetry cannot be announced from the outside. It alone can promise *itself.* At the same time, it announces nothing, nothing else, nothing that could be extracted from it like its meaning or its essence. The promise announces neither the realm of God nor that of Being, but *only* the promise. Nothing other than the promise is promised. "Only" and "nothing else" seem put there to disappoint. Perhaps. Poetic experience, to take up Lacoue-Labarthe again, differs from the philosophical concept in that it relates to the "*decept*," the deposition, and is not a matter of enunciations. Rather, we should say that it makes only *renunciations*. Nothing awaits us there, neither fortune nor glory. There is no [*pas*] gain, but a step [*pas*] is won—and *held* onto, and said, if saying is always also holding, although there is nothing to hold onto, nothing but the promise, only the promise. That is the generosity of this *untenable*, ungraspable, solitude. There is nothing else, and that is nonetheless what poetic experience holds onto tightest and what constitutes the singularity of its dwelling: it holds to [*tient*] this there, will go no further. For now, we'll leave it at that (point), taking the place of a ground: groundlessness, again.

Poetic experience is to hold, to say—but how? Poetic experience here touches upon the limits of language, that trembling place in which the cutting *between* sense and the insane parts. It touches precisely upon this between that is less something between two people than an interview, a holding(-forth)-between [*entre-tien*]: how the one relates to the other, who is not the other except for the one, yet for all that without being reduced to him. Therein lies all the difference from "philosophic" reappropriation. I have said that *there is no sense of sense*, no meaning of meaning, and that is in no way because there is no sense, but because this sense, here (always here), makes no sense except in exceeding itself, except in relation to the insane, the without-sense, to name it improperly (but since it is without name, it can only be named improperly). The completely-other approaches, and yet this is nothing other than the same coming from the other border of its limit. That the other approaches (to the point of burning) does not mean that it presents itself. On the contrary, it withdraws and, as though it were empty, therefore shows the "thing itself," which is always about to be touched, on the verge of being. . . . But it remains differed, deferred, delaying, dying-in-dwelling [*de-meurante*].

Ἡ ὁδὸς – μήποτε μέθοδος: "The path is never a method" (GA13 233). A path, Heidegger repeats, is not only there for the love of taking a walk through the forest, is never a means of arriving somewhere, by which we understand someplace other than *there* (and it is a question of this very "there," of what there is, there). The path is already the thing itself, what we keep *going* on (about). Thus, Heidegger's poetics opens up onto nothing else, not even a new "interpretation" of Heidegger. It opens up onto nothing, for even if we took this poetics from Heidegger's own "mouth," it will never be able to return to him. In the beginning *was* the Word (or Being): the impossibility of a perfect presentation is exposed in the form of this past tense. In the beginning the beginning will have been lacking and this lack will have given the beginning: word*s*, language*s*, everything that ruins unity and self-identity. Therefore, neither a plan nor a method is appropriate for this poetics. In fact, this poetics will begin with and *leave* off from Heidegger. But I emphasize "leave" because it is first of all a question of leaving.

What is at stake in this departure is simply leaving, not going someplace else. However, by the very fact that there is no point of departure, that this point is anything but a point, the step already runs up against its impossibility. It cannot leave from itself but only begin from the other, who is not the self but who, nonetheless, gives the self its departure. Just as there is no concept-point, not only as pure (of all alterity) but *as* concept (which implies the self-identity of the concept and its name), so too, if we must begin, leave off from, a point, we will have to begin to say it, and that saying (saying itself) will always be excessive. In this sense, we could maintain that Heideggerian-language (a construction that appears to me at once legitimate and problematic) constitutes an impossible point of departure to the extent that it *simultaneously* identifies itself with the essence of language and an absolutely singular idiom. It's all Greek to us, an idiolect Heidegger coined for himself in order to block all immediate comprehension.[14] We might understand this in a more enlightening way by taking this manner of speaking literally (which is already more Heideggerian). Thus Beda Allemann, taking up an indication by Lohmann, asks "if a language like the Chinese language, which is characterized by an isolative linguistics because of its nominal nature, would not be more appropriate for Heidegger's language, because it anticipates its tendency to isolate words" (Allemann 114–15).[15] This is also why we will have to deconstruct the privilege of the name, particularly of the name as the sacred name.

If the sacred names have become unpronounceable, including the name "sacred" (*Heilig*, saved or holy, unharmed or intact), that implies that an enormous part of Heidegger is ruined. We will have to take his side, mourn him, which will not be a mourning. Not only will nothing save onto-theology, not even the negative path, but the very care to "save" (even to "save the phenomena") takes part in the very thing that has given way, around an event that is unspeakable, even "as such" (and that thus cannot be said even under the name "Auschwitz"). It is the very bond that relates the sacred (or the saved) to the "as such" that is at stake in the attempt for an arche-phenomono-logy and that unbinds (and delivers) itself the moment that, and in the very place in which, the impossibility of an "appropriation" of Being (even in the most originary instance of an *Es gibt*) and the withdrawal of its saying are experienced. Impropriety is at the departure; it is general and generative precisely for translating itself, always differently, into the untranslatable singularity—that calls for translation, or retranslation.

The name liberates the thing inasmuch as it at the same time redresses it in a skin with which the thing can make a body in order to have figure, countenance, allure, dress. However, the bestowed name disfigures the thing as well, not to give it a figure other than its own, but simply because it figures it and *thus* disfigures it. Perhaps the only way to play out this play of veiling by unveiling that exposes itself in every work of figuration or of imagination (and every work is a work of these) will be to de-posit, to set down, names, at least to undo their property and propriety as substantives. To expose this play naked, however, is nothing other than to play it once again without delivering the ultimate content, "truth." Except in no longer playing the game, it is no longer possible to escape the disillusion that always delivers us over to the other instead of to the One. There is no way to avoid the game, if only because the game alone makes sense. Heidegger will not be able to escape it either: it is in the nature of things, these things that are not things any more than there is a "true" nature. The game is all there is. But the *there is* is not a thing, a new substance; in not showing itself, it shows only what is. There are names, things, but these *are* only inasmuch as they show themselves to each other, show themselves *in* each other. Made for this fold, intersecting each other in the interview, the holding(-forth)-between [*entretien*] of *that is to say*, they deploy what we can therefore call a *thinking* poetics. And if we must say this of Heidegger, then this signature will have to be countersigned by an other. Heidegger, perhaps, will have been but a pseudonym for what must remain without name: "they are lacking, the sacred names."

No mistake about it, we will have to submit a (written) deposition of this lack. To finish, we must to begin to speak it. Or begin again.

§ 1 Hermes' Gift

> Everything we designate as "found," we ordinarily call "a gift from Hermes" (ἕρμαιον). . . . He reigns over paths. On the borders of paths are found the piles of stones (ἕρμαιον) from which he received his name. The passerby threw a stone upon them.   Walter F. Otto, *Les Dieux de la Grèce* 130, 137

Hermes, the proper name of a god of paths, of passages, of accesses granted or refused, takes his name from a simple pile of stones, the significance of which we do not know. A passerby threw a stone there to win his favor. Hermes brings luck. He is the god of chance and of encounters, both good and bad, the god of highway robbers. In our time, he is known as the name of a telecommunications program, of a satellite.[1] In a play of thought he declares more binding and more compelling than the rigor of science, Heidegger says that he is also the guardian angel of hermeneutics.[2] This bond passes by way of the message. Hermes is the postman of the gods. He is their messenger, and in Greek the messenger was said to be an angel (ἄγγελος). He carries their word, their *dict*, and is also called "the radiant look-out," for he has wings and (like a satellite) in a single bound can traverse the immensity of the bitter waves to the island of the End-of-the-World, where Calypso keeps the shipwrecked survivor of Troy and of the furors of Poseidon hostage. Without Hermes, there would be no adventures of Ulysses, no *Odyssey*. But Ulysses himself, wherever he lands, relates his own adventures. He is his own speaker, even if he disguises himself in the coat of a poor bard.

The poets, Plato will therefore say, are the messengers of the gods. But without these winged messengers, who would speak of the gods? The gods are the inventions of the poets, and thus their own, proper messengers. Thus, the messenger finds on his path (and this is the sense of *invenire*) what it was his mission to announce. In other words, the only god here is the path. It is the path that sends everything: the messenger, the message, and the addressee (us). On the path, there is the hermes. A passerby threw a stone there, a white stone, a milestone, a mark(er). A passerby finds the hermes on his path. He knows he is on the *right* path, gives thanks, throws another stone in the same direction. Sense and the sense of direction precede. The sense or direction of the path is to be a path. It is pre-sense, which has already been given even *before* being "interpreted," explained, shown—hermeneutized. Thus, it is before the word. Sense, meaning, speaks in that it gives hearing, understanding.

Like so many other philosophical words, like the word "philosophy" itself, the word *hermeneutics* is Greek. At the beginning of *What Is That—Philosophy?*, Heidegger writes:

> We have already pronounced the word "philosophy" enough. But if we no longer employ it like a hackneyed term, if, on the contrary, we hear it from its origin, then it resonates: φιλοσοφία. Now the word "philosophy" speaks Greek. The Greek word, as *Greek*, is a path [*What* 6].

Where does this privilege of the Greek come from? From a proximity to the origin. But this proximity is not given by the antique character of Greek, Greek being by no means the most ancient of languages. At a decisive moment in his course *What Is Called Thinking?*, of which the second part is devoted to the interpretation (and thus translation) of the first eight words of fragment VI of Parmenides' *Poem*, Heidegger writes: "It is in fact superfluous to translate ἔον ἔμμεναι into Latin or German. But it is necessary finally to translate these words into Greek" (*Thinking* 140). Translate the Greek words *into Greek*? Does that make sense? Or rather would there be no philosophy except in speaking Greek? We might believe so from reading the "first" philosopher (at least the first to be named as such). Socrates was preparing to demonstrate that all knowledge is *anamnesis* (recollection)—another Greek word. The experiment therefore had to be conducted on someone ignorant, and Socrates asked Menon to show him one of his slaves. However, the ignorant slave had to know at least one thing: "Is he Greek and does he speak Greek?" All this is expressed in a single word in the text, as though it were enough to speak Greek to be Greek. Why is Greek a condition *sine qua non* of philosophy, although philosophy is at the same time initiated upon its declarations of universality? Even Heidegger (at least the "early" Heidegger) subscribes to the credo, repeated from Plato to Kant and beyond, that to philosophize is proper to the human species, is what signs the human as such, and is inscribed for all time as its "nature." Must we deduce from this that in order to be human, one must be Greek? It would be absurd to pretend that geometry, under the pretext that it is a Greek word, is a Greek science and nothing but. In the same way, the word "poetry" has Greek origins, but it is possible that in translating it into Greek we transport it onto completely different ground: *poiesis* names technique [*facture*] and production in general, and in no way a poetic specificity. Perhaps the specificity of poetry has very little to do with matters of production, even if we interpret that specificity philosophically. In any case, whether or not this word is proper, the thing did not wait for the Greeks in order to show itself, and did not stop with Homer or Pindar, who, moreover, were not yet called poets. Why would it not be the same for philosophy? Must philosophy be assigned a Greek origin in order to be authenticated? Or is this concern for assigning an origin not already a Greek characteristic? If every myth is the myth of the origin, then we can call this trait mythic. But must we reserve the privilege of the invention of mythic thought to the Greeks alone, even though philosophy is characterized (too summarily, in my opinion) as a rupture with myth and the dawn of "reason" or *logos*?

Upon first sight, Heidegger seems to repeat schemes that bring back bad memories. To be sure, every isolated human group thinks of itself mythically, in the first place, as the only humanity worthy of the name. It is a question of cohesion. The Cashinahuas call themselves (and names are always at issue) "the true men." In the same way, one could say that the Greeks, although less isolated, divided the human species in two: humanity properly speaking, composed of Greeks and of all those who speak Greek, and the others, the *barbarians*, those who talk gibberish, since there is but one language worthy of the name—Greek. Philosophy would thus be born from an exacerbated but also singular ethnocentrism, since the Greeks will have been the only people to have tied the idea of humanity to language, to *a* language elevated to a universal status because it alone would be *more* than a language: *logos*. Oddly, this word has never signified "language" [*langue*], and there is not even a word in Greek to name *that*. At least not *one* word:

> A Greek word for the word is δ μῦθος. Another word for "word" is ἔπος. ... Again another word for "word" is λόγος. We have to think that the Greeks from early on had several words for "word." On the other hand, they do not have a word for "language" (*Sprache*). They have, of course, the word γλῶσσα, "tongue" (*Zunge*). But they never think the word on the basis of the "tongue" by which it is spoken. Thus, their determination of the essence of man is not ἄνθρωπος ζῷον γλῶσσαν ἔχον, a living being that has a "tongue." Cows and mules also have a tongue. If, however, it is the essential feature of man to have the word and to appropriate it, and if the Greeks experience and understand the human being in this way, then is it not necessary that they, when they distinguish themselves and their humanity versus others, take as a point of reference for the distinction this essential feature?[3]

If saying, like Being, "is said" (λέγεται) in many ways, these different modes dwell, like Being in its ana-*logy*, in the unity of the word that designates "the Word," *das Wort*. Heidegger would undoubtedly have refuted this translation. The singularity of this "word," in German, is to split itself into two plurals: *Worte* are "statements," and *Wörter* simple words. "The Greeks had several words (*Wörter*) for the 'Word' (*für das 'Wort'*)": several words for a single word, that is, for the Word in the proper sense of the word. ... But what is this *proper* sense? To determine it, the proper sense must first be distinguished from all the other, *im*-

proper, senses. The ability to make this distinction constitutes the privilege of the human being and is conferred upon humans by their determination as the "living beings endowed with *logos*" (that is, with the "word" in the proper sense). Is this a circular argument? If *logos* gives the human this proper and distinctive trait, it is because *logos* is itself the ability to differentiate, to class, to give order—what we call "reason." Differentiation functions like a language system in which each word is given in relation to the others as not being the others, but also in referring to them, in always being capable of being substituted for by another or of itself substituting for another: *logos*, that is to say "word" [*parole*]; "word," that is to say . . . *etcetera*. *Etcetera* is again a translation for *all the others*, all those that remain. It implies the innumerability of the plural and as such might well be the word par excellence for language. It *might be* this word, yet it cannot be it any more than *logos* or *word* can, because there is *no* Word par excellence, no pure word that contains its meaning in itself, separate from the others, without necessarily taking part in them. The pure or proper *Word* is not a word, it is a barbarism.

By its very exclusion, the word "barbarian" gives the trait proper to the definition of the proper word. We could even say that it is the *absolutely* proper word. Unarticulated (if articulation is the pivotal point of language as an *infinite and living speech*), it precedes and makes possible the appearance of a language as articulation and the putting into relation of differences, as the specific and "proper" (relatively proper) community of *a determinate* language (and thus of a people). The word *barbarian* precedes the appearance of such a language exactly inasmuch as it can *never* appear except in *a* language (here Greek) which thus defines itself by the exclusion of its *other*, the unarticulated. Greek defines itself and appears *as such* solely in tearing itself from the undifferentiated non-appearing of the "barbarian," at least of what is named thus by those who "have" the word, properly. For the word βάρβαροι is still, and first of all, a *Greek* word. The so-called [*soi-disant*] barbarians never called themselves this. Or, to put it differently, the barbarian is always the name of the other: there are no self-named [*soi-disant*] barbarians, and perhaps no self-naming plain and simple. *The name always comes from the other.* The other is excluded or, on the contrary, appropriated: the movement is the same, assimilation being no less a form of exclusion.

Heidegger would like to efface this impure origin in positing a sort of self-appearance of language to itself. That is supposed to have taken place, mythically, with the Greeks, the first to have defined themselves in relation to others (people and animals) according to the privilege of the "Word," *that is to say,* of the Word proper. But the definition to which Heidegger has recourse (man is the living being who has, holds onto, possesses "language," or rather *logos*) presupposes, first, that language is structured like *logos* in order to formulate that definition, and, second, historically comes after the plural (though always unitary) structure *mythos-epos-logos*. If *logos* comes last, this is not by chance: it is a *philosophical* and thus belated definition. Heidegger uses the definition shamelessly here, even though elsewhere he will put it into question in order to overturn the inevitable ethno-anthropocentrism it implies. What is most astonishing is the justification of *logos* by its irreplaceable character. We cannot replace *logos* by "language" ["tongue," *langue*]. All animals have a tongue, even cattle. But they do not a tongue, language, *properly* speaking. It is a "simple" tongue, less than language, a tongue cut off from its *meaning*, without *logos*, that is to say, without *saying*. A cow, and by extension (in a relation only "sensible" humans, that is, those endowed with *logos*, can establish) an infant or a barbarian does not have (access to) language, because they have only a tongue.... They are lacking this decisive supplement: the *meaning* of the tongue, language, which ensures that language, properly speaking (*logos*, and not *tongue*), *makes sense*, that is to say, that it *says*, each time saying its sense, that of saying *itself.* The dream is of a self that is purely self-productive, but there is no pure (sense) unless it is purified of its other. Non-sense, however, cannot appear as such except *through* the sense that has appeared. But sense itself does not appear as such (as *so-called* / *self-named* "proper") except in demarcating itself from what precedes it or from what it rejects at the same time—cutting all impure descendance—as not being sense. The word must affirm itself in saying itself as such, that is, as *not* another [or an other], although it cannot be said except in taking the place of another [an other], and of another that could always, according to the law of the *that is to say*, take its place in turn.

The ethnic purification that Heidegger practices is all the more astonishing for its concern for a "milieu" or medium that authorizes no purity, at least no *absolute* purity. The worst exclusion concerns animals. Even in the "Greek" (Aristotelian) definition, man is *first of all* a living being. There again, a tour de force is necessary to re-translate the so-called meaning of "living" into Greek. First of all, to call for the translation of ζῷον as "animal" is just as erroneous and perverse as the translation of *logos* as *ratio*. Then, or at the same time, to carry "life" over to the side of *physis*, which is itself related back to *aletheia*? If we in this way avoid any biological or zoological connotations, this carrying over settles nothing, or rather settles its account with the "purely" living being (by which we understand the being that is *nothing but* living). Not having access to the "truth," to the Open, since he has no way to say it (to manifest that it is *there*, or is the "there"), how could this being give the human its proper characteristic? And, by the same token, does this being not become cut off from life? Endowed with *sense* (with this supplementary sense, that is, the ability to speak sense), must it also be *deprived* of all access to "pure" life, so that it would be the de-natured living being, in other words, *meta*-physical? Would he (perhaps she . . . if we push it) *alone* be able to have access to death (as such)? Pushing this logic to the extreme, we must remove the ability to die from animals, from "simple" living beings. They can only perish: is this a difference between words? No, it is the difference of *Being*, that is to say (this comes back to the same thing, if you will), a difference of saying, again. How, then, are we to conceive of this "pure" life without that which delimits it: death? And how are we to think death without life? The Heideggerian concept of death must itself be pure, *without a trace of life*. But perhaps therein lies the "being" of the concept: *in-born* death?

What is presupposed is that through language, traversing it bit by bit without, however, itself lodging there, Being *already* speaks, already sends its pre-sense. Is this a presupposition? Perhaps not, or only from the point of view of a preliminary *recollection*. Let us take as an example the Greek word *ousia*. In everyday language (we would again need to know if this is not already a philosophical distinction), *ousia* signifies possessions, property / propriety, what one *has*, and by no means what one "is."[4] It is only with Plato that the word takes on a completely different sense (which obliges Seneca to invent the word *essentia*). For the philosopher finds in the word a supplementary propriety, presence, and even the presence of the most-proper, that of the verb *to be* through its *present* participle. That Greek grammar *speaks* is just as much a privilege as an obstacle for us. The properly-proper becomes generality par excellence, what is most common. It is this loss of "Being" in the very name of Being that Heidegger marks at the beginning of ontotheology. Theology is added in order to make up for the defect of ontology, incapable of presenting what is proper to presence. Its rights [its propriety] must therefore be restored to it. All of philosophy can be read as a repeated combat against the usury of language, a usury that philosophy believes it is reducing even though it produces it as the language of generality, of essence. To that, Heidegger will say, it must be objected that "essence" is not a good (that is to say, proper) translation. In the same way, *veritas* alters the "original" (or literal) purity of ἀλήθεια. Perhaps. But if a word is not translatable by another, it is no longer a word at all. A word, whatever it be, is what it is only in referring *to* . . . and this structure of referral excludes all propriety *from the beginning*. But Heidegger's entire development aims to further "propriate" language, for example, to make the common word *Ereignis* say, *in the word itself,* appropriation. But this "event" would be so proper, so *idiomatic*, that nothing comparable could properly be named an *Ereignis*.

Logocentrism constitutes the essence of *logos*. Inborn Being, neither proceeding from nor produced by anything, is nothing but the self-manifestation to the self of self-saying [*soi-disant*], arche-

tautology (it being understood that tautology is not in the first place saying the same thing in just the same way, but saying itself). To deconstruct archetautology is not to call upon the illogical or the barbarian. On the contrary, *there is no other logic than that of identity to self(-saying)*. But this logic has itself come from the other of all selves. It is violent because it presupposes this other in the form of the excluded, of the "other" (or the barbarian). But the other *is* never the other. To put it in an*other* way, the barbarian is not an other; no, it is the same. A barbarian is a human being "just the same" (a human being is an animal "just the same," *etcetera*). But a barbarian is not a human being in the proper sense of Being. All that adheres to an impeccable, cutting logic, a logic that cuts *into* the same. "Just the same" is not *absolutely* the same (a human being), and thus is not the same *at all* (as regards the ground, that is to say, Being). But what does Being mean, what does it want to say: *Logos*? Is this to say that aside from speaking (being) Greek, there is nothing but the barbarian? It must be admitted that certain of Heidegger's propositions give this impression. Being would remain the first and last word, that is to say, the Greek "beginning." Yet that is only true for us. And who are we? Heirs, yes, but also the disinherited. But the Greeks were also disinherited. They are (I wonder if I can use the present tense) those who ask themselves what happened to them, what Being *was*, those to whom it *happened* for the first time (perhaps) in this strange "history of Being" no longer to know what Being (and equally: being "Greek," "philosophers," "men," etcetera) might signify. The Occident is born of this nightfall, of this fall in which sense (that of Being, of being a "there" of Being) falls *under* sense, at once brilliant and void. Now *passing over* all authority and all authorization, *without birth*, now burying itself under itself, under its own skin, it never ceases to oscillate between being the in-born and the living-dead, self-deliverance (the absolutely modern) and the return of the innumerable specters that it has become to itself. The Occident, I might say, were it not a bit too simple to give it but a *single* name, is this old man crying like a baby, looking to cut his own umbilical cord even in making himself his own gravedigger (or in writing his epithalamium in advance). It is the Republic giving itself as the year zero of a new age of the world, Hitler killing himself after the end of the world: a single figure with two heads, the obsession to be Being itself, and, if that is impossible, if we must necessarily share with the other, to be, all alone, nothingness itself. . . .

There is no point of departure because this point has *already* come, torn to itself in the coming that always exposes it as the other, so that it could not make itself appear except in the moment that it makes *itself* disappear. I will return to this. The structure of departure prevents all reappropriation, and that is why it must be called the *departure from belonging* [*départenance*]: the departure that does not belong to itself, no more so than does the *now*. The Greek departure can appear only to *us* at the moment that it has already withdrawn. What appears, then, is disappearance, cutting, and this is what unremittingly dis-orients the Occident. There are no "pure" Greeks; they were already withdrawing at the moment they came (were thrown) into the world. The translation of Greek *into Greek* (arche-Greek) that Heidegger dreamed of aims to overcome the gap in the so-called "origin" and to restore its mythic purity. Because the Greek that appears is always impure from the point of view of what has not appeared preceding it and throwing it *toward itself,* to fill this gap we must climb back beyond the Greek to what escaped it in its very springing forth (its departure: its cutting, its divorce from itself, which is its only possibility of being born). But that would also imply a supplementary ascending turn, surpassing us, since, fundamentally, we are taken up in the Greek decline. The other departure (*der andere Anfang*) invents another sense (direction) of (and from) the beginning. It says goodbye to *itself* as if, in this ultimate and probably impossible gesture, it could finally say itself *at the point of departure of the departure.*

Let us return to hermeneutics, a name for this departure that seeks to place itself at its very point of departure. Philosophy parts from what is given to it, Being or language, but will never recognize this. I take as an example the Hegelian "itinerary." First of all, only the Absolute is, is pure departure. But this purity must show itself as such, showing or manifestation being the very *telos* of the Absolute. But self-manifestation demands passing by way of the other, but not just any other. No, an other proper to the self is necessary, an other that abolishes itself in itself and does not *remain* other (a remainder would destroy the absoluteness of the Self-Same). A same-other that effaces itself in its alterity is necessary to serve as liaison, as a point of passage, as a milieu for the production *of self*. This ideal milieu (that of ideality itself) is language, which alone is capable of serving as a pure mirror of reflection. For example (we know that it is the example Hegel says manifests the "naturally" speculative character of the German language) *aufheben* is a speculative word, not only because it at once signifies to posit, to cancel, and to sublate, but because it *does* what it signifies as the mirror of the spirit of language itself. All language is *performatively* speculative, as the examination of the speculative proposition through the operation of the "sublation" of the copula attempts to demonstrate. The word posits itself, effaces itself, and maintains itself in ideality. It shows through, *trans-appears the absolute*. Thus, no matter how hard it tries to disguise its real "nature," it always returns to that nature, or rather, it comes back to *us*, with increased capital, an excess of meaning, probably because the so-called "natural" is already an invention of speculative thought for which "natives" will suffer the consequences. Thought always puts the language *before* language to work, and that, even though thought, *without* language, is incapable of showing itself *as* such, that is, of thinking *itself*, of being "itself." Thought must make *itself* appear and thus must alienate itself in the medium of language, from which it can always extricate itself in sublating this medium to its own absolute light: language thinks "despite itself."

I had to set out this classic itinerary (set out by Derrida in *Glas*) summarily in order to bring out, in contrast, the Heideggerian procedure, which could be presented as the reverse. Far from meaning preexisting language, which would be but a mirror of meaning, it is language that presides over the birth of meaning, on the condition, of course, that we know which language is in question. It certainly cannot be the "ordinary" language we use and abuse more or less like a tool that is appropriated to express what we believe to be "our" thoughts. This is so not only because this dominant conception of language as a means of expression is, in Heidegger's eyes, a monstrosity against nature, a true *Unwesen*, but because it supposes that language is in some way a *being*. But language, if it is the "depository" (the "house") of Being, cannot in turn be a being, otherwise it would lead us to a sort of ontotheology *literally speaking*, in the manner of an absolute tautology in which the *logos* "is" the same. In the same way that simple ontotheology is the system that folds Being back into *a* being, the Supreme Being (God), absolute ontotheology, that of *logos* as Being, would make *logos* the folding of Being upon itself(-*saying*). I propose completing George's line, "Where the word is lacking, no thing may be," with the following: "Where the thing is lacking, no word may be." This disconcerting proposition throws us off the path and demands a thinking of the *thing* that would be completely other than that of ontotheology. We would, for example, have to return to the piles of pebbles on the path.[5]

Heidegger himself corrected George's line as follows: "An 'is' arises where the word breaks off" (*Way* 108, 216). Saying (*Sage*) gives the "is" to the thing. This Saying is not the property / propriety of the human subject. Rather, it appropriates the human subject as subject *to* the word, and yet even there it seems that this power is refused to animals, exactly as, even more radically, it is refused to the thing, which could not even be mute. Heidegger then clarifies: "The essential relation between death and language flashes up before us but it still remains unthought" (*Way* 107, 215). Only those who are capable of speaking are capable of dying. We should even say that only those capable of speaking are capable of being . . . if it is true that *Dasein* is above all the capacity for Being. This is a may-be, but also a relation *to* being and *to* saying, *to* the world and *to* death. This possibility is thus not a simple eventuality; even less is it a faculty. It is more a matter of duty, of a debt. We must speak, simply because speaking is a matter of a *failing* or a lapse that is not a human failing; but already in the structure of speech itself, the step (not) of Being for which a "there," a place in which to take place, is *necessary* marks itself. This lapse is not reducible to a simple negativity, since it is first of all a call *to*. . . . But it cannot be evacuated in the name of a superior "positivity" of Being either. As such, everything having to do with a "foundation" by speech (even poetic speech) precisely cannot be *sublated* or reappropriated, but always remains in debt—as is the translator faced with the original to be translated. Consequently, we would even have to revise the canonical definition of *poiesis* as making-being. Language makes absolutely nothing be that was not there *before*, simply because Being is not *made*. It gives itself or refuses itself, comes or does not come; but even when it is lacking, and perhaps precisely then, it is always already sent, not as a *being*, but as what is *to be, to be said*.

I spoke of translation as an example. Yet we must also understand that there is *nothing but* translation as soon as it is a matter of "rendering" what is *to be said*. Everything, *to begin* with the very event of a *first time*, is translation [*traduction*] or, better, *trans-lation* ["translation," in French].[6] That is to say that saying means . . . translating. What is going on here . . . is precisely *going*, going *toward*, *to*—as one goes to the sea or to war? In that case, saying would be a goal, an end, a *telos*. But there is essentially no end to this advancing, no final word. We could even say that what approaches (but can always only approach, even though this is no "reservation": to approach is already to touch) the thing itself (to be said) most closely is also what *remains*, in the said itself, to be said, to be *re*said, that is to say, in an other way, to be exposed to the other.

Translation as trans-lation toward the to-be-said is in no way a simple technical question. We might even say that it is not a matter for professional translators. It is a question of nothing less than *finding a language*, as Rimbaud writes, and that also always means finding *more than one*. It seems that in Heidegger's eyes there was but one language *worthy of the name*, Greek at the exclusion of all other ("barbarian") languages, but at the same time we must add that this name ("language") is improper or "unworthy" of the Greek. Greek *is* not one language among others because it carries the mark of the *first time* it sent itself Being, be this in the form of this small, empty word "is." But this first can appear only for us others, "moderns," and consequently in the original repetition that is precisely translation as the "ordeal of the foreigner."[7] Thus, only the "literal" translation of what was the master-word of Greek experience, ἀλήθεια, will permit not only to open *us* to what is proper to this specific "foreigner" (not just any foreigner, since he is our source but also our future), but to open to the other what was at his heart, but occulted from him. The strange thing is not to have called what we name "truth" by such a name, but never to have thought what is said there, literally. Even in dwelling in the Open of this "clearing," not a single Greek heard [or understood] what his own language said, not one perceived *in the word itself* what Pindar named the "signless cloud of concealment," the *lethe* that *a-letheia* suspends.[8] Whether the etymology proposed by Heidegger is "true" or not is not the question. What is the truth of our word "truth"? According to Heidegger, it is but a Roman falsity. Latin translation is a complete catastrophe, perhaps even *the* major catastrophe in history for Heidegger. It re-covers precisely what is the very heart (though already occulted from the Greeks) of *aletheia*, that is, what Heidegger dis-covered: the *precedence* of the withdrawal, the *retrait*, of all "presence" (that is true, effective, has appeared, etcetera). *Veritas* is a defensive and even *obstructive* word.[9] It is therefore an *arche-false* word, so to speak, not only because it makes of "truth" a compact organization, an impermeable block, like a bunker in the place that the Greeks experienced everything in the lightness of bestowed grace, of dispersing fog, of the "clearing," but because it forbids all access to what, in the event of the coming to light, is also the secret hidden from view—say, what denotes the privative, and not "positive," structure of the word *aletheia*. Once again, the question is not to know if the Heideggerian translation is "true" or not (which perhaps no longer even makes sense: what truth can one authorize oneself when it is a question of its *essence*?). The question is to understand how, thanks to this translation (a reconstruction that passes, first of all, by way of a deconstruction of the Roman translation, according to the very principle of "destruction" posited at the threshold of *Being and Time*), the original appears more original, so to speak, even more Greek than the first time. We could almost say that the "true" Greek word is only possible by passing through the translation into that language called German (*Unverborgenheit* is henceforth the *proper* name of *aletheia*), or at least that German reinvented for the cause of translation. This German, therefore, far from coming *second*, as a simple "servant" (*ancilla* was long its title of nobility), commands absolutely the access to the thing itself. The translator is then that creator Heidegger defined as he who "advances toward the un-said and pierces toward the un-thought, drives out what has not come to pass and makes the un-heard emerge" (EM 123).

Differing from the "true" creator, however, does the translator not have something that has been *said* at his disposal, a model under his eyes that he should content himself with *resaying*, putting differently, rendering "differently" and yet in the same way—simply in another language? This is what we normally call translation: establishing the equation between one statement and another in a theoretically reversible equivalence. *Brot* is *bread*, and vice versa. Just the same, we might say, *aletheia*, that is, "truth," and not *Unverborgenheit* or non-occultation (if we can agree that this word might be the "good" translation of the Heideggerian word). The test is to replace *aletheia* by "non-occultation" in any non-philosophical Greek text (and yet what is a non-philosophical text?), and that produces gibberish. . . . A translation is "good" (just, adequate, true) when we can return from the riverbank we have arrived at to the one from which we departed, from the translation to the original, with a minimum of loss. There will always be loss—something untranslatable, we say, without thinking too much about it. But if we limit this damage to the minimum, we will obtain, at the most, an approximation, a more or less faithful copy. Such is the most frequent result, and such is the normative, "scientific" conception of translation. A copy supposes a model. But where does the model come from?

The theory of translation follows that of imitation, of mimesis, which in turn determines every theory of Occidental art. Without entering into a debate with a long tradition that has its grounding in Plato's (and Aristotle's) metaphysics, let us recall the *aporia* constitutive of mimesis: it presupposes a first, inimitable term that nonetheless makes possible and to a certain point even demands imitation. This will be "nature" for art, and the original text for translation. To be capable of being imitated, the one like the other must begin by withdrawing itself from the imitation even in authorizing it. An entirely untranslatable text is quite simply not a text at all; but a text that is entirely translatable, *without remainder*, is no more of a text. This means that *translation exists from the beginning*, and it is precisely this *original* translation that constitutes the untranslatability of the original. "From the beginning" means that there is translation in the original itself and that is why translation does not simply move from one language to another; it begins in language "proper," or the "mother" tongue. Translation begins precisely as soon as *it is to be said*, and that is never entirely sayable.

> To speak and to say is in itself translation, the essence of which can by no means be divided without remainder into those situations where translating and translated words belong to different languages. In every dialogue and in every soliloquy an original translation holds sway. We do not here have in mind primarily the operation of substituting one turn of phrase for another in the same language or the use of "paraphrase" (*Umschreibung*). Such a change in the choice of words is a consequence deriving from the fact that what is to be said has already been transported for us into another truth and clarity—perhaps obscurity. This transporting can occur without a change in linguistic expression. The poetry of a poet or the treatise of a thinker stands within its own proper unique word. It compels us to perceive this word again and again as if we were hearing it for the first time. These newborn words transpose us in every case to a new shore [*Parm.* 12; GA54 17–18].

To translate is to displace sense, and this is what Heidegger demonstrates performatively in translating the word for "translate." He displaces the accent from über*setzen* to *über*setzen, and makes translation a movement of passing over and nearly vertiginous ascension. The ordinary translation from one language to another that the linguist Jakobson renders as translation "properly speaking," "interlingual" translation, is at the lowest level. Then there is that translation Jakobson names "intralingual," rewording, the reformulation of turns of phrase by others in the same language, which supposes, as Derrida, from whom I borrow these scientific references, writes, "that one can know in the final analysis how to determine rigorously the unity and identity of a language, the decidable form of its limits" ("Tours" 173). Heidegger calls this second translation *Umschreibung*, but leaves the word in quotation marks, which makes one think he finds it improper (in effect, there is rewriting around the word). At the same time, he concedes a certain "originality" (*ein ursprüngliches Übersetzen*) to it, but an originality that is inferior to the *absolute* originality proper to translation properly speaking, reserved for the heights of the couple *Dichten-Denken*. Only there is the Word characterized by a first time, an absolute first ("man walked on the moon"), so that not only is this first not altered in repeating itself, it in a certain way demands a constant virginal repetition ("the act is virginal, even when repeated" [René Char]). But it demands that of *us*, the readers. Each time, we must hear this absolutely unheard of Word as though it were always the first time it was re-sonating, which is impossible in the case of intralingual translation, a simple re-formulation, replacement (*ersetzen*). With the translation (*übersetzen*) of the to-be-said into a unique and first Said there is no possibility of replacement, of substitution, or of *Ersatz*—thus of "translation" in the common sense of the word. From the very first word, the word is first, always already unique, irreplaceable, as though it belonged to no language, to the point that we might well ask if it is still really a *word*.[10]

Translation does not have, as its essential destination, to communicate, and that is so even if Heidegger speaks of a "message." But this word must be retranslated into Greek, must pass over (tele)communications to the angel Hermes. We do not even have to resort to the Greek. If we closely reread Walter Benjamin's text,

"The Task of the Translator," we will see a strange collusion (which does not exclude some essential gaps, I was about to say, gaps in the translation) taking shape between Heidegger and Benjamin. Both take as a "model" of the to-translate the "sacred" (or poetic) text. Heidegger explicitly declares many a time that ("essential") poetry expresses nothing, does not aim to communicate a *content*. It is not communication as such that is aimed at (even though it is made problematic in Hölderlin as in Trakl), but the difference between the content to be communicated and the linguistic act of communication. Put differently (an illicit rewording), the difference between a signified (which could be outside-language) and the very act of *saying it*—which is itself already the whole sense— effaces itself.

"If there is indeed between the translated text and the translating text a relation of 'original' to version, it could not be *representative* or *reproductive*. Translation is neither an image nor a copy," Derrida says, taking up Benjamin ("Tours" 201). But we must also be able to say that of Heidegger, all the more so since he always destroyed the essence of truth as adequation. That does not mean that the very notion of the original loses its rights, even if the original can no longer lay claim to the slightest right. We have left the sphere of the law, like that of representation. Derrida devotes numerous developments to dissecting (ironically) juridical manuals concerning the "rights" of translators (to make original, though "derived," works). He remains perplexed faced with this claim of an originality, despite everything, of the text to be translated. If there is no longer a model, why could the translation not be called *more* original than the original itself? Why stop at a first time, when the original is itself already nothing but a translation? But this formulation already betrays the secondary role traditionally attributed to translation: "to be but a" (translation) is to occult the "cardinal" word—to be *already* (in advance) a translation. Heidegger names the irrecuperable advance of that *jump* the "origin." Or rather, to retranslate, the *Ur-Sprung* is found in this "already."

In Benjamin as in Heidegger, the advance of the original is translated as "presence" (or rather by pre-sense, for the origin is never present *to itself*) of what could be taken for a "fiction," and even a myth: "pure language" (*die reine Sprache*, for Benjamin) or "arche-language" (*Ursprache*, for Heidegger). As Derrida again indicates, this originary language is not a theoretical construction like a universal language in the Leibnizian sense; it is not even a poetic dream like that of Rimbaud ("soul for the soul"), but is "the being-language of the language, tongue [*la langue*] or language [le langage] *as such*, that unity without self-identity, which makes for the fact that there are languages and that they are languages [langues]" ("Tours" 201). It is to that mysterious preliminary unity that Heidegger's three essays, entitled *The Essence of Language*, are devoted. The central formulation, the guiding or translating word (*das Leitwort*) that implements the reversal of *The Essence of Language* into *The Language of the Essence* gives, Heidegger writes (*Way* 94, 200), *die Ur-Kunde vom Sprachwesen*, not the "original document" [*document original*] of being-language, as this is translated in French, the original being in no way an archive (or, in that case, in the literal sense—the origin is "in need of the archive"[11]) but the promise, the announcement of the original, and of the original as pure promise. For Benjamin, translation's *mission* is to announce, almost messianically, the reign of pure language in the reconciliation of the divided languages, this language being nothing other than *the promise of language itself*. (This formulation, in turn, is in no way a restriction: not only is a promise not nothing, but the "Being" of language, or better, its *may be(ing)*, maybe, is given in the promise.) Just the same, for Heidegger whatever the diversity of languages (which are secondary, as regards the to-be-said), the *task* of thought (*die Aufgabe*: its debt, but also the gift that there is promise in this lapse) consists in letting this announcement before all message be said, this "before-saying" in an absolutely *literal* sense, even in re-nouncing, as the poet in the poem "The Word" renounces the gem to find the word for the Word itself to the extent that it is *by* (through and thanks to) this renunciation that it is announced as promised *and* forbidden. Thus, for Benjamin there is a kinship between languages, a kinship that in no way implies resemblance or imitation, but only a common filiation *leaving* from a "point of departure," which is nevertheless never present (or past, which comes down to the same thing), a point that could be defined as parting itself, or derivation as such; in the same way, for Heidegger there is, this time, an affinity not of resemblance but of cohabitation in the original neighborhood of *Saying*, an affinity not between languages but between thought and poetry, a proximity in the always unique manner of being *toward* this saying. The relation of Being *to* saying, however, can itself never be present to itself, but can only be capable of being shown beginning with the demand (that is to say, always differently).[12]

This saying must be understood *literally*, without changing the slightest comma. The task of the hermeneut (or the translator), be he thinker or poet, is not to lend a meaning to what does not immediately have one, but to make a sign toward what properly signs the *original*. An original *re*marks itself in that it can, and even must, be *re*said, in that it calls for replication, although it makes no sense to copy a copy (just as one does not translate a translation). Precisely because the original does not make itself understood (by itself), but always *through the other*, through this other that will be its unique and yet always repeated translation, and because, taken to the extreme, it therefore makes no sense *in itself*, each time it opens, in its own way, the *path* of sense, "sensibility," if we can understand this word literally: the pure possibility of sense. It is thus that Derrida, in the guise of a conclusion, writes of this limit: "*Pas-de-sens*—that does not signify poverty of meaning but no meaning [*pas de sens*] that would be itself, meaning, beyond any 'literality.' And right there is the sacred" ("Tours" 235). "Literality" is in quotation marks: this is not and will never be the proper word, and will never revert to a simple matter of literality. For the letter, *obviously*, has no sense in itself, does not "make" sense but in referring to the other.

The "not-sense" is the opening of sense before all signification. It is *passance*.

Thus the *path* returns. Heidegger comes back, in the third essay on "The Being of Language," to the privilege of the path, thanks to or by way of the very word for "path," *Weg*, as though it were necessary to open the word "path" to find the path *of* the word: a properly hermeneutic circularity that, nonetheless, far from taking us to the same point, deports us to the far away (*weg*, adverbially, signifies "far from . . . "), from the far away toward the near. It is thus that, by way of the bias of the most near (the Alemanic dialect of the verb *wëgen*), Heidegger renders the ordinary word *bewegen* ("to move") strange. He sends it away to the point of making it signify a sending that sends everything, by parodying (but also subverting) a celebrated word: what is essential in a sending is not what is sent (the "message") but the sending itself, since the sending is already *in* the sent (the word). *Weg* becomes an archeword of language that belongs to the same domain "of source and of river" as the verbs *wiegen* ("to rock"), *wagen* ("to dare"), and *wogen* ("to sail / drift"). In English, the kinship is lost. Is this to say that an uncrossable limit marks itself there? But there is no limit to the crossing. Crossing leads by way of and beyond languages to this "Being"-language that belongs to no language inasmuch as it puts them all *on the way to Being*. On the way to saying the Word, but only on the way, *only* in the promise of Being on the way toward. . . .

What has been *said*, nonetheless remains *to be said*.

§ 2 The Eye of the Word

Since it is a question of speech, it is best to begin with what *Being and Time* has to say on the subject. Only one paragraph is devoted explicitly to "speech": paragraph 34, entitled *Da-sein and Speech. Language.*

But before taking up this paragraph, two words. (They will always be more than *two* words.) *Being and Time* is conceptualized according to an academic model in effect at the time of its writing. This model has a thoroughly Germanic rigor or rigidity that, in other fields and in other camps, have proven their validity.[1] There are therefore "parts" (I will not insist upon the fact that, ashamed, one—private—part was cut off[2]) divided into sections, chapters, and finally paragraphs. These divisions recall the dialectical method advocated by Plato to fish for the fisherman.[3] The problem of analysis (and it is really an analytic, even an "existential" analytic) is to arrive at the smallest possible indivisible unit. But the atom—*Da-sein*, with a hyphen, or perhaps *DasEin?*—finds itself always already divided, is never where it should be, in the One, but has already passed into the Other. Thus *Sein* is found in Dasein, but this latter is *not* Being, only its "there," and yet, never *in the first place*, never immediately: Dasein has to be it (Being).[4] Dasein is the "indication" of Being in the sense that only it is capable of questioning the meaning of Being, which is at once there and not there, or there only in the trace, in the very word *Dasein*.

43

I now come to the place of paragraph 34 in the economy of *Being and Time*. It is part of an essential whole in which the three existentials composing the tripartite structure of Dasein take their place, and announces Dasein's tripartite temporality as state-of-mind, understanding, and speech. The situation of speech is not as clear as that of the two others; we can see this in the very title of the paragraph. Whereas, in the previous chapters, Heidegger wrote "*Da-sein* as state-of-mind" or "*Da-sein* as understanding," the "as" is now replaced by an "and," a conjunction that ties together in a manner much less strict than *als*, "as . . . ," which properly identifies what is in question. Moreover, where does this isolated addition come from, this supplement ("language") that, this time, seems to connect with nothing? We might think that it comes as an example, just as each of the preceding existentials was illustrated by concrete modes (fear and anxiety for state-of-mind; explication and exposition for understanding). But each time these examples constituted entire separate chapters. Here, "language" appears in the very title of the paragraph, literally as its *para-graph*: written off to the side, more juxtaposed than connected. What, then, is the *place* of language? Can this place be shown, especially *inside* "the constitution of the Being of Dasein" (BT 209, 166)? Can language be led back to the site, to the There of Being-there? And what speech could show (say) the place of this "phenomenon" without which no phenomono-*logy* is possible?

We find the same paradoxes that rule in the very word *Da-sein* again in the relation between Being and the human being. Language is a paragraph written beside speech, a paragraph without which there is neither speech nor a "speaking" Being-there. It is juxtaposed beside what it nevertheless makes possible, just as without Dasein no *Sein can be shown*, even as "not there," which is still the only manner, or at least the *primary* manner, of being there: we recall that the situation of Dasein is *not* to be there, is to be *improperly* (*Uneigentlichkeit*). This gap, which at once crosses out Dasein *and* gives it as being what *takes the place of Being*, is itself the *paraph* of Being, its signature *in absentia*. "Paraph" is the same word as "paragraph"; the written form is just altered, the *gra* of *graph* lost ("paraph: a flourish at the end of a signature").

Add *Da* to *Sein* and you will have distinguished the signature— countersigned what could never have signed except with the hand of the Other. For its beauty, I add the citation given by the dictionary, a quote from Jules Renard: "At the bottom of the page, he improvises a signature. The tail of the paraph loses itself in the paraph itself." Being loses itself in its signature, in this double that it nonetheless has in*cited*, that should have been but a lieu-tenant, a placeholder, a substitute, but that has played its role so well, has held the place of Being so well, that it has become Being, literally exempting Being from being *present*—as Being.

This is the end of my two opening words (words of paraphrase?). No, one more word, which will take on the appearance of a translator's note.[5] In the concern to return to the original (Greek) acceptance of the word, Heidegger begins by translating *logos* "literally" as *Rede*, clarifying that this "literal translation can only receive its validity from the determination of what *Rede* means" (BT 55, 32). And what does it mean? For that, *Rede* must be *re*translated into Greek, this time by a word borrowed from Aristotle: δηλοῦν or ἀποφαίνεσθαι, to manifest, make seen. But what will be named "apophantic," according to a literal translation of the Greek, is a derivative mode of explication and thus of understanding, and not of *Rede*. Things are complicated if we recall that "the Greeks had no word for *Sprache* (language); they understood this word 'in the first place' as *Rede*" (BT 209, 165). Did the Greeks speak German *in the first place*? But a German purified, it goes without saying, of the word *Sprache*, among other things.

And us? How are we going to translate? For example, the central sentence: *Das existential-ontologische Fundament der Sprache ist die Rede* (BT 203/160)?; "The existential-ontological foundation of speech is speaking"? This is a ridiculous and precious tautology. . . . If we write "the foundation of language is speaking," we obtain a formulation that is barely less hollow. Do we say, "the foundation (and why not add existential-ontological) of sleep is sleeping"? We say nothing as long as we do not know what speaking and meaning *mean*. To speak does not necessarily mean speaking or even meaning, but—*apophainesthai*?

And language? *Does it mean*? The text is clear on this point: *Sprache* is language and only language. The reference to Wilhelm von Humboldt at the end of the paragraph suffices to assure this univocal sense. But to understand it correctly, we ought to "forget" what Heidegger will say later when he has "turned" in *On the Way to Language*. For the moment, it is not to say that "language speaks." No, only Dasein speaks—but another *word*: it speaks in a *Rede*, which is not a language, but a manner of being "there." And as for language, the whole question is to arrive at situating it, *there*.

In *On the Way to Language*, Heidegger returns to hermeneutics, a word that, along with the word phenomenology, had almost disappeared from his language. On this occasion, the Japanese man expresses his regret that the "discussion" (or "situation," if you prefer: *Erörtung*) of language remained "quite sparse," to which Heidegger responds that he should read paragraph 34 more closely (*Way* 41–42, 137). But his interlocutor does not allow himself to be sent back to his studies so easily, and does nothing but express his regrets about the brevity of the text. The fact is that Heidegger is not very talkative [*bavard*] about speech (although he is more talkative about . . . chattering [*bavardage*]). *Being and Time* is not entitled *Being and Speech* of course; but speech is implied in it from the beginning, that is, from the exposition of the pre-concept of phenomenology (paragraph 7), a problematic concept in the literal sense of the Greek word: that which is thrown before and thus responds to the project of Dasein. Discovering from the beginning that the very *word* phenomenology already projects phenomenology "as such," the analysis operates according to the hermeneutic path: meaning is anticipated in the word. It is always a question of the concept of *logos*. Heidegger does not stop after having retranslated *logos into Greek*, or rather λέγειν as ἀποφαίνεσθαι. This "original" meaning, he says, is always already second and derived: "*Logos* precisely would *not* be taken for the primary 'place' of truth" (BT 57, 33).

Let us recall the difficulty in assigning a *place* to language. One could take language for the "natural" place of *logos*, and this latter, in turn, for the place of truth. But Heidegger, inverting that, first thinks *logos* as the place of language, at least as its ground, its "base," and, second, thinks truth as the place of *logos*, which from then on becomes second. In the meantime, "truth" must have changed meaning, or place, and emigrated from the spoken to . . . what? The thing itself? That is to say?

> *Aisthesis*, perception pure and simple, sensible of something, is "true" in the Greek sense, and indeed more originally than the *logos* in question ["judgment"]. Inasmuch as an *aisthesis* aims at its *idia*, or the being who is not properly accessible except *by* it and *for* it, for example the sight of colors, then perception is always true. Sight always discovers colors, hearing always discovers sounds. The pure *noein* is "true" in the most pure and original sense (that is, doing nothing but discovering, so that it can never cover over), is perception which looks purely and simply, takes in the simplest determinations of the Being of beings as such. This *noein* can never cover over, never be false, it can at the very most remain *non-perceiving*, an *agnoein*, insufficient to give access pure, simple, and appropriate [BT 57, 33].

What is a "pure and simple" perception? If perception, be it sensible or non-sensible, suffices to give access to a being ("as such"), to phenomena, what is the need, *in addition*, of a phenomenology or of a *logos*? Are they not but supplements? Can we say just as simply that there is a "phenomenon pure and simple"? Since it is a question of seeing colors, one thinks of Wittgenstein's aporias: how can we see blue if not as blue? But this "as" introduces a distance into the relation *to* the self, the very difference of Being, like that difference of saying-as.

It is not a matter of privileging seeing for itself, for each sense, in its proper domain, carries out a discovering of beings, and thus hearing discovers (is "true") no less than does sight. The philosophic tradition from the beginning (Plato and even Heraclitus) has simply privileged seeing as the "mode of access to the being *and to Being*" (BT 187, 147). Being can be seen (according to Aristotle, it can even be touched), but it is important to see that "to see," here, is to understand (touch, grasp). Moreover, this is what everyday language says when we say, "I see that . . . " Heidegger cites Saint Augustine's *Confessions*, where it is a question of *concupiscientia* as the "desire of the eyes." Even though, rigorously speaking, it is a matter of the eye, seeing applies to all the senses as soon as the knowledge of things as they appear is at stake. To see is to know (εἰδέναι)—to have *already seen*. And yet this "sight" of Being is by no means evident, even when it is expressed as evidence itself: the *idea*, that which one always already has "in" view. To see is to see *as* (this or that). The seen being *returns* to us from that "as" which it is seen; it *concerns* us only in this form. Let us imagine for an instant that the seen thing is *not* discovered. Heidegger would say that this, by nature, is an impossible experience, for in this case nothing would be seen and there would be nothing *nameable*. There is no "blue" unless it can be said *as such*. Of course, it is not speech that produces blue materially in its blueness, but without it, that is also to say, without *seeing* it, which is never seeing *blue* but seeing *as* blue, there is no blue. The priority of seeing *in this sense* comes from the absolute precedence of Dasein in that it has the *sense of sense*. Dasein is always already thrown into a world that makes (or does not make) sense; it always already *understands*, even if in *not* understanding. We could even say that not understanding is already a possibility of Dasein, and of it alone. An animal [*bête*] can never be stupid [*bête*] in the sense of the stupidity [*bêtise*] that, paradoxically, would constitute the sad privilege of the human. Of course, we would have to question again this "evidence" that removes all sense from animality as a result of the elevation of *aisthesis* to the height of truth. We could almost say, and this is what Heidegger will say in his course on Parmenides, that the animal does not see. We do not see because we have eyes but, as in the old evangelical saying, we have eyes with which to see.

> Just as an eye without the capacity to see is nothing, so too the capacity to see remains for its part an incapacity if it does not already bathe

The Eye of the Word 49

in a relation of man to the discoverable being of the look. But how can a being appear to man, if the latter does not in its essence already relate to beings as such? But how can this relation be established if man does not establish himself in relation to Being? If man did not already have Being in view (*im Blick*), he could not think the nothing even once, not to mention an experience of beings [GA54 217].

The privilege of the human is that of the relation *to* . . . in general (and even with the most general—Being—but also the most empty—nothingness). Before being this or that, the human is already in view of Being, in that the human is in relation *to*. . . . There is no intellectual tension in "grasping" the sense of this or that about understanding. Rather, understanding has *to see* what *already* addresses itself *to* us, even before we have expressly paid attention. Understanding can usually do without words; that goes, as we say, *without saying*. I walk down the street and I have already understood everything without having to say anything—without saying "sidewalk," "road," "passersby," etcetera. I have already seen all that, and *thus* have explained and understood it, without having had the need to articulate it. To translate this phenomenologically (which should not be necessary either, it goes without saying): "A pre-predicative seeing pure and simple of that toward which we are oriented understands and explicates" (BT 189, 149). This signifies that understanding is anterior to enunciation, but also that there is no seeing "pure and simple," if by that we understand a mechanical operation. The eye is, as simple eye, blind. For example, how could it see the *absence* of anything whatsoever? To see an absence (a thing or a person *as* absent), we must already have what hides itself from optical "vision" *in* view. But this thing that hides itself, even inasmuch as it does *not* appear, nevertheless appears *as such*—as "lacking" or having disappeared. This "as," writes Jean-Luc Nancy, "is not second, derived, added in an ulterior step to the first grasp of the being. In particular, it does not depend upon linguistic enunciation. It is rather it that makes this enunciation possible. . . . Language as articulation is not first, here; a sort of beyond-language that is no other than the articulation of the *Auslegung in* comprehension is first" (Nancy, *Partage* 32). This coming of sense to its anticipation defines the very structure of Dasein as *Being toward* . . . ("I follow": I understand). We should not believe that sense exists outside of this coming, that it subsists somewhere as something waiting to be captured. But sense is also not the effect, the production, of a Dasein that would have sense in itself the way it carries something in a pocket. Neither transcendent nor immanent, sense comes, gives itself in announcing itself "as," but gives only its announcing. There is no sense except in *pre-sense*. Yet we must ask how this announcing can be anterior to language and even "beyond-language." That it precedes enunciation and makes it possible, perhaps; all of paragraph 33 demonstrates a second and derivative mode of making explicit in what is enunciated. To enunciate is, first of all, to make seen; then, in relation to what is already shown, it is to say something, which is the stage of predication; and finally, it is to communicate what is said to others, that is, to make it seen in common (*Mitsehenlassen*). If we examine this triptych closely, we see that speaking always arrives *after*—sense. We might say that the word remains, in all this matter (of seeing, making seen, taking into view, understanding), in the position of a supplement. Sense always already arrives *before* the word and does nothing but express itself in it. It expresses itself there, signifies: speech always signifies, even when it is "insignificant." (On this point, Heidegger agrees with Freud: the insignificant already signifies, sometimes is even what is most significant.) There is no word (provided that it be a word) that is not, in advance, traversed by sense. Even when we do not articulate well, or when the language spoken to us is foreign, "we first of all hear *incomprehensible* words and not a sonorous babbling" (BT 207/164).[6] Sense has always already arrived ahead of speech. Only that being with the structure of Being to . . . , Dasein, and it alone, can make (or *not* make) sense.

If this strictly existential conception of speech does not confirm absolutely the canonical definition of language as the *property / propriety* of the human being (especially if thought as subject), it leads back to its major prejudice (its pre-judgment) in that it denies all access to language to other living, and *a fortiori* inanimate, beings, and does so in the name of sense. In view of language itself, this conception refuses language all autonomy, all "identity" proper, contrary to what the same Heidegger will affirm later. This can be seen in the choice of the very word for "speech," *die Rede*. It can indeed be said that language (*die Sprache*) "speaks" (*spricht*), not that it "chatters" (*redet*).[7] "One" always chatters, and this permanent chattering defines the everyday state of spoken existence: *Gerede*, the "one-says," chattering. But chattering [*causer*] does not take place by itself; it has a "cause," even if it is not necessarily causal, a cause in the sense of the cause to be debated. To speak is always to relate oneself *to* something; it is to speak "about" something ("let's talk about it"), even if this subject does not need to be pronounced expressly, as such. It is enough that it be *in view*, and we always take it up from a certain point of view (*Hinsicht*). It makes up part of the common world *to* which we relate. That is why speech always takes the form of a communication. Being to . . . is always a Being-with, Being-there is always a "common place." Even when it is impossible for me to communicate with the other because I do not know his language, for example, I communicate with him in advance, being of the (same) world, while with a seal or an oyster I could not complain of not being understood. This shows once more that it is first of all a question of meaning.

This communication can do without words. We understand each other better in half-words or even in silence. Thus, the strange praise of silence that breaks out in the very middle of a paragraph devoted to speech. Those who remain silent in the presence of the other not only do not say nothing, they say more than those who are never short of words. Their silence *speaks*. But how are we to distinguish the silence laden with sense from the silence that simply has nothing to say, especially when we hear [or understand] that the mute absolutely cannot remain silent. (Does he remain a Dasein then? Has he not fallen to the status of a stone? And what are we to think of this "powerful" silence that reigns in the stone, as Trakl says? So many questions remained unanswered at the time of *Being and Time*.)

To speak (or to remain silent) is, properly speaking, to have something *to say*. Even when we have nothing to say, and thus speak "to say nothing," we *say that*. Speaking, or remaining silent, *spricht das Dasein aus* (BT 205, 162). We translate this as "Dasein expresses itself." But Dasein does not express itself like a lemon that ex-presses its own juice from itself. Dasein has no juice, no interior; it is always already *aus*, outside. It is *toward*... and it is as such that it is (exposed) to speaking. Dasein is disposed to speech because speech is a disposition (*Stimmung*) to which one always already feels oneself disposed—even when not "in the mood to talk." Expression is not a matter of the exteriorization of internal feelings that could otherwise remain unexpressed without damage. There are no feelings "in themselves"; all feeling is *affected*, a feeling "oneself" in which the "self" designates nothing other than the harmony (or the touching) of he or she who feels and of the felt according to a certain *sense*. This is what the intonation (and in *Stimmung* there is *Stimme*, the voice), the modulation, and the tempo of a speech manifest, Heidegger writes. Nothing except extreme artifice can speak in an absolutely neutral manner. The voice always *betrays*. It always allows sense to pass through, but in another way, as though it flowed back from the pure throw to the being-thrown. Understanding, then, is not excluded. On the contrary, every disposition, joy or melancholy, and even the "neutral" disposition of those who have "nothing to say" indeed gives something to be understood, something of existence itself. But we should rather say that every disposition gives something to be *heard / understood* [*entendre*], and this is not exactly the same thing. This inflection of sense could well be the place of poetic speech that Heidegger curiously mentions in a short sentence, to my knowledge the only one in the entire treatise to define the poetic mission: "The communication of the existential possibilities of state-of-mind, that is, the disclosing of existence, can become the specific goal of 'poetic' speech" (BT 205, 162). That poetry be associated with the reign of affections is nothing new; but that as such it be a revelation of the possibilities (*existential,* and not simply *existentiel*) of Dasein is not evident in the context of *Being and*

Time, a treatise that pretends to be scientific and whose "style" is nothing less than poetic. Dasein is its own *Erschlossenheit*, its own illumination: it illuminates itself, is its own torch, if I can put it thus. Poetry is one of the flashes that opens the "fundamental mood" (*Grundstimmung*). And yet this flash no longer appeals primarily to *sight*. It even seems lost from sight. One page later, Heidegger writes: "Hearing (*Hören*) constitutes even the primary and proper opening of Dasein for its most proper capacity for Being as the understanding of the voice of the friend that every Dasein carries with it" (BT 206, 163).

The "voice of the friend"? This is not yet the still more secret voice of Being (*Stimme des Seins*). *Der Freund* remains masculine, not feminine and not neuter. Is this voice the call (the silent cry that each time does not say a *word*[8]) of conscience, of that "knowledge" that wants to call us back to our radical "nothingness" (*Nichtigkeit*) in order to awaken us to our most proper capacity for Being—the ability to die? No doubt the topos of the interior voice will recall the voice of the *daimon* that haunts Socrates, stopping him every time he goes too far: a voice that says nothing, or rather that says nothing unless it is to *prohibit*, and that accordingly, like silence, always has more to say than the voice of the one-says. In any case, should we identify the friend? One of Rimbaud's poems says: "He is the friend neither ardent nor weak. The friend." Because Dasein is always a Being-with, a being haunted by its *other*, we change registers with this voice. It is not only that this strange but all the more insistent e-vocation stands out against the preceding expositions that gave preference to seeing at the expense of hearing, but that with the indissoluble conjunction (true fold) of speaking and hearing [or understanding], Heidegger approaches the dark continent of speech. At the same time, he insists upon solidly fastening this hidden face to the privilege of sense (evidence itself) and thus insists upon making hearing depend upon understanding. *Das Dasein hört, weil es versteht* ("Dasein hears because it understands"): Dasein does not hear because it has ears, otherwise every living being endowed with ears would be a Dasein (the same reasoning follows for sight). Dasein hears because it knows what it is listening to, because it is *there*, because it understands. Hearing is thus always already *more* than hearing; it is to be (thrown) in(to) a world, next to things, a world that always already makes sense. It is almost not necessary to have ears to hear [understand]. A deaf person can obey—listen (*horchen, oboedire*)—in lip-reading the "sense" that must be followed. Words are always, as simple substitutes for the thing itself, subsidiary. One can understand by the sight of a simple gesture, a hand sign, for example.

If to hear is to understand, then we can "understand" better Heidegger's statement about Mozart in *Der Satz vom Grund*: "To hear is to see" (118). It is not to have eyes for the invisible, but to have regard and eyes for what addresses itself *in advance*, in an "instant" (*Augenblick*) that is the flash of vision, the flash of the coming of sense. This instant has already preceded itself: sense must have gotten ahead of itself. In that it is analogous to being "to" death as that getting ahead of the repetition upon "itself." This explains that most of the time we understand only what is *already* "seen," understood, come. To understand, in this case, is nothing other than collecting what is lying around, as it were, "under" our eyes. On the other hand, authentic understanding in no way appeals to something *present*, but announces itself as what has already *passed* itself (over) in an "absolute" past. In the same way, Dasein does not understand "itself" except in getting ahead of its end, in understanding it as *already* come, which alone permits it properly to repeat its end.

Speech should be the medium par excellence of sense, even more so than music, which always makes us hear . . . sounds. Unfortunately, if I can say so, speech also makes us hear something other than *pure* sense: it makes a noise of words, and so is often deafening. It can no longer hear itself . . . speak; or rather, *we* do nothing but speak. This is the phenomenon analyzed by Heidegger under the name *Gerede*. We chatter and chatter. . . . About what? Well, about nothing—nothing special, we say. It's already enough just to chatter, because, most often, there is nothing to say, and even for that reason we chatter. If not, if we always had to "think before speaking" to find meaning or sense . . . very quickly no one would open his mouth. But the average being does not need to rediscover this sense all the time. He has always already expressed and understood himself. This self-understanding is his very existence as evidence, as what is self-evident and *goes without saying*. Moreover, that "we" do not know, and do not want to know, about such "evidence" can only reenforce this evidence in its so-called [self-named] legitimacy: it does not need to be elucidated, being clear as day already. (It follows just the same for Being, whose "sense" is lost in unquestionable evidence.) Just as evidence is the perversion of seeing, language alters speech: far from making the thing itself seen directly, it becomes a screen. Just as there are no pure sounds, but always sonorous things, there is no pure word, every word being always already signifying (referring to . . .). Even though a sound (almost always) refers immediately to the thing that produces it (the wind, a Mercedes, etcetera[9]), a word is far from being this transparent. Not only does it refer to more than one thing; it begins by referring to other words, which themselves refer to more than one thing (and to more than one word), so that the "thing itself" ends up being dissolved in an infinity of references. The worst thing is that in the end the very distinction between the "thing" and the "word" is obscured, the word unduly taking the place of, and in turn functioning like, a thing itself (which constitutes a fetish). In these conditions, how could the word act as transparency, as a sign showing a "pure" sense and effacing itself in this showing? For Saying, there always remain too many words. Put differently, no words should (should have) remained. Does the eye, instead of making the phenomenon seen, show the "optic nerves"? The eye must not make *itself* seen, just as hearing must not make *itself* heard (otherwise one has, as we say, "visions"—or voices). The principle of Dasein is the transparence of the self, *Durchsichtigkeit* (in which sight still has something to say).

The struggle against what we call the "misuse" of words in order to reestablish their (so-called) purity in fact ends by resembling a struggle *against* words themselves. To tear "live" speech from language, we must rid it of all parasites, of all those innumerable deposits that ruin its claims to transparence. This leads to a paradoxical result: the "purest" word is the *silent* word, the word that no longer allows any other resonance to murmur in itself except that of the extinction of every "other," of all alterity to its proper self. It is the arche-word that resembles the most used up and *extinguished* word like two peas in a pod. . . . Forcing this somewhat, I would say that (at least in the reading of *Being and Time*) language is a major obstacle to the transparency of the analysis, that in certain respects it is even the *tomb of sense*. Sense is perhaps maintained in language, but it is buried there just as well. Words are like the successive shrouds of the thing itself: they conserve it even in veiling and enveloping it in a fold that is so intricate that the thing itself becomes indiscernible, never entirely able to be laid bare without remainder. At the end of a phenomenological dance of Salome, there will never be the ecstasy of finally "seeing"—the naked truth. But that is inscribed in the very structure of revealing, which is at the same time always (and perhaps even *first of all*) re-veiling.

If speech is an existential, language has no clear ontological status. On the one hand, it appears on the side of the thing as the "depository" of words that seem to subsist there. On the other hand, a language lives and can evolve or even die. Dasein, even, or especially, because it is in relation to death as such, is not in the first instance a living being; it cannot *be* dead. And finally, does not language, as a natural process analogous to a forest or a river ("Nature is a temple where living pillars / Sometimes let out confused words"[10]), escape the existential project of sense? Are the "confused words" of "living pillars" any less words than those we pronounce in a public speech? Do the oracles rendered by the leaves of the oaks of Dodona have less or more meaning than a treatise on ontology? If we focus everything on the side of sense (and if we reduce sense to simple signification), do we not evacuate everything terrestrial (though not necessarily human) from speech: sonority, musicality, but also the geographic and even geological character of every language as "speaking" of the land?

Paragraph 34 of *Being and Time* closes with an admission of failure: "We possess a science of language and yet the Being of beings that it takes as its theme remains obscure; better yet: the horizon of a possible questioning of its subject remains veiled" (BT 209, 166). When we speak of the "Being" of language, we presuppose that it is a being. The question of the Being of beings is the question of ontology. Every *logos* presupposes language, even if this is not in the form of *a* determinate language. With language and the question of its Being, the whole enterprise, whether it calls itself phenomenology or ontology, finds itself shaken—put into motion at the same time that its foundation is hit. Heidegger knew this, and near the beginning of *Being and Time* writes: "For this task [grasping beings in their Being], it is not only words that are lacking, but most of all 'grammar' . . . " (BT 63, 39). In paragraph 34, he evokes the necessity of "*liberating* grammar from logic" (BT 209, 165). This liberation passes by way of a deconstruction of the entire ontology underlying Greek logic, which served as the guiding thread for the elaboration of the "fundamental structures of the forms and elements of speech"—the doctrine of the categories and of predication. This deconstruction calls for the construction of a more fundamental ontology in which the preeminence of *logos* over Being is reversed. Following this path, we arrive at the *foundation* of the phenomenon of sense (as the anticipating structure of Dasein); but we also and in advance find language, *already* constituted, before sense (as making-explicit and understanding). If speech as existential is withdrawn from the ontology of the subsisting being, language remains and dwells a being whose kind of being is not clear, to say the least. *Sense* does not show through there. It seems to escape all control in words themselves and make a, *one*, body with the "flesh" of the word, to the point that to say *Brot* and *bread*, even if one *wants* to say the same thing, is still to say two irreducibly different things. This holds true to the point that meaning, wanting to say [*vouloir-dire*], is never assured of itself, never certain that it is not betrayed by what it *says*. The letter can always betray, even when it is (according to an ancient tradition going back to Greek grammar) most reliable:

> Essent (*Seiend*) is that which is permanent and presents itself as such: appearing, phenomenon. The latter manifests itself primarily to view.

The Greeks considered language optically, in a certain broad sense, that is, from the point of view of writing. It is there that what is spoken acquires appearance. Language is, that is to say that it maintains itself in the image of writing (*im Schriftbild*; "*l'oeil du mot*"; "the eye of the word"), in the signs of writing, in letters, *grammata*. This is why grammar represents language as being, while through the flux of speaking, language loses itself in the impermanent [EM 64, 49].

In French, *Schriftbild* is translated as "the eye of the word," literally the image of writing. It is not a question of an eye proper, at least if we understand by that the physical organ of seeing, which Heidegger would challenge. Earlier, he described the decadence of the eye when it passes from original vision that "for the *first* time intuitioned (*hineinschaute*)" what ruled a preliminary sense, and considering the eye *in this manner* (as seeing), puts it to work—as work. The eye is decadent, then, when it passes from this original vision to the degraded view that is nothing more than "pure and simple contemplation or looking over or *gap*ing at."[11] To see is not to contemplate, mouth hanging open, wide-eyed (the eye of Cyclops, which, because it does nothing but see, is blind). To see is to project, in a flash, the very thing that gives sight.

Language takes on consistency, appearance and stability, in short, a body, in writing and only there. There, it *sets itself down*, but also remarks itself. This indifferent remark that permits every word to be similar to itself and thus to differ from every other word is first of all the τύπος, the typographical character. It *is seen*; it is the eye of the word. This eye remains at the same time absolutely blind: the letter sees nothing for itself. Yet it permits recognition; it is this very mark that gives consistency to a speech that, otherwise, constantly risks taking flight (*verba volent, scripta manent*). Thus, the consideration of the "letter" corresponds to the metaphysical tradition. If writing seems rehabilitated here, it is in the name of Being as a stable presence, and not in the name of difference that is unassignable as such.[12] Everything remains in the horizon of the "as such." *Good* grammar, the "grammar of Being," therefore fails to say its meaning. The word is not sufficiently *visionary*, including the word "Being" itself, which says (and does) nothing *remarkable*—that is the word or mark for it. We would have to invent another glance, another trait inscribed in the very body of language and that would be different from this blind and indifferent vision that is the letter. We would have to surpass the letter and finally touch the *spirit* (of language). But is that itself not already a blind word? "King Oedipus has *one eye too many*, perhaps" . . . the eye for what is not to be seen.

But if it is only in light that what appears can allow itself to be seen, "light itself remains in a dimension of opening and of *liberty*" that Heidegger will name *die Lichtung* or *das Ereignis*: the flash that makes come (but also the coming-as-event). In *Ereignis*, in the "eye" of this word, there would be (though as a distant trace, already become *tain*) the *Aug*, the eye. The word gives us the eye at the very moment in which it no longer gives anything to be seen, nothing but the in-visible that is *in* the visible without residing there, *in* the letter, just as silence always returns to (re)sound in every word when it is left to go on its way, returns to haunt it in its *body*: the dead body of a live language, ready to be reanimated every time a fresh breath is lent it, as though we (those "endowed with speech") were but the puppets of a theater of shadows. This is the moment in which *language speaks*. At this moment, everything is reversed. But has philosophy not always carried out this reversal of the glance? From beings to Being—and now, from Being to what?

§ 3 The Path to Language

The phrase "the path to language" sounds like "the route to Compostela": a pilgrimage with a precise goal. But if we can arrive at Compostela sooner or later, we cannot arrive at language. We, the beings "endowed with speech," are already there. Yet are we there properly *speaking*? Are we the There of speech, or do we rather still have to be it (this There)?

The path of language does not lead toward us. On the contrary, we must travel *far* to find this "near," this There, that we have to be. The path of the most near is also the longest path. Those who wish to follow it are from the beginning caught in an interlacing of knots that are peculiar in that they coil upon one another more and more tightly, as Heidegger's formulation shows: *Die Sprache als die Sprache zur Sprache bringen* ("To bring language as language to language" [*Way* 112, 242]). It is a question of language; language is what must be "brought to language" (*zur Sprache bringen*). We cannot consider anything but in speaking. But speaking supposes the capacity to speak and thus *already* supposes language. The entire question turns around this "already," the gift and the possibility of speaking this gift, which is itself the gift of speaking. The path resembles a serpent biting its tail: it is a hermeneutic circle, or what I call the advance of pre-sense. As Heidegger writes in a phrase strangely omitted by the French translator, "the circle is a particular case of interlacing."[1] The figure of the circle is the kind of metaphor proper for the kind of trans-lation and relation that takes place in language—it always *returns* to the Same. But in returning there in the formulation, it necessarily complicates itself. The same to which language returns is not exactly the same, since it must be repeated *textually* by the conjunction *als*, "as," the marker or distinctive sign of meaning. To carry language *as* language to language is not simply to speak of language as one thing among others. This is so not only because what is aimed at and thematized is the same, but because to carry to language, here, is to speak as such, because what is *proper* to language is to say *as*; it is *to propriate* (*eignen*).

But to propriate as what? As *die Sprache*. We translate *die Sprache* as "language," but language is no longer the same, no longer the original, the *German*, language. Here we are once again stopped short by a problem of translation. Can't we leave the difference between languages aside, especially if there is nothing but language? The French reader risks being completely lost, for he will almost never find the word "language" [*langue*] in the translation published under the title *Acheminement vers la parole*. Why? Because in translating *Sprache* as "language" [*langue*], we would lose the play that recurs everywhere in Heidegger's language: *Die Sprache spricht*. Translating this as "speech speaks" brings out the tautology implicit in the German more clearly. Still, this translation will only be provisional, for *Sprache* is first of all language. The translator adds, in the form of an "it goes without saying" that seems completely unproblematic: "It goes without saying that *no* linguistic notion, definition, or distinction *whatsoever* has its place here." True, Heidegger has *displaced* just about everything, so that linguistics will not find its offspring, notably the famous distinction between *parole* [speech] and *langue* [language], in his work. But does mimetically renewing this *ignorance* (in the sense of the verb *to ignore*) of linguistics not risk proving right all those who critique "Heideggerianism" for its lack of rigor? Thus, Meschonnic writes:

> Heideggerianism, which is a cult of language, cannot, however, say "*langue*" for *Sprache*. Instead of "*langue*" it says "*parole*," or the rela-

tively neutral "*langage*" [language]. It says the opposite of what would be necessary. It says exactly the word that language hides. For the entire conceptual organization of *Sprache* is turned toward the elimination of *parole* [speech] in Saussure's sense and of discourse in Benvéniste's sense [282].

On the one hand, Meschonnic is right to denounce an "absence of technical rigor" that comes from a will to dissimulate in the translation of *Sprache* as "*parole*" [speech], because this translation in effect masks the turning from *Being and Time* to *On the Way to Language*. This turning is "characterized by the disappearance of discourse (*Rede*) and the gathering together of the reflection on language in the single word *Sprache*." Speech as *Rede* remains an existential of *Dasein*, while *Sprache* (of which we have seen how little its *place* is assured) overflows the framework of the existential analytic on all sides. On the other hand, it is always a question of speech, except that speech does not in the first place return to those who speak it (even if they are *Daseins* and not subjects) but to itself. We might well regret the absence of all consideration for linguistics, and notably for the distinction *parole / langue*, by Heidegger, but this position, in my opinion, is just as lacking in rigor as the incriminated translation. We forget what foundations linguistics (and grammar) rest upon and act as though this distinction were self-evident (without even questioning the "language" spoken by linguistics, for example). This distinction cannot work, however, unless we presuppose *parole* as an activity emanating from a human subject.

Nonetheless, in saying *language*, does Heidegger not essentialize the "thing," and does he not do so through *a* language (German, itself originally linked to Greek), as though this language were the only language, but most of all, as though that *went without saying*? This essentialization even seems to be made absolute, since it is a question of the language of *essence*, though of an other essence, it is true, of an other *Wesen* than that named "essence," *quidditas*, by ontology. Language "has" no essence because it is not in the first place a *being*, and *a fortiori*, not an enunciator. In this sense, it does not "speak," pronounces nothing. And when we say (or utter), "language speaks," we utter nothing either. This is not a valid utterance because *no one* utters it, no one is at the base of this utterance to support it. But then again, who said that in order to speak a subject was necessary *underneath* what is said?

Let us be sure to understand this: it is not a question of withdrawing speech from us to transfer it magically to an other—here, "language." No, it is always we who speak, and even who speak *all the time,* "even when we do not utter a single word aloud, but merely listen or read, or even when we are not particularly listening or reading, but are attending to some work or taking a rest" (*Poetry* 189; UZS 11). Not to (be able to) speak, for the human being, would be like not (being capable of) being. Man is subject to speech precisely because it furnishes him with the ideal element of presence, the constant support that permits him to relate *to* everything. But speech is not language. In a sense, language never speaks, at least not in the way we speak; it *alone* speaks, in an other, though differently. This gap must be maintained to understand what speaking is *as such.* This "as such" signs the speaking "of" language as the place of a gap, a gap in language, an unassignable place in speech as utterance, a place essentially *not* phenomenolizable—and that is why *Being and Time* cannot "situate" it in the structure of *Dasein.* A "phenomenology of language" will be, if not a square circle, at least a monstrous construction: where is the phenomenon in language? And yet, offering itself to *no* present intuition, but no longer being hidden, language becomes *the* phenomenon par excellence, a *monstrous Showing* [*Mon(s)tre*]: theratology before ontology. . . . (A monstrous, but also simple, phenomenon, there is nothing *external* to language. If something remains "outside" speech, it is not as a domain foreign to language but remains withdrawn from speaking in speech itself—"un-said." What is withdrawn remains of the same "stuff" as language; or more exactly, there is no material, nothing but language. Language and language alone can speak—not the stuff, not the sound of language, not even its mouth.)[2]

A *unique* and solitary phenomenon, language speaks, does *nothing but speak.* It *alone* speaks (properly), speaks *for the sake of speaking*. This monologue, however, must not be thought, as Novalis (who is cited at the beginning of "The Way to Language") thinks it, according to the model of human speech. This is not an internal monologue or the voiceless dialogue of the soul with itself that defines the discourse of thought since Plato. Language does not hold a monologue for lack of an interlocutor or in doubling itself to become its own interlocutor, for it is not a speaker at all. But it needs to be spoken, and thus needs interlocutors, *others*. Or rather, it needs *an* other who would be ap-propriate to it, who becomes properly himself by way of this speech that language gives him, that he will only *re*say, first of all in hearing it speak. There is no speaking proper to this other (the speaker in general); there is only the resaid. Paradoxically, the purer the resaid, the *closer* the (pronounced, human) speech to speaking properly, without adding anything of its "own." It is thus that language, this non-subject without presence, alone speaks properly: speaking, properly, comes from it as (ap)propriation.

This interlacing of relations that makes human speaking first of all a relation *to* speech is at the same time extremely simple: to speak is to hear [or understand] the *voiceless* speaking of language spoken, a speaking that cannot *re*sonate except in the *re*said returning to "itself." Therefore, "at its origin" all speech would be *tautology*. But here we stumble upon the inability properly to think "the Same" that characterizes philosophy from the beginning. If, for example, we define the Same in relation to the "other," which inversely would refer to the Same as its "other," nothing will say the Same in its *propriety / property*, if, that is, it *has* property / propriety and *is* not rather that *propriety / property*. But then is the Same not the same as the Proper? Is the Same tautological, and, first of all, logical? *Is* it even? Must we renounce saying anything whatsoever about it, except in *resaying* it ("language *as* language," "Being as Being," etcetera)? Is it in this original resaid that an unassignable *difference* opens itself in terms of identity *to* self, in terms of the "same" or the "other"? This difference would even precede "Being" and thus could no longer be qualified as ontological, no more than, in all rigor, we could speak of a *Being* of language. If, as an annotation in the margin of the integral edition puts it (GA12 230), "the language of all languages" is the *is* (of the *that is to say*), whether "uttered or on the contrary mute," can we still say of a language *without* the verb "to be" that it *is* a language? Does not all speech come down to (re)saying, "It is"? "Such is the question," Derrida writes:

> ... the alliance of speech and Being in the unique word, in the finally proper name. And such is the question inscribed in the simulated affirmation of *différance*. It bears (on) each member of this sentence: "Being / speaks / always and everywhere / throughout / language" [*Margins* 27].

The generalization of the "is" to the structure of *every* language reflects the becoming-planetary of the logocentric Occident. But at the same time can we forget what Heidegger was the first to name "the forgetting of Being," that is, that Being speaks neither everywhere nor always, that it speaks only with a mute voice, in a silence that nevertheless *resonates* through and *as* the *resaid* speech? To hear [or understand] this silence would already be a first step. For that, we would have to renounce the enunciation, including that utterance that says that Being speaks "through" every language. Renouncing the enunciation does not amount to remaining silent, as Wittgenstein believed. This renunciation must still be a *reply*, must already be language's announcement *to* itself, its resaying of the "finally proper" name—*die Sage*. That is to say? That is to say, Saying. I will not linger over the meaning of the name *Sage*, not that it is insignificant that in spoken language it means legend, but because we go astray in looking for the meaning of this or that proper name in Heidegger's language, like in every language, for that matter. A proper name is not proper except in showing, designating, and not in meaning. That is also why it is untranslatable, or translatable only by the same, since it is the very name for saying the Same. One of the particularities of the German language, which did not fail to overdetermine Heidegger's own language, is that *all* nouns are endowed with capitals and thus are readable as proper names. The capital initializes the word according to a paradoxical trope of originality, since nothing is more common and essentially reproducible than the letter. But it is also on this double scene that Heidegger plays: *die Sage*, the proper name of language, which says even more properly than *die Sprache* what speaking properly speaking is, is also, in common use, a legend. If Heidegger makes an issue of this, it is because this name is the name of the verb that *says* what saying wants to say: *sagen*, "to say." For us, a legend is but a manner of saying, and is precisely not the most proper one: it is only an "it is said," a story, a rumor (*fabula*). But the proper trait of a legend is that it has no author proper, a lack that we ordinarily interpret as an effect of community. "It is said" [*On dit*].... This *on* [we, one] is the *vox populi*, and the legend is always popular. However, the people, far from only producing the legend, is itself legendary in the sense that it says "itself" and thus makes itself appear as people through and by the legend. The Greek people is born of the Homeric myths; it recognizes itself and reads its "proper" Being, its *genius*, there, even though Homer's existence remains legendary. Myth is without author because, like language, it is not a speaker. A myth comes *before* being said; it is only resaid. It comes before the separation of discourse into two antithetical poles: the transmitter (active, producing) and receiver (passive, accepting the said that has become simple information). Those who speak the legend, far from being inventors, always already *receive* it (and yet, receiving it, invent or reinvent it), not only from an other, himself having received it from an other in a chain that loses itself in the darkness of the ages, a chain that we call oral transmission. The very act of reception is at the origin of legend: it is the *originary resaid*. Even though information is always exterior in a discourse, what *forms* itself, in myth, is nothing other than the language for saying it, *that is to say, for resaying (it)*. Language precedes all content as self-formation, if the fatal categories of "form" and "content" still apply. Saying itself as coming *from* the Greek language, which itself (re)says itself in myths, the Greek "people" takes form *as* Greek. Every myth is the myth of an origin, that is, a process of identification.

We must also emphasize that in Heidegger's particular (almost idiomatic) usage of *Sage* to designate what is "proper" to language nothing refers to *a* myth in particular (or even to myth in general, if there is such a thing as myth "in general"). It is more a matter of a structural analogy: every word, whatever it be and whatever we undertake to make it mean, is a word *of* language, including that word chosen to designate language "itself." That language *says* is never in our power, and it is in this that language says *before* meaning [or wanting to say]; or rather, we can only want-to-say, *beginning with* this saying "of" language. But what does saying mean to say? Saying, that is to say, showing. This is said and shown in the very word—in Greek (*dicere* comes from δείκνυμι) as in German (the old *sagan*). And to show is to make seen, to let appear. But is this not already indicated in the "apophantic" function of discourse? Is there a difference, phenomenologically speaking, between the "showing" speech of *Being and Time* and what is named "Showing" (*die Zeige*) in *On the Way to Language*? In what way does "showing" constitute the arche-original ground of saying, that is, of language?

To respond, let us examine the way in which Heidegger treats the canonical representation of language, the one that is put in place from the beginning of Aristotle's *Peri Hermeneias* and that, nearly unchanged, remains the theoretical matrix for every Occidental philosophy of language. First of all, he writes that "only a careful exegesis would permit an adequate translation of this text" (*Way* 114, 244). In order to translate, we must interpret. And reciprocally—to begin with the title—*hermeneia* names translation as much as it does interpretation. After having translated the passage in his own way, Heidegger emphasizes that each of the words used by Aristotle to name the complex and differentiated relations of voice to the passions of the soul, of writing to the voice, and finally of the passions of the soul to things, each of these words, different in Aristotle's text, is here translated by *a single* German term, because they are understood *through* it. This means that "the translation does not take into account the diversity of the three modes of showing (*Zeigen*) that the text distinguishes." With one word and only one—*Zeigen*, "showing"—Heidegger destroys the entire structure of relations that lays out the conceptual architectonics of language for philosophy as well as for occidental linguistics. And he does so, according to his custom, in the name of the origin, returning the "sign" (*Zeichen*) to showing (*Zeigen*), first, then returning showing to *aletheia* (the first and ultimate point), which permits him in turn to discredit, in the name of this source, all that is downstream, that is to say, the *whole* tradition, as a same and single decadence: "Designation is no longer a showing in the sense of making-appear. The transformation of the sign from that which shows to that which designates rests in a change of the essence of truth" (*Way* 115, 245). In a note, Heidegger refers to his 1942 work, *Plato's Teaching on Truth*, which clearly exposes this mutation as a degeneration of "original" truth. But if already with Plato truth was no longer the *aletheia* of Parmenides, then it seems difficult to maintain that Aristotle, who comes after Plato, was closer to the origin than his master. What's more, Heidegger was later compelled to recognize that his thesis of a mutation in the essence of the truth could not be defended.[3]

The sign, in the sense of what signifies, designates, is thus derived from the sign that shows directly, that is to say, makes enter into presence. What happens, in history and as history, is that what is derived, the offspring, far from *showing* the origin, the father, takes its [his] place. Out of the inability to present him directly, it *re*-presents him. But that is the very definition of the sign in classical rhetoric: that which holds the place of something else, takes its place because this thing is absent and because it must therefore be re-presented. But this question remains: in what way is representing less a presenting than showing? In what way does the "signifying" (linguistic) sign show less than a direct sign—a pointing finger, "for example"? Heidegger does not respond and would even seem to take the question as not having been posed since it is self-evident that metaphysics (in the—decadent—species of grammar and rhetoric) has lost view of the "thing itself," even though the sign (whether written or not) is entirely oriented toward the latter—*ta pragmata*, in Aristotle's text. Most commentators follow Heidegger blindly in this penchant (for declining the question). For example, François Fédier, who devotes about a hundred pages to the "interpretation" of the first lines of *Peri Hermeneias*, attempts very courageously, but also very imprudently, to return to a mythically "pure" and purely phenomenological source. Inevitably he stumbles on the taboo word, "sign," since we read σημεῖα in the text. The contortions he goes through in order to avoid the word "sign" coming to signify "sign" and thus signification, in short, to *purify* the sign of any conventional and arbitrary representative element are sufficiently symptomatic (or amusing) to be cited:

> In a sense, this is very much our word sign—but as it is employed in everyday language, not as it has been taken up by linguistic science. We know that linguistics distinguishes the "signifier" from the "signified" in a "sign" (we could even naïvely believe that it is a question of a phenomenological type of distinction). But when I hear said, "These clouds are a sign of rain," there is no means whatsoever of applying the above scheme. In effect, a certain type of cloudy sky does not signify; it does not *make* a "sign"; even less is rain thus "signified." We say on the contrary: "These clouds announce rain," which simply means that when the sky looks like this, rain is not far off [Fédier 49–50].

But there is *no* pure sign; there can only be signs *of . . .* , and that is rigorously inscribed in the beginning of phenomenology, so that a sign that does not signify would quite simply not be a sign. To want to eliminate the signification of the sign is to try to reduce the gap between the sign and what it "shows": in the example cited (in everyday speech), clouds are not a *sign* of rain, they are *already* the rain. They are, at any rate, made of the same "stuff," if I can put it this way. According to Saussure, signifier and signified are conceived as "two faces of one and the same leaf" (Derrida, *Grammatology* 11). But the signified as *referent* remains, in the Aristotelian tradition, irreducibly heterogeneous, and without this *leap* from one to the other, there is no signifying relation (or else signs are conceived as "reproductions" of things, imitations that must nevertheless be produced by the things themselves, though we do not really know why or how). What we always try to reject is the sign of the sign, which does not refer directly to the thing itself in its simple and immediate presence to itself, but "only" to another sign, exactly as the letter refers to voice, which refers to states of the soul, these being the only direct signs of things. (But are they not also already *inscriptions*?) This structure makes all of language (voice, like writing) a supplement, a simple convention for re-presenting the thing *affecting* the soul. And if voice seems more immediate than the letter, it is because we can imagine a voice being affected more easily than a letter . . .

Nonetheless, it must be reaffirmed that the sign does not come *after* the thing. *Everything is a sign*, just as "everything is sensible" (Nerval, *Vers dorés*). Contrary to what we hear taken abusively from Heidegger's considerations on the forgetting of Being (that is to say, of difference), the thinking of the sign remains faithful to the "original" phenomenology. The quotation marks impose themselves as soon as the origin is seen as precisely nothing but an effect of a time-lag, as soon as phenomenology is seen as never original, but always derived, without, for all that, it being possible to *show* from what it is derived: *that* is its point (not) of origin. The "old" difference (between signifier and signified, between beings and Being, etcetera) does not exist in general unless it *appears*, and it does not appear unless it is shown, said—though always *in the name of the other*. Thus, the sensible is not named except by its other, the sense that gives it the power to be sensed / sensing, but that *itself* is never sensible except through that to which it gives sense—we can never sense "pure" sense. We cannot even show it; for that it would have to coincide entirely and without remainder with what it shows, the sign, to the point that there would no longer be any *difference* precisely at the origin of sense and yet never showable as such (neither as origin nor even as sense). It is nevertheless toward this supreme identification that all of metaphysics tends, in a hyperbolic process that rejects, with the same stroke, all "artificial" signs (letters or even voice) in the in-significant exteriority that, according to a "pharmaceutical" turn we are now familiar with, returns to affect and infect the purportedly pure interiority of the "thing itself." Is this not what Heidegger attempts in postulating an "intact" origin of saying as showing delivered from all supplementarity of the sign?

Let us return, however, to what Heidegger said about the *sign* in *Being and Time* (paragraph 17, "Reference and the Sign"). Signs, we read, "are themselves first of all tools whose specific character as tool consists in *showing*" (BT 108, 77). At the time, Heidegger in no way dissociated the sign from showing. Every sign has its specific manner of showing and of enumerating in itself, "traces, vestiges, monuments, documents, witnessing, symbols, expressions, appearances, significations" (BT 108, 78). (The fact that signification comes last is certainly not insignificant.) The example is of course exemplary: "Recently [during the '20s], motor cars have been equipped with an adjustable red arrow whose position, at an intersection, for example, shows the direction the car is going to take" (BT 108–9, 78). Heidegger speaks of the indicator that was still moved by the driver himself. It is first of all a tool that has a certain utility, but this utility does not characterize the sign itself. One can, in fact, always replace the indicator by an arm stuck out the window. Even in this case, the arm alone does not suffice to indicate direction. A code is still necessary; the *meaning* of the gesture must be *understood*, and thus the sign already *signifies*. That it signifies means that it is never immediately accessible: an arm might be stuck out the window to hang one's hand outside, to wave to a friend, or . . . to indicate direction. Thus, it cannot be seized "properly," as the sign *of the sign*, as a sign showing direction [*sens*], except by a being who *already* understands what it refers to, a being who has a "sense" [*sens*] of direction [*sens*]—if I can put it thus—which is spatial in the sense of the spatiality of *Dasein*: being endowed with de-distancing (placed at a distance that draws near) and of the "sense" of orientation. "The sign," Heidegger writes, "is *not* properly 'grasped' if we just stare at it and identify it as a showing-thing that occurs" (BT 110, 79). The "arrow" does not show itself (it is not the arrow we must look at, as in the story of the idiot who looked at the pointing finger and not the moon that it showed), no more than it shows a determinate thing (something odd, or a beautiful woman), but it shows its own sense or direction [*sens*], that is, "going toward." Oddly, this is *nowhere* readable, neither in the "tool" itself, whether artificial or human, nor in the "thing" shown. In this sense, this sign comes very close to the *word* that delivers its sense neither according to the signifier nor the signified, but only in what is called, very vaguely, "context" (in the language of *Being and Time*, one would say "the world").

A sign must be *instituted*. Why? Because things, in their ordinary use, tools in the broad sense (and anything *can* serve as a tool, even the sun), are not noticed, not remarked. The intention of the sign is to bring out the *Zuhanden* (ready to hand), which is ordinarily unapparent. The sign remarks the *Zuhanden*, makes it appear as such or such a thing. That is also why *anything* can become a sign. There is no "pure" phenomenon that is non-signifying from the beginning and to which the value of being a sign would be added later. The question, then, is to understand what could be there *before* the institution of signs (as such).[4] If, on the one hand, there is no non-signifying phenomenon, signification, on the other hand, never comes from the thing: there is no necessary and intrinsic link between them. The example of tying a string around one's finger demonstrates this. A well known mnemonic sign, it seeks to remind us that we must not forget; but since it does not say *what* we must not forget, it is by itself incapable of presenting what it is the sign of, so that a *second* string is often necessary to signify what the first "means." And yet the second knot might very well signify something completely different, or even signify nothing at all (if it was tied mechanically). But the string, whatever its signification, which is not *attached* to it materially, and which it can therefore lose, nevertheless does not lose its status as sign. A sign without sense or having lost its sense (of direction) is called an enigma. We will return to that.

If we understand the word as the sign par excellence, as what refers to . . . but that, considered in itself, is incapable of presenting the thing to which it refers, then the institution of signs is essentially nothing but the institution of language, with all the aporias that that institution does not fail to raise at its origin. A language is necessary to institute a language, just as one must know the sense of the sign in advance to institute it as such. And since there is no sign except *as such*, we must conceive of a self-institution that, nevertheless, has nothing natural about it rigorously speaking. The privilege of the sign, then, comes from what I have called *pre-sense*. But there is still another type of "sign." This time, the word is not *Zeichen* but *Wink*. It appears, for example, in the dialogue with the Japanese friend, when he says that the turn of phrase "language is the house of Being" "makes a sign" ([*fait signe*]; *Winken*). The translator once again regrets the very word *sign*; he even sees it as "the most patent failure of his translation," because *On the Way to Language* "literally leaves behind the notion of *sign* (that notion that, throughout the history of metaphysics, is key for understanding speech)." According to him, the "sign" in question is infinitely more *immediate*: "*Winken* means saying without words, but rather 'directly' with the body."[5] But in what follows in the interview, Heidegger expresses his reservations as to the use of this word as the key concept (*Leitbegriff*) for language. How to prevent this conceptual drift? To prevent it in the sense of excluding it is impossible, Heidegger insists. We cannot, in fact, get around the concept, even when we "in a certain way" think without a concept (as Heidegger himself attempts to do), because the concept is part of experience, or because all experience is conceptual, beginning with the concept of experience (and thus of the "path"). The return of the "sign" in the translation of *Wink* is a sign of this closure. It is also why the *Wink* does not leave behind the notion of sign. It is always a sign, since it leads from one place to another, but not in the same sense; far from being rendered more present, the other place, what would be called the "signified," on the contrary remains essentially distant and concealed, and it is as such, in its "absence," that it makes a sign. Therein lies its difference from the traditional sign, and this has nothing to do with what is visible and does without words, and thus would be "closer" and also more proper. On the contrary, there is nothing less immediate than the *Wink*. Thus, the phrase "the house of Being" that is used to qualify language is not comprehensible in an obvious way; it presents nothing self-evident. But it makes a *sign* toward what *signs* language, that is, precisely a dwelling [*demeurance*] that is always more enigmatic inasmuch as we consider that Being *resides* nowhere. It does nothing but *haunt*. . . . It haunts or "inhabits" (these are the same word) language. Every word carries a (half-effaced) *trace* of its "passage" or *passance*, which is ungraspable in itself. This "sign" is of the same order as the oracle of Delphi, of which Heraclitus says that it "neither shows (unveils, says clearly) nor hides, but *makes a sign* (σημαίνει)." The oracle calls for an interpretation but refuses it as well, at the risk of appearing as nothing but gibberish. But the *sign* it gives—in the way one gives "signs of life"—precedes signification. Hegel, who summarized all of Occidental thought, would say that it is impossible for a sign not to end up by signifying, even if it has no determinate signification. It is in this way that metaphysics will always be right [*avoir raison*], having by definition "reason" [*raison*] in advance. But that does not rule out envisaging a sign that would not have its "sense" in the signified but only in the fact of *making* a sign, in calling. To what? Not a what, but rather a "where," and precisely that "where" *from where* it makes a sign. This place is not an origin (not a single point), is neither sense nor foundation, and perhaps does not even exist. But it so happens that it makes a sign, or *gives its word*, in the manner of a promise. Language has all the traits of a promise: it calls, makes eyes at us, says, "*Come!*" but with an "obscure mouth" (*Trakl*). But it says this inasmuch as it comes even in this calling and maintains itself in it, going no further. In this sense, it is not the sign of something else, and thus is not completely a sign. But no more is it something else. It is a *cut off* sign, cut off from its other half, always calling it, but from its absence, from this very cut. The word is not, properly speaking, because it would signify totally, present its transparent sense without obstacles, but because, cut off, it remains open to . . . (The ellipses mark what remains to be said.) The word is dedicated, promised, and yet, in this promise, *nothing else* promises itself, neither the kingdom of Being nor that of God—nothing but the promise.

We will return to the promise, or rather it will return to us, ungraspable and yet *thus* to be held onto. For the moment, let us defer the promise (which will be still another way of holding onto it) and return upon the path of language that we will never have left (how could we, if we are always already there?). Let us return there to retrace the path. The second moment of the text begins with a return to language as language, to the "as" that marks its return, properly speaking. Language alone speaks properly, or *as*. This experience (of the return to the self that defines experience as such) is not a simple "return," not a flashback. It would not be a question of gathering together the diverse traits after the fact in order to arrange them syntactically; it is rather a matter of an *a priori* synthesis in language itself. This synthesis links language indissociably to our speaking so that our speaking is taken in advance and initiated in the speaking of language. Speaking thus enters into presence *as* that to which presence "speaks," that with which presence is concerned. "That includes fellow men and things; it is all that conditions things and determines others" (*Way* 120, 250). Language is this common place, an "open house," Rimbaud will say, and is open onto the mode of pre-sense *to* . . . , or more exactly of the *loan*. The rules of the loan characterize presence just as well as speech. "To lend" comes from the Latin *praestare*, to "furnish." This verb is constructed in the same way as *praesentare*, with the prefix *prae*, "next to." Presence or speech are only ever loaned. But in general a loan is subject to recall. But to whom is speech (or presence) to be refunded? It cannot even be returned to *itself* if it is not a responsible person. This failing is nonetheless the structure of the promise. Because it cannot answer for itself but requires an *other* to do so, to respond to this loan, a response, then, that pays into appropriation without return to sender, to the forwarding party, speech does not let itself be gathered up in a single unifying trait. It will only ever be able to let itself be resaid, named, that is to say, *re*named.

> The nature of language exhibits a multiplicity of elements and relations. We counted them but did not string them together in a series. In going through them, that is, in the original count (*Zählen*), but

that does not yet count with numbers (*Zahlen*), the announcement of a belonging together was given. Counting is a recounting that anticipates the unifying element in the belonging together and nonetheless cannot bring it out and make it appear [*Way* 121, 251].

Why cannot this unifying trait appear? Is it because of an incapacity in thought? Thought does not succeed in producing the experience of unity, but this failure is nothing new; it *stems from the beginning* and that is why this unity remained "unnamed" (*unbenannt*). All names for what is aimed at under the title *Sprache* fail, are missing *from* the name and lack *a* name. This unity, however, is not a number. As we know, Heidegger considers everything marked by the sign of calculating, if not worthless, at least *secondary* in relation to the original, which alone *counts*. But in this evaluation of the principle, there is already a(n) (ac)count. It counts "without numerals." How is this possible? The numeral is taken as secondary, in the same way as the letter in the composition of words: but what would a word be *without letters*? How, above all, could it remain present and identical to itself?

Chiffre [numeral] is a word that comes from the Arabic *sifr*, zero. The zero is unknown to Antiquity, but also to Heidegger, it seems. The zero is like the sign: it can be anything because it has *nothing proper* to itself. For Heidegger, counting begins with unity and not before, a unity that *already* gathers multiplicity together onto itself. Before, there is nothing—or there is the zero, which, however, is neither known nor named. From this point on, we understand why Heidegger considers numerals to be harmful to thought. Not only do they reduce all unity to the indifference of number, but they threaten the closure of the One, its *a priori* operation of synthesizing the multiple. The multiple can always be gathered together in the fold (of the) One (*Einfalt*), even though the zero escapes it. Gathering nothing together, neither unifying nor initiating, neither closing nor totalizing, the zero puts the privilege of *logos* into danger. (This privilege is always an "account" as well, but first of all a *gathering together* upon the self: *theology*, even "negative" theology.)

Heidegger dictates that the unity he seeks be called *Aufriss*. This is indeed a dictation: in our inability to find the One of being-language, we give it a name, acting as though it too were not one name among others in language, conferring upon it a governing status when, like all words, it is ruled by what it is charged with saying. I will translate *Aufriss*[6] as "cutting-up" or simply "cut," thinking of the cut in a fabric or a verse (". . . virgin verse / Indicating only the cut"), or, still more precisely, the cutting of woods, a "clear cut" that is more severe than the "thinning out" of a forest that gestures in the direction of "clearing" (*Lichtung*). But the word for the One of the cut of this fabric or this forest that is language must itself be cut to make the woods of which it is made appear: *Riss*, the tearing or breach that can be a crevice but that always follows a layout. *Riss*, Heidegger writes, is the same word as *ritzen*, "to make lines" (or to cross out), for example, to score a line on a wall. But this example (which has made so many artists dream, from Leonardo da Vinci to Rauschenberg) is immediately described as a "devalued form." That tracing (a sign or a word) be in effect *crossing out*, that deletion or the effacement of the trace be at the beginning of literature, cannot but disturb the scheme of a *full* unity that is dear to Heidegger.

> The cutting-up is the unity of the traits of this drawing of the being of language, the structure of a showing in which those who speak and their speaking, what is in speech and what is not, are assembled through what is addressed (to saying) [*Way* 121, 252].

The gathering together is carried out through what is addressed or called for, *assigned*. This definition of the cutting-up of language thus repeats exactly that of the sign, the only difference being that what orients, guides, and gives sense is here reintegrated *into* the structure. Ordinarily we think what is to be said as external to saying itself, which becomes indifferent to the former. Any manner of speaking will be good as long as it serves its objective: to make seen, to present what is at issue, what is to be said. The signature of Being-language, on the contrary, is to gather together everything (what is said and what is not; those who speak and their speaking) upon this assigning. If this assigning comes from language, if as a consequence it "propriates" everything, folds every element (even what is not put into speech but remains maintained in itself) into the fold of the proper that it puts to work, the demand does not remain any less enigmatic, almost the effect of a magic trick. How can *we* say that it is language itself that carries out this assigning? With what speech? Is it language or us lending this goldsmith's hand? Does the wall mark its own lines, the earth trace its own furrows? Even if this were the case, an other would always be necessary to *re*mark it. And it is there that everything vacillates. It is possible that without the re-mark or the re-said there is no mark, even no original mark, at least no mark *as such*. The mark will always have remarked itself and thus appeared; but it only appears on the basis of the non-mark, of a non-mark not even speakable as such (and especially not under the improper name of a "nothing"), on an *asemic* space that at once makes the first mark possible and impossible. Remarking itself, the mark crosses itself out in its originality. It is always already repeated, the mark's double, the sign of the sign. At the origin, there is the crossing out of the origin, the line on the wall, the tain of the mirror. Propriation happens (as event) on a ground (improperly named *as* ground) of general and *generative* impropriety. To say, to show, to sign: these verbs are all in agreement, but never return to themselves. They leave toward . . . the departure from belonging [*départenance*] that is at the point of departure of all as*sign*ing. In the beginning was neither the word nor even Being, but the departure, the *not-to-itself* of departure. We will have to cross this departure out, however, in order to imagine what will have presented itself and been lent to presence only as a departure and not as a return to (the) self. No one will come to reclaim his goods; the to-say belongs neither to one (he who says) nor the other (the saying "itself"); it *departs belonging* [*départient*] from the self. Neither language (which has no address and is not in a position to receive) nor anyone will again find their "(ac)count" there.

But Heidegger will not loosen his grip. He does not want to abandon language to its *wandering*, which never renders it appropriated and even thereby renders it "speaking." Let us read a brief passage from the end of "The Way to Language." At question is the transformation of language into information under the influence of the mechanisms of technical equipment. On this path, that language said to be "natural" is threatened by a growing formalization that is a putting into arrangement, putting it *under arrest*. The *Gestell*, its "fable" (*Sage*), is the final word of the sending of Being; but since it is still a word breathed into language by Heidegger, it is not the end (of the word and of language). The introduction of this (proper, that is, also strange) name immediately follows this evocation of silence: "Thus even remaining silent (*Schweigen*), willingly reattached to speaking as being its origin, is from the beginning a response (*Entsprechen*)" (*Way* 121, 252). There are thus nothing but responses, responses to the "silent" assigning of the to-be-said. Our speech is this silence of language in that it makes language resound (*läuten*) without, however, making it signify (*lauten*) anything. The difference is that of an *Umlaut*: as such, *Gestell*, as a noun coming from language, returns to language again, is reappropriated there. It is in this way that language "has" us (but also dupes us): every word returns to language, even though we think we are its initiators. We need language to speak, even though it gives nothing in giving itself. If it requires us, this is not because it ceases to be the only one to speak, but because it remains the only one that *properly* speaks. Language always has the last word.

At least, Heidegger says so. Or resays it? Resays what? Something resaid?

§ 4 The Essence of Poetry

The first lecture Heidegger gave with the intention of "clarifying" Hölderlin's poetry is entitled "Hölderlin and the Essence (*Wesen*) of Poetry." As often happens in Heidegger (above all in *Being and Time*), the "and," far from juxtaposing one thing with another, is an "is": Hölderlin, *that is to say*, the essence of poetry. Thus, if we cut this title off so that it says nothing but "the essence of poetry," we mutilate the explication at its heart, as if we wanted to understand nothing of the specificity of this choice, this election, in which the name of a singular poet finds itself associated with the *essence* of poetry. This association is a suturing that demands rethinking the essence as other than a generality that is valid for everything and thus for nothing. If *Wesen* designates something other than an abstraction, it is only thanks to what precedes it. Without Hölderlin, we remain riveted to universal discourse and "criticism."

And yet, let us ask what role Hölderlin plays in this "interpretation." His role is that of a guide: he leads from one place to another. He is a bridge. What is proper to an artist, we read in "The Origin of the Work of Art," is to be that passage that destroys itself, or almost, in the passage itself. Nothing more than a "something" remains (*etwas*: not even a human being), a something that is indifferent in relation to the work, which alone *counts*. We must therefore acknowledge, with Heidegger, that it cannot be Hölderlin *himself*, any more than any other poet, who is at issue. We can pass him over, since we do nothing but pass by way of him; he is there only to give place to his poem. The poet effaces himself before the poem, which alone remains, alone rises up there, in its abrupt presence, like a temple. The name of its architect, which marks a false origin, can be passed over in silence. And thus we must say simply, "the essence of poetry."

And yet, a name such as that of Hölderlin is not so easily effaced. There will always be something left over from it. Take, for example, Heidegger's text entitled, ". . . Poetically Man Dwells . . ." This title is a citation taken from a poem "by" Hölderlin, or rather a poem that was *attributed* to him. This attribution is controversial. We find a trace of the debate in the first sentence of Heidegger's commentary, where he acknowledges his debt: "This line is *borrowed* from a late poem by Hölderlin, which comes to us by a curious route," (*Way* 213; emphasis added), a transmission so particular Heidegger does not breathe a word of it. Must we say that it is a matter of literary history and that, as such, it is not essential? It could then be explained that the transmission is a simple avatar. The poem is attributed to Hölderlin by the person who has "transcribed" it, cited it, and given it as a citation, exactly as though it were a poem by Empedocles transmitted by a late scholastic. The scribe was called Waiblinger, and he never claimed the poem as his own. At any rate, he would have been incapable of writing it. Everything, we are told, carries the mark and signature of Hölderlin, and no one would contest this seriously. We can thus suppose that Waiblinger was but a copyist who took *dictation* of the "very" words of the poet, that he was a simple scribe or clerk. Perhaps, but on two conditions. One is that Hölderlin was really "himself." But the unfortunate man was already, if not completely "insane," at least sufficiently "other" to sign most of his poems with another name ("Scardinelli" for example). The other condition is that this poem be a poem. But it has been transmitted to us *in prose* and, whatever the efforts of the editors to attempt to restore it to its "original" (or supposedly original) poetic form, it remains in prose. But what remains, then, of this pseudo "poem by Hölderlin"?

What remains is . . . the interpretation, Heidegger's commentary, which properly identifies the "contents" of the poem as being *by* Hölderlin. After having "borrowed" a phrase from this "poem," the interpreter immediately moves on to what it *means*. The expression of meaning will in effect be all the easier for the fact that nothing else remains. To be sure, Heidegger specifies that it will be necessary to "restore [the phrase] to the poem with caution," but on what grounds can we restore a statement to what will never have been a poem except by attribution? What is this restitution that seems to proceed from a pure and simple *in*stitution? In the same spirit, if I borrow a fake van Gogh, how am I going to restore it to the "true" van Gogh who never painted it?[1]

But, before even knowing to whom the writing of this poem falls, whether Waiblinger or Hölderlin, the poem must first return *to itself*. It is for having heard this *internal echo* that Heidegger will be able to identify and authenticate the poem, not only this poem as being *the same* (poem), but, absolutely speaking, as being *the* poem, the poem of the poem. Let us therefore read the text entitled "The Poem," which begins by explaining that it is not possible to speak "about the poem" from a superior and external position. We are only permitted to articulate the poem's specificity *as poem* through the poem. But such a speaking is reserved for the poet alone. He does not speak about his poetry, even to say the same thing about it in another form. Rather, he poeticizes *through* what gives the poem its specificity, its "voice." In other times, poets attributed this voice to the Muses, and this is also why we can speak of the *vocation* of a poet. But to speak through such a voice as a poet is one thing; to hear it *as such* and put that voice itself into a poem is another, and is rare, even impossible. This would be more than hearing oneself speak. It would be to hear the *source* of poetic speech; it would be being at this very source. However, Heidegger affirms in the form of three brief sentences that crack like bolts of lightning that there is a poet to whom that has happened: "A singular, and even enigmatic, poet. There is one. His name is Hölderlin" (GA4 182). We might ask how Heidegger can know this. Has he heard voices? Yet that is not the strangest thing. That there was such a poet or not, the "poet of the poet," is less remarkable than the fact that he *keeps* his name: "His name is Hölderlin." We should not be able to name him other than as himself, *the* poet, the only one, since he identifies himself completely with that voice that makes him what he is (supposing that one could be a poet, that this were a "state" . . .). This is an absolute identification analogous to the one Heidegger has already made with language. The identification surprises here by the fact that Hölderlin is a notable name but all the same is only one name among all the other names of poets. If we can envisage a "pure" language and therefore a pure poem, how can the name Hölderlin be hoisted to such heights?

We must begin by agreeing on the meaning of the word "the poem" (or "the poet") by separating the two meanings at its essence. The scalpel passes into the duplicity of the definite article, which can signify either the universal or the demonstrative:

> "The poem" can signify the poem in general, the concept of the poem, which is valid for all poems in world literature. But "the poem" can also signify the poem that is notable (*ausgezeichnete*), that is, signed (*gezeichnete*) in that it alone suits us in being assigned to us, because it dictates affinity from itself, the destiny in which we stand, whether we know it or not, whether or not we are ready to submit ourselves to it [GA4 182–83].

What is excluded from this division is nothing less (we will have to take its side) than the "concept" of the poem, such as it is valid for the entire history of "world literature." (This is no small matter, the inventor of the notion of *Weltliteratur* being none other than Goethe.) But the universal, being what is valid [*vaut*] for everything, is worthless [*vaut rien*]; it leads "the poem" back into the horizon of comparisons and values, or of literature (for Heidegger, an abusive term associated with cosmopolitanism, the dissolution of the Proper in the troubled waters of "culture," that is, of the market, etcetera). But it is not *just any* poem that is in question, but *this* unique poem, notable because it is signed by a drawing, a line that delimits an arche-proper figure. Its particularity is (in two words) that it is destined *for us*. But why it and not an other poem? Is not every poem addressed to us? But it, the poem "by" Hölderlin, and it alone, says, and says in the form of a poem, as its own poem, this destiny itself, to begin with its proper destiny, but also with ours. It is this very suitability or affinity that it would be suitable for us to consider first. This affinity precedes *us*; just as "the poet never invented" the voice that dictates the poem, he only submits himself to this *assigning* (GA4 183). By the same token, we are nothing before this affinity; there is no "we" unless we belong and respond to the poem thus addressed and addressing. But how do we belong to it? In hearing or reading it? Is that sufficient if, "whether we know it or not," accept it or not, this destiny is assigned in advance? And why would reading Hölderlin—and him alone—be a destiny?

Part of our difficulty comes from restricting ourselves to the horizon of reading "in general," to the concept of universality, instead of following the sense *this* poem manifests literally. Max Kommerell understood this, reuniting the two lessons of Heideggerian "interpretation":

> What we must learn from you [Heidegger] is that Hölderlin is a destiny: equally in the sense that it is in him, or better, in his language, that our destiny, the dissolution and institution of a world that concerns us, takes place. And we must also learn that Hölderlin is a destiny for those who encounter him: like Empedocles, he leaves nothing without metamorphosis [Kommerell 113].

It is also a question of the hermeneutic relation to a language that can give itself only if it is received, and that can only be received if in advance the possibility is open that it come to *speak* to us. As Kommerell puts it, it would thus be "pedantic" to agree with any particular part of Heidegger's interpretation. In a sense, it's all or nothing: either everything is unacceptable or nothing is. But, *before* everything, "to accept" will have changed meaning. It is not simply a matter of accepting this poem as what gives itself as "a" poem in order eventually to measure it against a kind of preexisting essence ("poetry") and thus judge, pronounce something about this poem. This poem will always come to tell us what *poetry* is, but only on the condition of opening the space for this coming, that is to say, of thinking that space. Heidegger affirms quite plainly that what the phrase "man dwells poetically," which has been *attributed* to Hölderlin, says "does not speak our thought. Despite this, we are thinking the same thing that Hölderlin is saying poetically" (*Poetry* 218). In his response to Kommerell, who described his essay on "As on the Day of Celebration" as a "disaster," Heidegger will say: "Unlike that of poets, all direct thought is a disastrous accident in its immediate effect. From that, you see that I *cannot* identify myself with Hölderlin in any way. An exposition of the thought of a poet is under way here, in which the exposition goes even so far as to posit what is opposed to it. Is this arbitrary or is it supreme liberty?"[2] In a sense, we could respond that it is *both*. But this response would short-circuit the Heideggerian notion of "liberty," which excludes the arbitrary. In any case, if there is no identification with the poet, there is an identification, that is, of what poetry is, of its "essence," a destining identification insofar as the poem is not only destined for "us" but first of all *destines* us. Let us emphasize, however, that this "destiny" of the poem (to be readable as destiny) comes from its *own* possibilities. As a poem addressed to us, it calls for our con-sent [*con-venance*], a division, and thus a sometimes violent taking of sides. Liberty is not the abstention from all bias, and the "objectivity," or at least what criticism presents as such, of a neutral reading that would not engage itself is nothing but cowardice disguised as method. We could then speak, as Nietzsche does, of a "factalism of facts," [*faitalisme des faits*] if "texts" are too often taken as intangible golden calves.

One example among others of an *oriented* reading is the text entitled "Hölderlin's Earth and Sky." It takes as its point of departure Hölderlin's late poem "Greece." Along the way, Heidegger makes much of the following lines:

"Zu Geringem auch kann kommen / Grosser Anfang" ("Toward a Lesser can also reach / A great beginning") [*Sämtliche Werke* 2:1 257].

The lines are largely undetermined; there is no indication of the nature of this "Lesser" (*Geringem*), any more than there is of the "great beginning" (*Grosser Anfang*). To be sure, the outline carries the title "Greece" and begins with the evocation of the "voices of destiny." It would be simply puerile to deny the poet's meditation on destiny. This meditation passes by way of a reflection on the relations between "Greece" and the "Hesperides." We find these relations explained in the *Remarks* on Sophocles' tragedies, of which Hölderlin undertook a translation that was his final work before his collapse. Heidegger lingers over this at the beginning of his commentary, even going so far as to indicate in a long note that "Hölderlin's meditation on the 'return to the homeland' and on the '*nationel*' will not be the object of our attention here," not only because "many things remain difficult to interpret and because the whole is not univocally assured as to its meaning (. . .) but because Hölderlin finished by leaving this stage of the path behind him, having gotten over it" (GA4 159). But in the name of what can he affirm this with so much assurance, since "Hölderlin's poetic path," to take up Kommerell, is interrupted at precisely that point? There are the late poems, of course, those said to be written in his madness. And it is even because "Greece" is one of these, and because it is *named* thus, that Heidegger can predict the sense of a path that is hidden in obscurity. It is only in the name of the title ("Greece") that he can identify the "site" of the poem. But he does not question the legitimacy of having recourse to such a proper name that perhaps designates nothing identifiable, at least nothing that could lead back to the thematics of the return to the homeland, as Heidegger comes to admit, moreover. And yet, seeing everything through the "philosophic window," he does not stop calling upon the context of the *Remarks* to explain what Greece is for Hölderlin.³ Greece then, is given as "the oriental" or the non-Greek but *original* element that Hölderlin sought to accentuate in his translation of *Antigone*, as he wrote in his letter to Wimans of 28 September 1803:

> I hope to show Greek art, which is foreign to us by national conformism and the faults to which it has always known to adapt itself,

to the public in a more lively manner than is habitual by accenting the oriental that it renounced and in correcting its artistic faults when they take place [*Sämtliche Werke* 6:1 434].

This correction must be an "improvement" of the *original* text that through translation will become *even more* original. This is madness, if we follow Goethe and all those who are learned and "objective".... But as Reinhardt writes, Hölderlin in no way acts thus from a taste for "orientalism, to say nothing of the exotic."[4] It is a question of correcting the Greek cultural tendency (become "second nature"), which consisted in a struggle for differentiation, and thus against the Asian (the Dionysian, the "aorgic"), and, thus, of restoring the natal Greek that was, as a poem puts it, "lamentably idle."

Once the "great beginning" is identified with Greece as orient(ation), it is no longer difficult to situate the other pole toward which it tends: "The Lesser one is the occidental. But Greece, the oriental, is the great beginning whose coming still takes place in the mode of the possible" (GA4 176). It is true that Heidegger does not understand the occident as a cultural or geographic notion, and especially not as reduced to Europe, this "little point on the Asian continent" that Valéry described, but as what is *called* to become the "country of the evening" (*Abendland*) in the meeting with the Greek "great beginning," itself less past than fallen into the future or the possible. And we could follow Heidegger here in his meditation on the *origin* ("*Herkunft ist Zukunft*," "origin is future") of what reigns at present, the globalization of technique as *Gestell* [equipment] in which the enlightening trait of Being flashes, be it as *retrait*, withdrawal. In this, *Besinnung* (a thought on the trail of sense, *Sinn*) always remains well beyond commentary, even the most "exact" commentary. At the same time, in this movement of the identification of *sense*, not only are the limits of the "explanatory" genre surpassed, but the text (in case we could still speak of a "text" when dealing with Hölderlin) is no longer anything but a pretext for a still more original text that is unwritten and to come, as is this "country of the evening" exposed in its re-turning origin. There is perhaps nothing to deplore here, except from the point of view of "literary" criticism; it is in fact a matter of a destiny, of a meeting, that is to say, again, of a trans-lation. As Kommerell so precisely put it, Hölderlin—*that is to say, Heidegger as well*—leaves nothing without metamorphosis.

The poem has no need of translation into pseudo-common language since it is that translation that, miraculously, changes nothing in the original, or rather is that original as pure language. There is no loss in passing from one medium to the other, since the poem is this medium, but is it immediately, an immediacy that does not exclude mediation, however, inasmuch as it carries it out, opens it. The poem makes a sign in the double sense that it gives the sign and remarks itself, *this* poem as *the* poem properly speaking, but also transmits the sign. Its making-sign is at once pure and common: pure inasmuch as it is suitable and cannot be changed, unlike the arbitrary signal, and common because it makes its reception come with its coming, and thus suits us, makes us its addressees. This sign is the double mark of poetic destiny; it is what Hölderlin's poem gives and what renders the poem, and with it his signature, notable [*in-signe*]: he is the poet of the poet because he bears witness that he has received the Sign, is— poet, *poet and nothing else*. This is an absolute vocation or calling, not to this or that, but to the calling itself. Every poem by Hölderlin will carry this sign and, by this very fact, no longer even needs to be signed. Yet the name *remains*. . . . Why? Because an other must remark it, an other who will be marked by this sign of election. An other is always necessary, but not just any other, not a reader in general, but one who would already be *elected* to read in himself the very sign. He cannot be this unless he is already inscribed in the poem, called by it to such a destiny. And yet, let us read the final two lines of *Heimkunft*:

> Such concerns must, whether he wishes it or not,
>   Be carried in the soul of a poet (*Sänger*), and often—
> [but in] the others no!
>
> Sorgen, wie diese, muss, gern oder nicht, in der Seele
>   Tragen ein Sänger und oft, aber die anderen nicht.
>
> *Sämtliche Werke* 2:1 99

The Essence of Poetry 89

The poet disburdens the others of all worries, at least of "such" worries. Is this to say that he expects nothing of them? In "The Poet's Vocation," we read that a poet willingly associates himself with others, so that they help to understand. When it is a matter of understanding, the poet willingly associates himself with others; but when it is a matter of his *mission* proper, he is alone before his god, alone in being able to grasp his sign with a firm hand or letter. It is thus that the poet questions whether he must name the god:

> Will I name the High? A god does not like the unseemly.
> To grasp him our joy is almost too small.
> Often we must remain silent. They are lacking, the sacred names.
> Hearts beat, and yet discourse remains behind?
>
> Nenn' ich den Hohen dabei? Unschikliches liebet ein Gott nicht,
>   Ihn zu fassen, ist fast unsere Freude zu klein.
> Schweigen müssen wir oft; es fehlen heilige Nahmen,
>   Herzen schlagen und doch bleibet die Rede zurük?
>
> *Sämtliche Werke* 2:1 99

"Will *I* name": this task does not fall to another. Naming risks being unseemly (*unschickliches*), it being a matter of the Very-High. "He," this god that "In lovely blueness . . ." declares "unknown" and yet "manifest like the sky," has no name, or is named only by attribution, a name that always remains improper, because the "sacred names" are "lacking." Or is it because a name is but a name? Joy has no need of naming and thus seems closer to being suitable, even if it is *too* close ("Close and difficult to seize, the god"). Joy makes us speak (in) "madness." It is the sign par excellence of that proximity that is incomprehensible in terms of distance, space, and even measurement.

Let us now read what Heidegger says of nomination. There is a double bind (*zweifach gebunden*) at the origin of the poetic vocation:

> *Dichten* is the original naming of the gods. But its nominative force is conferred to the poetic word only when the gods bring us to speech. How do the gods speak?
>
> > "and since ancient times the Signs (*Winke*) are
> > the language of the gods". . . .

The saying of the poet is to take these signs by surprise in order to send them back in making a sign to his people. To thus surprise the signs is a receiving and yet at the same time a giving; for the poet already sees in a flash (*erblickt*) the Accomplished in the "first sign" (*Zeichen*) and hardly installs this perception in his language to predict what is as yet unaccomplished [GA4 45–46].

The signs of the gods are neither signals nor significations. Far from presenting or representing, they have the property of making everything "foreign." They must be discovered, taken by surprise, like a robbery, a pickpocket. But this taking must first of all be a reception that allows the very thing that it must take to be given. The divine sign, in all rigor, does not make sense, and yet, if only to be taken *as sign*, it is *already received* and thus, if not "understood," at least translated into a language, that is, a language of signs. The poet divines not the "sense" of words actually pronounced by a god who would *already* speak a language similar to the common language of mortals, but the *sense of being a sign* of what is addressed: the flash *as* the sign of a god. Here the sacred tradition of the Greeks is found again: the poet, the "robber of fire," the hermeneut of the gods. Situating himself between men and the gods, he can thus with right be described as a "demigod," not half god and half man, like a mythological monster, but *in-between*, so that for the first time the dimension in which men and the gods turn toward (and against) each other and thus inhabit the same region is opened. That is why Heidegger will say of the poet that his proper being is to take measure—but this is a "taking" that is itself *first of all* a gift. Just as the unknown god nonetheless manifests himself *as such* (as unknown) in the blueness of the sky, in the same way the god appears, in poetic speech, unknown *and* manifest, unknown and thus *all the more* manifest. This also means that the poem *measures up to* this "taking measure" in that what gives measure is itself what hides all possibility of measuring it. What gives (the "there is," the *es gibt*) is precisely never a given. Taking measure is a *relation of in(ex)scription*. Just as the god "delegates" himself in the foreign or the invisible *in* the visible, so is the divine sign *in* the word of the poet. Poetic speech is an *ex*perience in accordance with that ex(ap)propriation. It holds everything in a relation, as in this solitary phrase Heidegger cites as the *Leitwort*, the guiding word, for the reading of Hölderlin: *Alles ist innig*, "everything is intimate." Heidegger comments upon the phrase as follows:

> The one is appropriated in the other, but so that it remains properly itself, and only in this way does it achieve this proper: gods and men, earth and sky. This intimacy (*Innigkeit*) does not signify a mixture and a dissolution of differences. Intimacy names the co-habitation of what is foreign, the reign of estrangement, and the demand for a sense of modesty (*Scheu*) [GA4 196].[5]

That means that without an enduring poet no one can perceive the signs of the gods, but also that without an other who would perceive (*vernehmen*) the language of the poet, it would fall into the void. This other *must not* himself be a poet. And yet he must be sensitive to poetry, must say it *in* its difference. Thus, it is always difference that gathers together: "The equal always moves toward the absence of difference, so that everything may agree in it. The same, by contrast, is the belonging together of what differs through a gathering together by way of difference. We can say the same when we think difference" (*Poetry* 218). Despite the abrupt *nicht* that closes *Heimkunft*, Heidegger will be able to explain why others are nonetheless necessary to share the concerns proper to the poet. These others are not only a people, but first of all exceptional (and chosen) individuals who are "meditative" and "patient," who would be companions on the voyage, neighbors who are nonetheless different from the poet. And because the Germans are the "people of poetry *and* thought," there must *first of all* (*zuvor*) be thinkers "in order that the language of the poets become perceptible" (*vernehmbar*: takeable, receivable) (GA4 30). This fantastical operation that comes down to effacing the name of Hölderlin in enlightening (or purifying) it beforehand, that is to say, in renaming it with the stamp of thought: such is the *Zauberkraft*, the "magic force" that will have marked the reading signed Martin Heidegger, a sleight of hand [*tour de passe*] from which we are not close to returning.

Nonetheless, we must do so in the very name of Hölderlin, though not to bring guarantees of his word and its exactitude. "In the name of Hölderlin" will always be *in the name of the other*, of the other he has become, urged on by a necessity he qualifies as "sacred." If it is sacred, this necessity is such for always coming from the other, from what calls for a name and yet refuses it, calls *to saying*, but saying is not always naming. The "sacred" exceeds the name, even the proper name, by virtue of the very logic of the name, which identifies but at the same time substitutes itself for what it names and, taking its place in its name enslaves it, or at least reduces all its *proper* strangeness. In a sense, all nomination is a burial in beauty. If we consider language from the point of view of the name, as Heidegger often seems to do, thereby remaining faithful to Occidental philosophy and grammar, we make of language a(n) (empty) tomb: the name is all that remains of the dead. Mourning is the celebration of the name, and that is why Heidegger (perhaps following Hölderlin) accords such importance to the "sacred mourning" that marks the *Grundstimmung* (basic mood) of the poet in a time of *Not* (need, crisis: a time of the lack of sacred names). We might even ask if he did not retain the name of Hölderlin only in order to crown it with a burial wreath.

We should remember that in the beginning Heidegger seems to recognize that no one has the right to speak in the name of the poet. It is the poet who makes experience, and he alone should be able to speak of that experience, if anyone can do so. But at the same time, it is an other who says that; it is Heidegger who gives this law of poetic experience. Not only does the poet take dictation of a poem breathed by the voice of another, not only is it yet another who says it, but this voice that dictates is no one's voice, but the voice of "the Poem." This is a strange subject, difficult to recognize as a subject of (and to) the law. If the poem is really the "author," rather than the poet, who is all the more faithful in that he will have effaced himself and added nothing of his own to the poem, then the poem should hold the copyright! What remains, then, of the part due to the poet? Only exactitude: the poet is *closer* to the "original," as though he were but a more faithful or literal translator, as if, especially, this "Poem" had already been *written before having been written*.

Heidegger often invokes the neighborhood of thought and poetry. Both have a "common place," the same element—language. Thinking does not take place without saying, and poetry also says. The country in which each of the neighbors lives in its own way is language, since it is the dwelling par excellence, the "house of Being." It remains to be known where difference, that from which the "same" carries out its gathering, is situated. Difference does not reside in the form (of saying), and thus does not reside in that ancient difference between poetry and prose. Hölderlin thought every bit as well as a philosopher, perhaps even better, but he always thought "poetically."[6] The difference is (roughly) that only the thinker can *say* it, the difference. The thinker will say, and even *assign*, poetry its place. But this assigning, the putting into dwelling or "situation" (*Erörterung*), so that poetry will not be the effect of the arbitrary, must always be carried out in the name of poetry itself. That the poet lives as neighbor in the same country does not suffice. The place from which he speaks must still be localized, identified exactly, which is not easy, because in general poets hardly concern themselves with exactitude and too often pass for vague spirits. Their words must therefore be taken from them and made into a fate, a fate that renders them "worthy" of being thought. Adding a hyphen to *Abendland* to make of the word a "country of the evening," for example, signs the word with the princely stamp of thought.

Fortunately, there exists a poet—only *one*—who concerns himself with exactitude, above all the exactitude for marking what is "his": "his name is Hölderlin." With him, the neighborhood poses no difficulty. He in fact accomplishes the work reserved for thought: he wants to delimit *more closely* the specificity of poetry, what marks the "vocation of the poet" as such. At least, this is what *Das Gedicht*, "The Poem" . . . by Heidegger affirms. This is not a poem signed "Heidegger," since he never claimed this vocation, but is "the poem" in the name of which Heidegger will be able to remark the poetic determination. Poetic determination is made, first, in the name of the name, since the poet's task is situated in nomination. But it is *in name of the poet* that the neighboring thinker can say this.

Of the name that it is the poet's mission (this time Stefan George is being considered) to find, Heidegger writes: "We do not right away understand 'name' in the sense of a pure and simple designation. Perhaps the name and the meaning word are here understood rather in the sense of the expressions: 'in the name of the king,' or 'in the name of God.' . . . 'In the name of' here signifies: 'at the call, by the command . . . '" (*Way* 61). The name gives authority; it has the force of law. He who acts or speaks "in the name of . . . " is discharged of all personal responsibility; he is no longer anything but an executor or a mouthpiece, a speaker carrying the word. But how could a poem make law?[7] To be sure, the voice that commands the poet and gives his poem its authenticity is not purely transcendent, not the voice of God. Still less is it the voice of an institution, even a supreme institution. And yet this voice remains foreign to the poet *precisely as* his source. But this source not only is not given to the poet, it must still be instituted *as* what commands him, enjoins him to be a poet. Such is the double bind.

Why would the determination of what is proper to the poem in the name of the name not be faithful? One (provisional and almost personal) answer is that it does not render the "echo" that others believe they have perceived in the flow of Hölderlin's language. Bettina von Arnim, for example, compares the poet with someone who would have been carried off by the current of a wild torrent, like the demigod of "The Rhein": "and this power is the language that has drowned his senses under its rapid, irresistible rush."[8] She then adds: "He says that it is language that informs all thought because it is larger than the human spirit, which is but a slave to language" (von Arnim 246). We could easily seize upon a kinship with the Heideggerian thinking of language here. Only language speaks; man is neither owner nor master of language, simply the "respondent." Nonetheless, the ascendancy of language in Hölderlin is translated in its *poetic* form: rhythm, which is first

The Essence of Poetry 95

of all a flux, flow, flood, a quasi-demonic carrying away. The poet must not abandon himself purely and simply to this current that comes to "drown his senses." On the contrary, he must resist, like the Ister that "reluctantly" abandons its source and would almost like to flow against the current. Hölderlin calls the moment of this resistance that bears witness to the presence of "spirit" to the point of falling "toward the high" a *caesura*: a suspension of language, or, again in von Arnim's terms, "this living suspense of the human spirit upon which the divine ray rests" (von Arnim 248). This is what gives the poems (especially the poems of the years preceding his madness) their striking character, their not only obscure but agonistic character, as if the poet had attempted, despairingly, to retain this stream, to maintain control of *his* speech. Heidegger again accentuates this tendency in cutting from the fabric of the poem only excerpts, fragments, but ones that, if possible, make sense in themselves. They are what appear most solid to him, most graspable, like the rocks emerging from a torrent, to take up that image again. These rocks are, precisely, names: more capable of being shown than the "rhythm" of the poem, they have the advantage of giving a grip, of being identifiable, since, resting below, they are those elements that always remain the same. For a long time now, grammar has called them *substantives*.[9] Let us take as an example the seven lines (the precision carries a certain weight: its value is that of an in-scission) without title, published for the first time in 1951. It is still a matter of the name of the gods:

> But since they are so close, the present gods,
> I must be as though they were far away and obscure in the clouds
> Must to myself be their name; only, before the morning
> Dawns, before life blazes up in noon
> I will name them silently to myself, so that the poet has his part,
> But when / if the celestial light goes down
> I willingly have that light of the past in mind, and say—flower nonetheless.

> Aber weil so nähe sie sind die gegenwärtige Götter
> Muss ich seyn, als wäre sie fern, und dunkel in Wolken
> Muss ihr Name mir seyn, nur ehe der Morgen

Aufglanzt, ehe das Leben im Mittag glühet
Nenn' ich stille sie mir, damit der Dichter das seine
Habe, wenn aber hinab das himmlische Licht geht
Denk' ich das vergangenen gern, und sage—blühet indess.

(GA4 192)

"I will name them silently to myself, so that the poet has his part": literally, this would simply be "has his." The "his" is not clearly identified. It is the share or part reserved for the poet. But does that mean that the role of the poet is restricted to naming? And what does naming *oneself*, for oneself, "in silence" signify? Heidegger begins by emphasizing the repetition, with an interval of two lines, of a verb: *muss*, "must." He moves on immediately to the "necessity" (*Not*) that will even become, at the end of a vertiginous ascension of the gods to the divine to finish at the sacred, the "sacred necessity." This is the "unspoken demand that reigns everywhere and under which his poeticizing upholds itself" (GA4 187). The force of this sentence stems from the conjunction of *Anspruch*, a statement that has the force of law, an injunction (in the name of the sacred), and *ungesprochen*, unspoken. The statement uttered here does not breathe a word; it commands in and to silence. In the name of the sacred, in the name of sacred necessity, naming is an utter necessity, but naming in silence. Naming is necessary, and yet "they are lacking, the sacred names." Or should we rather say that the name is necessary *because* it causes a lack or failure. A name, even a sacred one, will always only be a name, not the sacred itself. Unless [*Sauf*]—it is saved [*sauf*], passed over in silence, a silence that, even more than any name, would witness the "lot" of the poet.

This silence is here a mark of modesty toward the Greek gods, who have "fled": they have had their time. It is a silence that responds to the silence of oracles, of dances, of celebration, and that thus corresponds with what, departing in the distance, addresses a final greeting: "I willingly have in mind the light of the past." Only a trace of the Greek gods remains—the name. And as for the name pronounced under the pressure of "sacred necessity," it remains, sacred though it be, improper for presenting what came forward *under* the name of "Nature." If this name is not entirely suitable, this is not so much by virtue of its Latin origin, improper for translating "true" *physis*, of which Hölderlin was not thinking anyway. "Nature" names birth. At birth, the new-born indeed receives a name, but it is not the name that gives birth to him. The name is even the part belonging to death and, most often, the name of the father, very rarely that of the mother. If the "illegitimate" [*naturel*] child can be distinguished from the legitimate one, it is precisely in not having received the name of the father. In the natural state (a fiction Hölderlin borrowed from Rousseau) there is absolutely no need of names. The necessity of naming what comes to the world without a name comes from the father, who wants the law (always his own) to be respected. "Nature," like the mother, always remains an improper name, even in that, as name, the without-name submits to the régime of the institution and transmissibility of a heritage, a "property / propriety." That does not mean that one could go without names in general. But what is naming in general?

> Does "naming" consist of something being endowed with a name? And how does one come to a name?
> The name tells what something is called, how it is customarily named. Naming is assigned (*angewiesen*) to a name. And the name results from naming. We turn in circles with this explication.
> The verb *to name* derives from the substantive *name, onomen,* ὄνομα [GA4 188].

This is an example of Heideggerian rhetoric: a vicious (and not even hermeneutic) circle responds to a false question. What is naming *in general*? Naming refers to a name and the name results from the act of naming! But this circle is only vicious if we are trying to determine an exact origin. At this point (of origin) there is no origin, neither verb nor noun. This circularity without origin (a name comes from the very thing it *calls*, makes come) is the very sign of an *other* originariness, say, of that birth or origination *from the other*. The name always comes from the other: it is received, but at the same time is irreducibly called by the very thing that has *no* name. But Heidegger does not understand it in this way. There must (in the name of what?) be a precise origin to nomination, and this origin is the name. Not the verb, which is said to be merely "derived," including the verb "to name." This derivation permits us to return to the origin of the name for "name," in which the Greek *onoma*, the root *gn-*, the same as that of *gnosis*, "knowledge," is embedded, driven like a stake into the soil of language. This entire process is, moreover, largely prepared for by German grammar, which permits the nominalization of verbs much more easily than French (which would never say "*le nommer*" [*naming*] as it says "*le dîner*" [*dinner*]). Yet, phenomenologically speaking, there is no way to demonstrate that the noun produces knowledge, to say nothing of the unveiling opening (*aletheia*) as Heidegger understands it. Heidegger is, moreover, obliged to agree a bit later, when it is a matter of the nonetheless supreme name of "Nature." But he does not concede this except for this very specific name that "must" veil. In this exceptional case, in effect, the thing to be named is too close, and the name must allow us to gain some distance. The name of this naming that advances in the distance is *calling*. But is not all nomination a calling (before being a designation)? In a sense, the name does procure an "access" to what it names. It does "ac-knowledge" but only in the sense of a bringing nearer for the one giving the name. When, at a party, so-and-so is "introduced" to me by name, having been "introduced," he is henceforth more accessible: I will be able to recall him *as so-and-so*. In the same way, the new born who receives a name at birth stops being a stranger to the world, but that does not mean that its *Being* is unveiled to me. It is simply "presentable" from that time on. *The name attributes an "its" but in no way a being.* It allows an entrance into the common dwelling place in which every thing and every being has its "place" (the name is first of all social). But it does not "communicate," and makes known only the most general character of what it "clothes," nothing of its proper being. It makes generality, and thus identification, possible. Everyone *must* have a name. It is the first sign of identity. (Let's imagine for an instant that no one had a name, or that our names changed from day to day: the entire State would collapse.) Identity always comes from the other, like an attribution that, whether we like it or not, and whether we know it or not, is always arbitrary: there is no natural name, nor, therefore, is there any natural identity. Not only nationality, but also gender (and sex), "man" (or "woman"), are arbitrary signs. This is also what makes the name of "Nature" all the more strange—and more appropriate. It manifests language as this radical *generative* impropriety of all appropriation. But Heidegger does not want to accommodate himself to the arbitrariness of the name. The name (especially for the most high) *must* itself be *geschickt*, suitable, naturally and almost magically appropriate. This constitutes a fetishism that is, moreover, the mark of the proper name: sacred! To tamper with the name is to tamper with Being. . . .

A fragment by Heraclitus says that the One refuses and yet accepts to be named Zeus. The refusal comes first: in the beginning is not the name. But what *calls for* a name, a name that would be in accordance with this call and thus always remains lacking, is all the more lacking the stronger the call. Heidegger says that the supreme Name, that of the "unknown" (and yet manifest like the sky) god, *must* remain secret. Not that the poet could keep it for himself, otherwise he would fail in his mission, determined as that of calling the gods, giving them their *proper* names. Is this name secret, then, like the name of God in the Jewish tradition? Heidegger makes no mention of that whatsoever. However, he cites an excerpt of the eighth strophe of the hymn "The Rhine" (a proper name?) where it is said that, since the gods feel nothing by themselves, "it is necessary, if such a thing / May be said, that in the name of the gods / An other feel compassionately. / Of this they have need" (" . . . Muss wohl, wenn solches zu sagen / Erlaubt ist, in der Götter Nahmen / Theilnehmend fühlen ein Andrer / Den brauchen sie") (*Sämtliche Werke* 2:1 145). We should feel that these lines verge on sacrilege. The gods feel nothing; an other is needed (this is perhaps nothing other than the other side of "sacred necessity") to feel in their place *and in their name*. In the name of the gods, an other is required. But not to name! No, to *feel*. The gods in fact feel nothing and, for example, neither suffer nor die. They *lack* that. It is to this experience (the experience of sense, of suffering, and of mortality) that men are *closer*. . . . For there to be sharing, "taking part," and, first of all, giving this "part" or role to he who, if it is permitted to speak thus of the gods, is *deprived* of it, is necessary. It is to this deprivation that the poet bears witness, and this is also why he *must* speak in the place and in the name of the gods. In a certain manner, he compensates for this "lack" with his divine (and divining) words.

With this evocation of the "need" of the gods, Heidegger recognizes that Hölderlin "touches upon the fundamental experience of his *Dichtertum*." This experience goes well beyond the simple nomination of the gods or of the Sacred. Not only are the sacred names lacking, not only do they give no feeling and are improper for "presenting" what does not want to be known in the first place, but their lack bears witness to the essence of poetic experience: precisely that *the lapse is already the announcement of the sacred*. This also emerges from the final lines of "The Poet's Vocation," on which Heidegger comments at length in his 1935 course. How can the "lack of god" (*Gottes Fehl*) come to "help" the poet? This is a strange, almost impious, affirmation in the mouth of a poet whose mission was to name the Sacred. Heidegger indeed remarks upon the difficulty, increased by the fact that an earlier version says precisely the opposite: as long as the god is not lacking, the poet has need of nothing. But since this version bothers him, Heidegger relegates it to the title of a simple outline (cf. GA39 233). This also permits him to reject Hellingrath's interpretation, which explains the about-face from the outline to the definitive text by means of a detour or a returning of the poet faced with the overly present divine, a return to natal "sobriety." For Heidegger, the "lack" in question is in no way a simple absence, a lack to be regained. To understand that, it suffices to place the accent differently, not on *Fehl*, which nonetheless carries the nominal group, but on its determinant, *Gottes*. This lack is not nothing, since it is (the lack) *of God*, belonging to him like his proper mark. Far from signifying a deficiency, this divine lack is the sign of an "excess," of the height of presence. But again, why is presence associated with the divine? Why would it be unthinkable that, on the contrary, the "lack of god," as lack, open something like another space for poetic language? This would be less a specifically atheistic language, even in the literal Greek sense, than another space of the sacred, another link of language to the divine in which the lapse would be the very place of a promise, of an other coming, of the coming of an *other* than he who, until now, has been named "god." The Greek gods remain irreducibly distant, inaccessible to the senses; the Christian God made himself human but by the same token put himself to death as God. Henceforth, not only is "God . . . dead" (he has been dead for two millennia, and yet nothing has changed), but the name of God is extinguished. Something else is necessary, not another name, but the other of the name.

To arrive at that point, we must say *farewell* to the very name of "poetry." The home—rather than the "essence"—of what is called poetry, *Dichtung*, is the call to come: "O Fire, come!" It is also what calls for calling what comes in the call to come by "its" name. But the name is lacking, and it is precisely because it fails to make come—to make enter into "presence"—that it calls for something else. For feeling? But the sensible is unspeakable, or the unspeakable is only sensible, not nameable or nameable only improperly: in the name of names, of their rule of appropriation by the other. The sensible and the unspeakable will always be given in the name of the other of the name, and the very name of poetry is an exemplary sign of this. Not of a call for a more *proper* name that, finally, would ward off this lack that always haunts language, but of a call to bear witness, to witness what, beyond "essence" and presence, *speaks*: an "unspoken demand."

§ 5   The Witness of Being (*Andenken*)

As the subtitle of this chapter indicates, I will be discussing "Andenken." But which "Andenken": Hölderlin's poem, Heidegger's exegesis, or both? Heidegger's text dispenses with having recourse to the poem, since it includes that poem integrally, first, and then includes it in the form of citations, so that the poem is doubled but also cut up and finally also recited inasmuch as the clarification recounts it to itself, word for word, so to speak. Heidegger's text is a true linear *explication de texte* that recalls the verse for verse exegeses of the Scriptures. This will come as no surprise if we consider that hermeneutics was born in the context of speculative theology, as Heidegger himself reminds us.[1] Reading "Andenken," by which I mean that of Heidegger, do we not get the feeling of going through a chapter of revealed theology? Hölderlin's (assigned) mission is not only to name the gods and the Sacred; his poem itself has become sacred. But for those who read (Hölderlin's) "Andenken" (the poem appeared, Heidegger recalls, in a "popular" review, "The Almanac of the Muses") nothing sacred (in the theological sense at least) immediately emerges. It is one of Hölderlin's rare "great" poems to mention the name of no gods, nor even of the heroes of antiquity. If we take an inventory of the proper names, we find, successively, Garonne, Bordeaux (written "Bourdeaux"), Bellarmin, the Indies, Dordogne, and once again Garonne. If we except Bellarmin (Arminius, the German hero), who is not a god but a romantic hero, there are only place names, all of which refer to the real situation of the poet, his stay in France. But Heidegger refuses such "prosaic" notations. "Andenken" does not recount the memories of Hölderlin the tutor (GA4 84); it says something completely different, which is what we would like to believe: if there were nothing but memories of a voyage put into verse, this would not be a poem *by* Hölderlin.

Andenken: thought in remembrance of.... The poet *thinks* and does not content himself with describing, even poetically. He thinks *about*.... But about what? About friends. Where are they? And, first of all, *who* are they? They are "Bellarmin and his companion," that is to say... Hyperion himself. Or should we say: Hölderlin? "*Hyperion* is the name of the poet. He himself is the *companion* of whom we now ask where he is situated. But the poet must know quite well where he himself is, especially now that he is the greeting party who makes himself recognized as he who has returned to the homeland to remain there" (GA4 128). But what if he had not truly returned to the homeland? What if he got lost on the way? What if he himself no longer knew where he was? Is this not what happened to Hölderlin, to the point that he even lost his proper name? If it is indeed a matter of a certain "return," this is perhaps not a return to his country, but first of all a return in time. Is Hölderlin-Hyperion (he who goes "beyond") thinking of his youth? Is he addressing an emotional memory to that youth? Is he thinking of his companion Diotima? Do the "brown women" (*braunen Frauen*) "of these places" remind him of her, even though she left for even farther away than the Indies, left for a place from which no one can return, if not in memory? Heidegger does not ask these questions. No doubt they would appear too naïve to him, or too biographical. Perhaps. But let us read a bit of what he says about "women":

> This name here has kept its earlier resonance when it designated the mistress or the protectress. However, in the present context it refers only to the birth of the poet in his Being [GA4 107].

Must "woman," and especially the women of these parts, brown women, be nothing but mothers? These women hardly seem to interest the thinker, at least in themselves. He will indeed note that there is something strange about the expression "of these places" (these are, in fact, strangers, foreigners). He justifies this expression "that to the modern ear has the brutal effect of being at the limits of juridical or commercial language" in advance by explaining that it is a matter of "maintaining this distant presence at a distance, which is its proximity" (GA4 108).[2] It still remains a question of *brown* women. I emphasize, because this adjective of color is immediately interpreted in a rather determinate sense. Brown "recalls the earth of the South, where the element of the fire of the skies shines with an excess or clarity." But the "fire of the skies," according to the poet, is the natal element of the Greeks. This is as much as saying that the brown women are there to refer to the Greeks (but not necessarily to Greek women), that they are simple signs of the stranger or foreigner who must be appropriated by the natal, that is to say . . . the German. From this arise two lines of another poem, "Gesang des Deutschen," as well:

> Thanks be to German women! They have kept
>   The friendly spirit of the images of our gods for us.
>
> Den deutschen Frauen danket! sie haben uns
>   Der Götter bilder freundlichen Geist bewahrt.
>
> *Sämtliche Werke* 2:1 4

A commentary follows that it would in fact be better to leave silent, but that I will cite pitilessly, if not in its entirety:

> German women save the appearance of the gods in order that they dwell as the instituting event of History. . . . German women save the coming of the gods in making it pass into the tenderness of a friendly light. . . . The safeguard of the coming of the gods is their constant contribution to the preparation of the Celebration.[3]

However, Heidegger recognizes that the praise of "Andenken" does not name German women but . . . the (brown) women of these places. These are no blonde protectresses. The others, in fact, must be monsters, like Antigone or Niobe, "become like the desert," or like Diotima, alias Suzette Gontard, an adulterous woman who

The Witness of Being ('Andenken') 105

wrote to her lover (it was her last letter): "Are you coming?—The whole land is mute and deserted without you!"[4] "Come!" is the very call of love. This poem is called "Andenken," "(In) Memory." But the expression is especially used for the memory of the dead. Of whom does Hölderlin want to preserve the memory? In order to answer, we must enter into a domain that Heidegger always held as rigorously insignificant: personal memories, biographical memory, and memoirs. Let us, then, enter into this domain that has been "forgotten" (or occulted) by pure thought. It has long been believed that it is only with his return from Bordeaux that the poet learns of the death of Suzette. Pierre Bertaux has contested this version and maintains, on the contrary, that Hölderlin had been notified (by his half-brother Karl) of the worsening of her illness (consumption, no doubt), which had eaten away at the young woman for a long time. This very news might have motivated Hölderlin's hurried departure from his position as tutor in the home of Consul Meyer. Perhaps he had time between 7 June 1802, when he was notified in Strasbourg, and 22 June, the date of Suzette's death, to visit her one last time. All that is very possible and would explain the state of absolute distraction in which he arrived at his mother's, and even his subsequent madness. As an ultimate proof, Bertaux gives the adventurous (to say the least) interpretation of a central verse of "Andenken," a poem he takes to be a Memorial to she who has Disappeared[5]: "*Nicht ist es gut / Seellos von sterblichen / Gedanken zu seyn*" ("It is not good / To be soulless / Of mortal thoughts") (*Sämtliche Werke* 2:1 189). The core of the lines would then be a cryptogram: *sterblichen Gedanken*, "mortal thoughts," would not name the thoughts proper to Mortals (as Heidegger interprets them), but thoughts of death, relating to death. These thoughts would not relate to death in general (or as death), but to the death of S.G., Suzette Gontard = s(*terblichen*) G(*edanken*). We must recall that at the end of *Hyperion* Diotima dies. Offering his book to his loved one (with this personal dedication: "To whom else but you?"), Hölderlin already presents it as the *memory* of his past happiness: "Here is our Hyperion, my dear! This fruit of our happy days will bring you, despite everything, a bit of joy. Pardon me for having made Diotima die."[6] The "general disposition (*Anlage*) of the book" demanded it, as though writing *called for* the death of its heroine. "Andenken," however, was written well after the death of "Diotima." We might think that at this point Hölderlin had forgotten it. But what would forgetting signify for a poet such as Hölderlin? The "valiant forgetting" that another poem celebrates is certainly not a simple negligence or an infidelity. "Andenken" does indeed speak the "faithful thought," *in memoriam*, and it is in this light that we should consider Sinclair's bitter remarks, complaining that his "friend" remains "married to a tomb." Bettina Brentano in turn takes up these remarks in a more romantic form: "Ah yes, he who marries the tomb, the living have quickly considered a madman: by day, he dreams, as we dream at night, but in the depths of sleep he is awake and full of compassion. He goes hand and hand beside the other who has long ago disappeared from the surface of the earth."[7] The final line of "In Lovely Blueness . . . " says: "Life is death, and death is also a living" ("Leben ist Tod, und Tod ist auch ein Leben") (*Sämtliche Werke* 2:1 374). Heidegger cites the line (GA4 165), but to pull it in the direction of a thinking of death "as such," as though death were not always the death of a *singular*, living, being.

Whatever this passion, be it encrypted in the poem or not, it is at least clear that there was nothing "soothing" about the "German" woman for Hölderlin. On the contrary, she ended up consuming him. Was he not her god, her idol? Did she not think much harder about his "image" than about that of the god of the church? In any case, "Andenken" never evokes the gods. That perhaps only renders the poem all the more divine in a sense that escapes every theology, but Heidegger just as much, it seems, even if he affirms that the Greeks had no religion (a Latin word). According to Heidegger, it is the evocation of the "days of celebration" that leads to "commemorating women." Perhaps. But is it because this celebration is that of the "engagement" of the gods and men, as a passage in the hymn "The Rhein" puts it, and thus, the celebration of the moment of equilibrium of "destiny"? Again, perhaps. But is this destiny "the hidden birth of History, *that is to say here* [my emphasis] of the History of the Germans"? That is taking the identification too far. It is not a question of Germans in this poem; what Germans could be at issue, those of 1800, those who, according to one of Hölderlin's letters, have nothing to do with the poet, so that he is forced to take the path of exile? Or those of 1942, who apparently still have nothing to do with his poetry, or indeed have something else to do? Or is it a question of a mythical Germany still "to come," at least as long as destiny has not come to hear and understand Hölderlin's words... or those of Heidegger? When Heidegger evokes the solitude of creators who "live near by / On the separate summits," this neighborhood of peaks separated by "abysses," he not only images the "neighborhood" of poets and thinkers in a nearly Wagnerian framework ("this time of peaks, this swell... only he who, like the shepherd, knows only the steep paths and the source, the mountain pastures and the clouds, the sun and the thunderstorm, can sense them"). He also gives this solitude more dreadfully "current" tones when he writes that the two, poetry and thought, spring forth the "actualization of the *Dasein* of a people as people through the State—politics" (GA39 51). A people—what people...? Between the first course on Hölderlin (1934) and "Andenken," which makes a *retrait* (withdrawal) toward the *polis* as "the place the Sacred assigns to History" (GA4 88), a great deal has happened in the "time of peoples." This probably explains the disappearance of any mention of "creators of States"... but not of the Germans. We must simply presume that "their" time has not yet come or that they must become themselves in "hearing" the "still unheard" words of the poem (that they will not hear except in lending an ear to its privileged interpreter). Let us try to hear then:

> The North-East wind blows.
> To me it is the most beloved of all winds
> For it announces the spirit of fire
> And promises sailors a good voyage.

> Der Nordost wehet,
> Der liebste unter den Winden
> Mir, weil er feurigen Geist
> Und gute Fahrt verheisset den Schiffern.
>
> *Sämtliche Werke* 2:1 188

The North-East wind, Heidegger writes, "is led out of its native country [Germany] in the only direction it indicates: toward the sky of the South-West and its *fire*" (GA4 84). To this point, everything is perfectly exact. We are even astonished to read such trivialities: Where could this wind carry but toward the "South-West," that is to say, toward the place the poet remembers, and about which he has "thoughts"?

> But go now, and greet
> The beautiful Garonne
> And the gardens of Bourdeaux.
>
> Geh aber nun und grüsse
> Die schöne Garonne
> Und die Gärten von Bourdeaux.
>
> *Sämtliche Werke* 2:1 188

For those who are familiar with the geography of France, "South-West" indeed names that Atlantic region, the Aquitaine (the region of water), that spreads from the Garonne to the Pyrenees; and the ocean can only be the Atlantic. If this wind continued its march like the "sailors" whose sails it fills, it would in effect go to the Indies... but the "West Indies," America then. "But at present the men / have left for the Indies," and that, the poem specifies clearly, "at the windswept point, / At the foot of the vines / Where Dordogne descends / And together with Garonne, / Broad like the sea, / The river pours out" ("Nun aber sind zu Indiern / Die Männer gegangen, / Dort an der luftigen Spiz' / An Traubenbergen, wo herab / Die Dordogne kommt, / Und zusammen mit der pracht'gen / Garonne meerbreit / Ausgehet der Strom") (*Sämtliche Werke* 2:1 189). The description is exact, an irreproachable topography, including the evocation of the "vine," of the famous Bordeaux wine.

The Witness of Being ('Andenken')

But Heidegger did not understand the poem in this way. Reading "the fire," he reads "Greece" under the pretext that elsewhere Hölderlin in fact says that the "fire of the sky" is proper to the Greeks. Reading "the Indies," he reads "beyond Greece [to] a more distant Orient." True, the earth is round . . . but the first person to experience this (painfully, of course) was Christopher Columbus, the discoverer of America. There is a poem by Hölderlin entitled "Columbus" of which only a few beautiful ruins remain for us. It begins with a breath at least as intense as the North-East wind:

> If I wished to be one of the heroes
> And might freely declare it,
> Then it would be a hero of the sea.
>
> Wünscht' ich der Helden einer zu seyn
> Und dürfte frei es bekennen
> So wär es ein Seeheld.
>
> *Sämtliche Werke* 2:1 242[8]

Another fragment consisting of only two stanzas is entitled "Diotima": "I could name the heroes / And make silence reign over the most beautiful heroine." To make silence reign over Diotima is what Hyperion-Hölderlin promises: a deathly silence, if I can put it thus, and a silence that "Andenken" cannot but keep. But "Andenken" will be able to name the heroes, the sailor friends, those who have left "for the Indies" and perhaps even farther, and who "fear to go to the source." Yet what source? The "fatherland"? Strangely, the poem does not breathe a word of this. Perhaps this silence has more to say about the "nature" of the source than any commentary. Speaking the source is perhaps never possible without speech at the same time failing, forbidding itself to speak. Perhaps this is the sign of "proximity," the sign that the source differs from itself in an infinite distance, that it only promises itself, but thus refuses itself to all immediate speech. The source, for the poem, would be this breaking (off) of speech at the source. The source of Heidegger's exegesis does not reside in the poem itself, however, but in his reading of five lines of another poem, "Bread and Wine":

> For spirit is not at home
> In the beginning, not at the source. It is the prey of the fatherland.
> Spirit loves the colony, and valiant forgetting.
> Our flowers and the shade of our forest delight him,
> The overcome. He who gives his soul was nearly burned.
>
>   zu Hauss ist der Geist
> Nicht am Anfang, nicht an der Quell. Ihn zehret die Heimat
> Kolonie liebt, und tapfer Vergessen der Geist.
> Unsere Blumen erfreun und die Schatten unserer Wälder
> Den Verschmachteten. Fast wär der Beseeler verbrandt.[9]

Heidegger reads in these lines "the fundamental law of history" that the poet is to found: "The historicity of history has its essence in the return to the Proper, a return that cannot be made except in the initial form of a voyage to the foreign" (GA4 95). This historicity, however, is but a transposition of the Hegelian dialectic. In order finally to be at home, in order finally to return to oneself in full *self-presence*, one must leave oneself, go and alienate oneself in the other. The other is not other except in already being in relation to *its* other (the "proper") and thus in being appropriated. Memory would be but a re-membering of the proper via the stranger, though not just any stranger: no, a stranger who already (from the beginning) recalls the proper. Thus, the not-being at home of the beginning is already being at home as the speculative result of the source that must, in order to know itself absolutely and as the absolute, produce an image—an other who, being other *for* the self, already in advance, in anticipation, becomes proximity to the self. If forgetting is necessary, this forgetting in fact forgets nothing. Nothing is lost, and we could say that the poet's exile, if it "is certainly less aggressive than a colonialism, in Heidegger's eyes, is, on the other hand, no riskier than tourism" (Fynsk 204). But the poetic experience of exile in Hölderlin is a thousand times more radical and exposed than what Heidegger makes of it. Let us recall the words of "Mnemosyne," the poem on Memory: " . . . we have almost lost language in the foreign." What does it mean for a poet to lose language? It is "almost" losing life. And yet it is possible that language must be lost in order to speak and live as a poet, to speak "as a madman."

Where does the source begin? It does not begin at the source, at the beginning, but at the end, the sea, where the horizon extends itself to the point that we *lose sight of it*. "But the sea / That takes memory, gives it" ("Es nehmet aber / Und giebt Gedachtniss die See") (*Sämtliche Werke* 2:1 189). What does it mean to take memory? Heidegger writes that "To the extent that taking memory is equally giving it, and giving is taking again, the sea that takes memory gives" (GA4 142). This is a variation on the theme of repatriation through the voyage to the foreign. In the same way, Heidegger wrote that those who have left "for the East" (since it is thus that he reads "the Indies") must always be more valiant in their forgetting (of the fatherland), since once they have arrived at the "Indies" they will have arrived "at the turning in which the voyage that led them to the colony changes into a return to the source" (GA4 142). A bit later, in a still more marked way in the identification, he writes: "The Indus marks the turning that leads to the *German* nation" (GA4 139; my emphasis). Nonetheless (and I do not make the remark in order to oppose a meaning different from the "Occidental" orientation that is a dis-orientation, a detour in the turning of the Orient), it might well be that the sea takes memory . . . and does *not* give it back. But does the sea not give memory also? Yes, but because it takes it, and takes it *in the first place*. "Taking" is before "giving" in the stanza. What is most disorienting in this "image," moreover, is indeed this anteriority of taking. What if, by chance, the sea takes in the same way that "love," which "rivets attentive eyes," takes, that is to say, carries away, transports, ravishes? Where would this theft leave us? What would it give, if it gave anything at all?

This question carries us beyond the classic scheme of the ordeal of the stranger that, whatever Heidegger says of it, faithfully reproduces the initial journey of Spirit in what Hegel named "the experience of consciousness."[10] This is to say that here Hölderlin would no longer be thinking in the framework of historicity, whether formulated in dialectical terms or not, that he would be thinking in other terms, without reference to historicity, or rather in the thinking of an other history, a history that is more legendary, more mythic, more poetic, more inflated with "golden dreams." He would be thinking a history with a more imaginary, more wayfaring geography, which removes nothing of its force; on the contrary, it is in fact this imagination (the march to the stars) that made Columbus a modern hero, rather than the assumption of a "destiny," whether national or not. (Columbus was Genoese and probably Jewish, and his discovery was confiscated from him by the Spanish sovereigns who had just expelled the Jews.) If Columbus is a *modern* hero, it is for having first accomplished the famous Hesperian "return to the homeland": he went looking for the Orient in the West, the origin in the end, "noon at two o'clock," Baudelaire would say. And he ended up finding the Hesperian islands. But at the same time, this was also the beginning of the end for this reign of the naïve or of the native that he discovered, and Columbus' return was anything but a salvation. The disorientation was only beginning, the sources drying up one after the other, and the poem is invaded more and more by the numerous frantic voices: "You are a know-nothing" [*tu es un sais rien*] is written about Columbus in French on the manuscript. Or about the tutor Hölderlin?

~

Does every lesson, like Hölderlin's poem, escape itself in the moment of concealment that is nothing other than the coming of speech promising and refusing itself? It is not our place to decide. Rigorously speaking, it is impossible to account for this, for to do so would necessarily mean doing exactly what Heidegger does, speak *in the name of* Hölderlin, even in the name of a truth of the text that would be forgotten and disfigured. In the name of what are we going to correct the Heideggerian exegesis, of an exactitude of the text? "Through erasures, drafts, his reworked fragments, Hölderlin seeks an ever truer and more correct expression," Paul de Man affirms in an article I will discuss for its methodological value.[11] It is this myth of exactitude that governs both philological and philosophical readings. Heidegger distinguishes between "correctness" (*Richtigkeit*), which is nothing other than adequation, and the truth that is disclosure: *Richtig, aber nicht wahr!* ("Correct, but not true!"). It is thus that he often puts critics in their place. But this is only to obey another type of presupposition (truth is a presupposition, we read already in *Being and Time*). After having enumerated a number of heresies Heidegger knowingly commits against "the most elementary rules of text analysis" (I have taken down some of them: the use of the apocryphal "poem" "In Lovely Blueness . . . "; ignoring contexts; isolating lines or single words to give them an absolute value, most often through information foreign to the original, etcetera), de Man concludes in a surprising manner: "However, these heresies are not arbitrary because of a lack of rigor but because they rely upon a poetics that permits, or even *requires*, arbitrariness" (250; emphasis added). The arbitrary corresponds to what I call the *dictation of pre-sense*. It has nothing to do with the arbitrariness of a simple convention (that of the "signifier," for example) but rather amounts to an absolute legitimation. In the name of the "same" that presides over the neighborhood of thought/poetry, *that is to say of the Same* as such, commentary must be appropriate to the poem from the moment that the poem already inscribes appropriateness in the Same . . .

Yet why have recourse to Hölderlin? Did Heidegger really need Hölderlin to say what he had *to say*? What need does he have to cover himself with such a reference (which is at once doubtful and prestigious), even though Heidegger "is the thinker who has shoved aside all available authorities" (de Man 252) (that is indeed what the phenomenological prescription to go straight to the things themselves signifies)? De Man is right in responding that it is not because Hölderlin is a poet. To see this, it is enough to see how Heidegger treated Rilke, who nonetheless said the same thing with his "Open". . . . No, a *witness* for this "presence" is necessary. In effect, all others have failed; the philosophers have fallen under the forgetting of Being, and Heidegger himself "is not sure he has seen Being and, in any case, he knows that he has nothing to say about it beyond the fact that it conceals itself" (de Man 253). (This is an abusive, though not entirely false, simplification.) A witness (and a *single one* suffices) is needed who could put before our eyes the deposition signed by the very hand of Being, the witnessing of its presence in the sense of evidence that is just as indisputable as the stigmata of Christ for Thomas. This deposition Heidegger found in Hölderlin's poetry, which carries the very signature of Being. Exaggerating a bit, de Man will even be able to affirm:

> There is nothing in his work, not an erasure, no obscurity, no ambiguity, that is not absolutely and totally willed by Being itself. Only one who has truly grasped this can become the "editor" of Being and impose commas that spring forth from "the very necessity of thought" [254].

That a witness is necessary, perhaps. But why have chosen Hölderlin? De Man begins by distancing "national" (read *German*) motives as "unrelated," although they seem relatively central if we remember that the *Heimat* is identified with "Being." For de Man, the principal reason for this choice lies elsewhere: "*Hölderlin says exactly the opposite of what Heidegger makes him say*" (254–55). The paradox only seems obvious. On this level, the opposites in fact meet up again: "To state the opposite is still to talk of the same thing though in an opposite sense" (255). And that is already a great deal, because that proves that this thing *is indeed the same*, if we recall the way in which Heidegger describes identity through the gathering together carried out by difference. But how can de Man establish that Heidegger does indeed make Hölderlin say the "opposite" of what he in effect says? For that, we must first of all know what Hölderlin "really" means. We must, like Heidegger, although in an opposite sense, identify Hölderlin's proper meaning as indeed being *that very meaning* . . . (the "opposite"). In this game, we risk being able to demonstrate nothing at all, if not the presupposition of a signified—X. But let us examine the de Manian demonstration more closely. It relies principally on a commentary of the hymn "As on the Day of Celebration . . . ," of which Kommerell had already said that it *could well* ("I'm not saying that it is") be a "disaster" (*Unglück*). It is no accident that this text is chosen by de Man, for it begins with an anti-philological affirmation characteristic of the Heideggerian exegetical "method," as Beda Allemann has already remarked: "The text that serves as the basis of the present commentaries, reviewed from the manuscript outlines, is founded upon the explication we are going to attempt" (GA4 51). Heidegger *established* the original text and did so according to his exegesis, which, however, should come "after" the text. . . .

The first difficulty with de Man's essay concerns the identification of the "signified" under the name of "Nature."[12] Through the adjective "omnipresent," de Man deduces that "Nature" signifies the "immediate" presence of Being. Elsewhere, de Man affirms: "its language is Being present." But the privilege of presence is not absolute in Hölderlin, and absence (of the fled gods, for example) is not a simple object to be lamented. As I said above, there is a "lack" at the heart of speech that *calls*, a lack that does not call so much to be filled in as it is already the *height* of the sacred, that is, of what passes by presence (the "Open"). In any case, this immediacy is never present in Heidegger's commentary, which says exactly the *opposite*: "Omnipresence maintains the extreme opposites of the highest sky and of the deepest abyss in opposition to one another. What thus maintains the one drawn up against the other in its adversity remains torn apart the one outside the other. It is thus that opposition emerges in the most extreme acuteness of its alterity" (GA4 53). De Man must not have read this passage very closely or he would not have imprudently assimilated Nature to the immediate. It is true that he could not read otherwise, since in the Hegelian manner he understands the immediate as the absence of mediation that immediately negates itself as such. This misunderstanding or presupposition led de Man to declare as contradictory the pivotal point of Heidegger's explication, which, however, relies upon the notion (borrowed directly from Hölderlin) of "rigorous mediacy." (In two words, this notion is not "contradictory" unless we take the principle of non-contradiction as being intangible, even in its dialectical version, that is, in the explication of a syllogism by the inclusion of the excluded third term.) "Heidegger's thesis can be considered as demonstrated if the following identification is granted: the intercession, which is language, is also the immediate itself" (de Man 260–61). De Man here touches upon the sensitive point I have tried to show: the identification of Nature (or a name for Being) with language or speech. This is the core of Heidegger's poetics, but it in turn rests upon the supreme identification that governs the identity of Being and thought, that of Being *as* Being. It is difficult to see how either Hegel or de Man could get out of this knot that binds Occidental thought from its beginning. Simply, instead of seeing in language the knot of identification, they consider it only as a "means" to an *exterior* end—the revelation of the Absolute to itself. It is as if this Absolute could be present (to itself) without language or even when the Absolute merely makes use of language as a middle term, a "medium"—without this medium, which is in the beginning thought of as doomed to effacing itself in the transparency of "sense," in fact coming to take the first place, as the "motor" of the machine that, otherwise, would remain nothing but inert oppositions, and even stammerings. But this identification (of Being *with* and *by* speech) is not only presupposed by Heidegger, it finds powerful motivation in Hölderlin himself. De Man relies upon the following line: *Was ich sah, das Heilige sei mein Wort!* ("What I saw, the Sacred be my word!"). He quite rightly remarks that the verb *sei* ("be") is not an indicative but a subjunctive with the value, here, of an optative marking a (mere) wish. Not only does the line express "the eternal poetic intention," but, he adds immediately, this cannot be anything but an intention, never a fact. In short, it is the moment of the "beautiful soul." The poet's word indeed calls *presence* but does not establish it. But on the one hand, is not *calling* nothing but a mere wish? Is it always and everywhere necessary that what is called enter into presence for the call to be "true"? Can we conceive of the poetic call based on the model of a simple desire that always wants its fulfillment? And, on the other hand, how are we to understand the final line of "Andenken": *Was bleibet aber stiften die Dichter* ("But what remains, the poets found") (*Sämtliche*

The Witness of Being ('Andenken')

Werke 2:1 189)? This statement, for Heidegger, constitutes one of the five traits qualifying the essence of poetry. Must we then say that he "invented" that essence, that he takes his desires for realities? No matter how we turn the formulation, the desire to found Being (in the very word, the word for Being, but a word that is other than the word for the Other) is not simply a mere wish. It is the poetic vocation such as it called upon Hölderlin but also destroyed him. In a sense, this wish has realized itself only too fully, and *my* word has become the *Sacred*, which is also to say, has ceased to be *my* word, in order no longer to be anything but *the* word, similar to the word of the oracle, no longer belonging to the person who proffers it.

We must still hear [or understand] this word. As Heidegger remarks, no information is given about "what remains," since for once the thing is not *named*. "He [the poet] does not name the thing upon which we would immediately like to put our finger, the 'content' of what remains" (GA4 145). Is there only content there? Or would what remains not characterize itself precisely in such a way as to escape the too easy distinction of container and contained, of signifier and signified, etcetera? Whatever we establish as the meaning of the poetic word, something excessive that is always persistent and even recalcitrant always remains (*das Übrigbleibende eines gerade noch verbleibenden Restes*) (GA4 144). This remainder is an unassimilable residue that is irreducible to a determinate signified. It is not the remainder in general, but *a* single remainder, Heidegger emphasizes, reading an earlier variant (for once). This is a remainder, then, that is "what remains of a proper remaining." And that fundamentally is what the poet "founds": nothing other than his own word, which as written bears witness as what remains (of the said event). The word is the letter itself, which must be kept, the source that "leaves" its place "with difficulty." It "remains" inasmuch as its "permanent" source, the source in which it dwells, is always springing forth. There is no other secret: the poem is the going to the source, since it comes from this very source. But how can what comes from the source return there again? What comes from the source moves only in one direction—toward the sea, and, even if it regrets leaving its native place, this can only be nostalgia. Or must we rather imagine that this "image" (of the source, the river, and the sea) is but an image that disfigures the movement of the proper precisely in figuring it? Does the Greek *physis* mean coming to the self in coming from the self? Is this once again poetry "as" *physis*, no longer as imitation but simply identification, though an identification that will always produce a remainder that cannot be appropriated? The text is what "remains" and what, no matter what happens, is never at itself, never at home. (To answer, it is enough to see how difficult it is to establish the variants in "what remains" itself!) Put differently, if by some extraordinary chance identification ever took place entirely, so that the word "were" the sacred without remainder, then there would quite simply no longer be any speech. No words would remain. There would no longer be anything but the "sacred," period, that's all. But if the Sacred and the word are two, separate, it is simply that, whatever the sacred character of the word, we must be able to say, to say—"the Sacred be my word!" Is this exclamation already the sacred? If it is but the announcement, the call, of the sacred, it should efface itself (just as commentary must disappear in the end Before the coming of the poem itself) so that the Sacred itself comes in person. This self-effacement might be the poet's vow [or wish], the very dream of art: to efface itself as art to the point of no longer appearing as art(ifice) but rather as "Being," come purely from itself to itself. At the same time, this vow must be said since it is the whole misfortune of even the "fortunate" word that a remainder, a trace of this effacement, always remains. Effacing is not nothing; it is perhaps a "supreme" writing (though there is no supreme writing). To this Hölderlin's manuscript bears witness, made as it is of deletions and an overabundance of corrections that we would like to efface. That is what all exegetes, philologists, and philosophers dream of in order to have a final state, a final word that would be the word of the end: a "remaining." But only the poets institute this "remainder": what remains (the text), only they establish that, in writing it. But since writing will always be leaving one trace too many, one remainder too many will always remain.

The Witness of Being ('Andenken')

The poem will never be sufficiently effaced, or it will only be sufficiently effaced in being rewritten, without end. The beginning, the source, will never be at the source. "The Sacred be my word" is still a statement that "remains." There is no full word or statement; there is no content in the remaining that the word remains, that is, in what always defers the coming through the very call to come. A remaining: a Requiem?

The "attempt undertaken to characterize dwelling and foundation without consideration for content," to cite Heidegger against himself (GA4 147), does not truly respond, as we have already seen, to Heidegger's attempted explication of the final statement of the poem. Does it respond more fully to this statement itself? We cannot answer this question: only poets can respond to their words. They keep their word, are above all men of their word. And Hölderlin was the first to promise to keep his word. His word demands that he keep his word. "The Sacred be my word!" concerns a sacred promise, a sermon (*sacramentum*), because the sacred is the promise itself, the word to be kept. At the same time, "they are lacking, the sacred names." Even the name of the "sacred" does not keep its word (none of these letters is sacred; they are not even letters of nobility). The name "sacred" lacks the name necessary to keep the sacred promise. But this lapse is not a simple failure. It can always appear to be such a failure, if we take the Sacred as acquired in advance or if we take the remainder as subsisting (whatever be the variations or variants). Here all the schemes of cause and effect are null and void. Remaining is not produced by poetic institution, no more than the Sacred is its result (which would, in effect, be sacrilege). The word's lapse is the very heart of its sacredness. It is the breaking and the price (and the hold) of poetry. Because it leaves this coming that remains to come without voice, poetry calls for a saying that would be entirely calling, and nothing but. We must stand fast in the very place of the failing that marks the promise of an ineffaceable debt. The word will not be in the sacred unless it defers the Sacred in calling it to come, which also means that the word will never be in the sacred, if by the future we understand an as yet unrealized present. It is a matter, here, of the sacred or of the promise, as it is of death. Death is not a possibility-to-be except in remaining in its pregnancy, continually growing fatter from its most proper and unrealizable, or rather, untenable possibility, that of impossibility. The promise cannot be kept, and that is what must be kept. But (*aber*) what remains, (only) the poets say. They live close to the source; that is why they are poorer, essentially poorer. They cannot take up residence there unless they keep their word. But the word cannot be kept in any appropriable way. It cannot be kept unless one renounces oneself, renounces standing for-oneself, just as the source keeps nothing for itself, but gives, lets what will distance itself spring forth irreversibly from this place. Irreversibly: *there is no return to the self,* and that is what escapes Heidegger just as much as it does Hegel. Hölderlin knew this and thus also knew that he was going to his ruin, without return. It is always already too late to be born or even reborn. Birth cannot but escape the mortal (and even the god, in another sense). It is omnipresent, the all-powerful, which, however, leads everyone to maturity and ruin "in its marvelously light arms." It is the Nature that gave man language (the most dangerous of goods), so that, "creating, destroying and disappearing, and (thus) returning to the eternally living" (a return not to the self, but to Nature), he *testifies* to "having inherited from [Nature] what he is": a man of his word, who keeps his word of Nature only out of love for Nature, and for love of the "Love that conserves the Universe," for the love of the Being of love [*l'être d'amour*], whose letter [*la lettre*] is a being-disappearing [*disparêtre*] in the very difference of the letter.[13]

It is possible that the poetic crisis exceeds every critique by reason, which does not mean that commentary is exempt from an elementary critical "spirit" (from a criticism of itself, in the first place, of its status as commentary). This crisis puts nothing less than identity itself at stake, beginning with the identity of criticism's own language. No one can entirely master the word. The word is ungraspable. Even that phrase, "the word is ungraspable," is ungraspable. *But* we are grasped by this ungraspable word—in the lack. *But* a poetic lack.

§ 6 In (the) Place of Being, Antigone (The *Retrait* of the Polis)

At the beginning of his 1943–44 course on Heraclitus, Heidegger relates two "anecdotes" (GA55 5–28). Both concern the site, the place [*lieu*] of philosophy in the city, or rather what the Greeks named *polis*. One of the anecdotes is famous, and Heidegger returned to it at length in the *Letter on Humanism*. Some visitors come to find Heraclitus and find him close to a bread oven warming his feet. Since they are amazed—there is nothing very interesting or "tragic" about a thinker who feels the cold—Heraclitus responds sharply: "the gods are even here." In this *very* place, close to the fire, in the ordinary light of day, in the home of the familiar dwell the gods, the Strangers / Foreigners. In the same way, *there*, in the habitual (place), is the in-habitual of Being.

The second story is less famous. It is told by Diogenes Laertes. Heraclitus had retired to the sacred enclosure of the temple of Artemis. But there, in the consecrated *place* [*lieu*] par excellence, his fellow citizens find him in the middle of playing knucklebones with children instead of [*au lieu de*] devoting himself to meditation. This time less friendly toward them (these are not foreigners but the inhabitants of the same *polis*, Ephese), Heraclitus questions them: "What are you amazed at, somber knaves? Isn't that more worthwhile than conducting politics with you?" The remark is stern, and *could* be applied to the fellow citizens of Heidegger, himself also retired to his sacred enclosure (the heights of Todtnau-

121

berg). One could then explain Heidegger's retreat after he had taken note of his "great stupidity" (the 1933 Rectorship) in the following manner: it is better to teach Heraclitus or play dice than to tangle oneself up in the political affairs of the day. That would support a judgment his former student Hannah Arendt has spread widely: Heidegger's error was less to have believed in National Socialism than to have occupied himself with politics, a typically, one could even say hereditarily, philosophical mistake. The philosopher is fundamentally unadapted to the everyday world of affairs, in the Greek sense of *pragmata*, because he dwells elsewhere, in clouds that make him fall into a pit as soon as he puts his feet back on the ground. This is the story of Thales and of the servant who laughed about his fall. Of course, blindness is never an excuse, all the less so since Heidegger otherwise pretended to have a piercing view on History. But it is true that since Socrates and Plato the ground is pulled out from under the feet of the philosopher uniquely preoccupied by the invisible world of Being.

Heidegger immediately challenges this interpretation of the position of the philosopher, however. He does not dwell elsewhere, but *in this very place*. One might be tempted, he writes, to interpret the "situation" ("*Situation*," in ironic quotation marks in the text) in a modern way: the philosopher would recognize himself *here* as an "a-political" man who is not completely at his task except in the enclosure of his private life. But beside the fact that the distinction public life / private life is not Greek and that it is only true in one way (the qualification of "private" shows in what sense the Greeks thought man as *essentially* political, political in his very being), we must still agree upon the sense of this small word, "political." This is *not*, despite its origin, an originally Greek word.

Since *An Introduction to Metaphysics*, that is, since 1935, Heidegger contested the translation of *polis* by State (*Staat*) or City-State (*Stadtstaat*).

> *Polis* means instead the place (*Stätte*), the there in which and as which Being-there (*das Da-sein*) is as taking place historically. The *polis* is the place of history, the there *in* which, *from* which, and *for* which history takes place. To this site of history belong the gods, temples, priests,

celebrations, games, poets, thinkers, the king, the council of the Ancients, the assembly of the people, the army, and the navy. All of that does not belong to the *polis*, is not first of all political, for having a relation with a man of state and a strategy and for relating to affairs of state. On the contrary, it is political, that is, historically situated, as far as, for example, the poet is *only* a poet, but then really a poet, the thinker *only* a thinker, but then truly a thinker [EM 117].

In other words, what is contested is the modern, and more particularly Hegelian, interpretation of the political as the matter, *above all*, and thus also *exclusively*, of the State, that "concrete universal" that would govern all human behavior. It is not because the philosopher would keep himself at a distance from political affairs that he can be qualified as "a-political." *As a thinker and only that* he might even be "more" political than any politician, by which I mean, more *originally* political, that is to say, concerned by what is at the beginning of politics—the *polis*.

Thus, Heidegger would have come back to the *polis* as to that place [*lieu*] which *makes a place for* [*donne lieu*] any politics and which, as such, "is absolutely not a 'political' concept" (GA53 99). This strange re-traction governs Heidegger's "position," a position that in a certain way is no longer one at all, but rather a de-position. If we can speak of a Heideggerian retreat, it is not the traditional one of the philosopher gliding in his metaphysical clouds; but no more does he espouse the position of the theoretician, of the thinker 226 226*of* the political (the position of Schmidt, for example) who situates himself above the mêlée and climbs back to this side of the political to delimit its foundation, its *principles*. Not only does Heidegger refuse to allow himself to consider the principle according to the consequences, he renounces establishing a principle. And he does so precisely because the principle is not a principle properly speaking, not original, but is already nothing but a consequence, a modern derivative.[1] A principle is what governs because it comes first: it is a translation of the Greek *arche*. A good prince must govern according to good principles, by which we understand principles that are philosophically proven. And that is why for Plato there are no good rulers except philosophers. But what if the principle of the political is erroneous as such? What if it is not the political (especially as State) that is at the *point of departure* of the *polis*, but, inversely, the *polis* that is at the point of departure of all politics? The *polis* is not and cannot itself ever be a principle, at least not in the sense of an indisputable principle that is sure and certain, *beyond question*. This explains as well that Heidegger, when he undertakes a dialogue with the Greeks on the essence of the *polis*, does not do so in the first place with the philosophers who wrote "Politics" (Plato, Aristotle), but with the poets that these same philosophers had excluded from the *polis* and, above all, with Sophocles. If *Antigone* is in question, it is without doubt for having given rise to the most radical philosophical interpretation, that of Hegel. But the singularity of Heidegger's questioning lies in that he does not at all situate himself on the same level as Hegel. The horizon is not the State, not even self-consciousness. *Antigone* does not come into question except through a very particular view of a dialogue with the Greeks in which it is the essence itself of "occidental destiny" that is in question and whose initiator is himself a very singular poet, the "poet of the poet": Hölderlin.[2]

Man is *essentially* political. Evidently, everything depends upon what we thus *call* and what is included in—and thus excluded from—the definition of the political. The Greeks, inventors, among others, of "democracy," excluded from the lot slaves, women, and even barbarians. The *polis* is, first of all, a belonging to the place proper. That is why banishment is a punishment worse than death; it deprives "man" of the place of Being. For us Moderns, that is to say, for a subject that thinks itself at the origin of itself, as at home (in itself) beforehand, the question of place makes practically no sense. On the spatial model, place is identified exactly with contingent exteriority. Above all, the subject determines all being, here or there, as self-consciousness, so that the here itself no longer refers to the presence or absence of the gods (of the Others) but gives itself as the immediacy of self-presence.

Heidegger never pretended to subtract the adjective "political" from the subject "man." On the contrary, he clearly affirms that *everything* must be political *for this subject*, but only if we consider it as being certain and resting upon an unshakable foundation that is nothing other than "man," *ego*, and / or the State (society). Put differently, this determination is valid only for the modern subject (itself a redundancy: there is no subject but the modern one). In this historial determination, there is no domain of reality that could be subtracted from this imperialism of the all-political, but also from the all-subject, where the essence of "political" totalitarianism originates. Heidegger goes so far as to give to the totalitarian the sense of the unique path possible for the "fulfillment of metaphysics," which corresponds to the "perfection of Technique."

> The fundamental modern form in which the specifically modern human self-consciousness organizes every being, all while relating it to itself [that is, self-consciousness], is the State. That is why the "political" becomes the normative self-certitude of historical consciousness. The political determines itself from History conceived according to consciousness, that is, History "technically" proven. The "political" is the fulfillment of History. Because thus the political is the fundamental technico-historical certitude of all acting, the "political" will be characterized by the unconditional putting out-of-question (*Fraglosigkeit*) of itself. The unquestionability of the "political" and its totality belong together. The foundation of this conjunction and its terms do not rest, however, as one naively believes, on the accidental arbitrariness of dictators, but founds itself in the metaphysical essence of modern reality in general [GA53 117–18].

All this development to end up at what? To explain or even justify modern totalitarianism straight out? It is rather to found not "the accidental arbitrariness of dictators" (a significant plural) but the very principle of dictatorship in "the metaphysical essence of modern reality"! To put this differently by retranslating concretely, if there were Hitlers or Stalins, are Descartes and his project of unconditional "certitude" at fault? When all is said and done, it is the connection itself, the order (in the sense of the chain of reasons but also of what orders, plans, and dictates its "reason") that would have to be questioned, even though it has sheltered itself from all questionability in self-certainty. It is to an *interpretation* of modern reality, however, that Heidegger in the final instance committed himself. He denounces the ignorance of those who did not have this "view into what is" and who attribute to abnormal and even pathological individualities what falls within the jurisdiction of the norm par excellence, even though it be in itself an enormity of the result of a radical wandering [*errance*] (of the forgetting of Being): the technicalization of all reality. Consequently, we can understand why he qualified National Socialism as the decisive encounter of modern man with planetary technology, and also how this explanation effaces the singularity of the Nazi "phenomenon" (anti-Semitism). For on the level of essence there is no essential difference between Nazism and Communism, or even democracy, to the extent that it too is modern and submits to the command of technology.

Against the modern model of the State, it would be necessary to erect the more "authentic" model of the Greek *polis*. We could interpret Heidegger's gesture in this way and, once again, would follow the wrong path, not only because he nowhere proposes to return to the Greeks, but also because the *polis* is anything but a model (which it never was, except from the modern point of view, from Rousseau to Hegel). It is not a model because it is highly questionable, and that for the Greeks themselves: the "worthy-of-question" par excellence, in contrast to modern politics, which shelters itself from every question in its principle of unconditional self-certainty. But if the *polis* is in no way *primarily* political, and if, moreover, there is nothing that could be removed from the political, what can we still say of the *polis*? Can we say that it is not a being and thus that it is a nothingness—a *utopia*? The projects for an ideal *polis* in Plato testify to the fact that, since the Greeks, the *polis* was already seen as such a utopia. But we can also think in a fundamentally Greek way that the *polis* announces the place of what is not a being without being pure nothingness: Being. It would be tempting to see it thus and follow similar disjunctions, at least rhetorically, in Heidegger: the essence of the technical is in no way technical; similarly, the essence of the political (the *polis*) is in no way political. The whole question remains in knowing if such a passage to the essence is possible, or if it does not content itself with repeating the metaphysical leap from the ontic to the ontological, from consequence to principle.

In order to accomplish the *retrait*[3] from the political to the *polis*, the recourse to an essence or a foundation (thus to all *founding* [*fondation*] by the originary, even "Being") must be avoided. This is what Heidegger will have understood (too late, of course) and it is why the look he casts upon *Antigone* in 1943 is fundamentally different from the one he cast in 1935. It is a *retracted* look, as though facing the horror of an error. How could he have identified the splendor of Being with what took place and for which Heidegger will have but a single word: *Unheil.* From now on, it is no longer a question of aligning "thinkers" (or "poets") and "creators of State" on the same side. But most of all, heroism has entirely changed meaning, if not camp. Before, the founders (including those of State: Hitler, for example) were called *apolis*, "without city (*Stadt*) and without place (*Stätte*), solitary (*Ein-same*), *Unheimliche*, trapped in the middle of nowhere, and by the same token, without status or borders, with neither hearth nor home," because *as creators* they first of all have to ground (*gründen*) all that. At present, it is rather Antigone (she who has no place, is *apolis*, and who, in the imagination of all of occidental history, has always symbolized the resistance to the arbitrariness of the reason of the State) who is perceived as the "witness of Being" and, as such, as the exemplarity par excellence of Greek "man": the most *Unheimliche*. This exemplarity is itself exemplary, that is, without example, absolutely inimitable, an exception literally speaking. It is what is withdrawn, subtracted from every law of figuration, from fictioning. Antigone prohibits all "fiction of the political."

This is no longer a foundation, *not even a poetic foundation* as Heidegger still conceived of it in his 1934 course on Hölderlin, because, especially as hearth, home, and dwelling, how could the "place" (since it is as "place" that *polis* must be translated) be founded, and how could it give place to a foundation? It is this failure (of refoundation) that carries the *re-trait* [retreat], here marked with a hyphen [*trait d'union*] because it is not simply a prudent withdrawal (not at all: it is difficult to reproach Heidegger for having been timid, he who will identify himself almost entirely with the supreme audacity of Antigone) but first of all a step upstream toward what conceals sense from (and thus gives it to) the political as such: *the* retrait *of the place*-polis. Heidegger's retreat comes from the *re-trait* of the *polis*, which can never establish itself as the foundation of political space. Every fundamental position is exposed to being but a wandering, all the more since it wishes it were solid and certain of itself and of its "truth."

> The *polis* is and remains the properly worthy-of-question (*Fragwürdige*), in the strict sense of the word, not simply what can be questioned (*Fragliche*) in any question or debate (*Frage*), but what relates to the highest and broadest contemplation. That it be thus is still evident from the late considerations that have been transmitted to us in the works of Plato and Aristotle. Amongst other things, Plato says this in his *Politeia* (book V, 473ff.): "If either the philosophers do not become masters in the *polis* or the so-called current rulers and holders of power do not 'philosophize' in an authentic and appropriate way—there will be no end to the disaster (*Unheil*) for the *polis*" [GA53 105].

Unheil: the word is strong and *could* well be the way Heidegger "salutes" the current "so-called rulers and governors." At least, we could read it this way, if we wished, to save Heidegger from the very disaster that he had saluted ten years earlier with a *Heil*. . . .

For the Moderns, this view of Plato will appear perfectly "Platonic," Heidegger continues. Everyone knows that philosophers glide in the clouds and that they lack all practical sense, all "contact with reality." How could they manage affairs of State? But it is not about that, since the *polis* is not the State, especially the modern State, and since the "affairs" are not the essential part of the State. But neither does Plato say that political leaders should occupy themselves with philosophy, "as if it were a matter of the type of a collection of beetles." It is not a matter of putting politicians *in the place of* [*au lieu de*] philosophers (or inversely), but of arriving *at the place of Being*. "According to another of Plato's statements, philosophers confine themselves to the brilliance and light of Being, and that is why it is so difficult for the ordinary eye to discern whether or not someone is a philosopher" (GA53 106). Being does not have a place any more than the *polis* does, which is "founded on the truth and essence of Being." We do not find it anywhere, like a thing that is or is not in its place. It is not a current affair, not an affair at all. It has nothing to do with that, nothing other than to dwell there, in its brilliance, sometimes, like Antigone, to the point of losing sight and life. That Heidegger also had taken Nonbeing (*Unheil*) for—in the place of—Being is certainly not pardonable, but bears witness that such a dwelling remains the most exposed to aberration and to loss. Heraclitus could still retire in the inviolate sanctuary of the inviolable Artemis, the goddess "of *physis*," Heidegger says. But today, at present, in this time of "distress" when there is no Present—no place in the wandering of the planet (earth) is inviolate or inviolable. A guest, the most "unheimlich" of all, the most disturbing because the most familiar (and the *least known*), is standing at the door: nihilism. He is already there; he has entered even before having knocked. He is everywhere and nowhere in particular because he is already confused with Being, because he takes the place of it, in the *form* of the "human." Everywhere "at home" (*pantoporos*), he nonetheless remains foreign to everyone, the *other*, he who must be excluded to reestablish the purity of a purely fantasized home / *Heim*. We could call him the "hôtre" (host, haunting, other), he who *haunts* the dwelling, that guest you never wanted to accommodate, who snuck in, fraudulently, by the same means that we believe ourselves sheltered "at home," the *only* master, "ourselves" and *no other*. Making the other nothing, we by the same token engender in our interior our other, our "interior enemy," Hegel would say (we will return to that), the Trojan horse that will have surrounded the place *beforehand* by the very fact that it is thanks to its exclusion, its annihilation, that, like a fantom, it can cross the most closed off walls of an intimate interior or of a nation (and even a "Europe") that we believe to be very much our own, cemented, like before, by a Wall.

The *polis* is first of all what *takes the place* of Being, what institutes itself as the place of Being in place and in lieu of Being—just exactly as *Da-sein* does. That means, first of all, that it is the first place in which Being shows itself under the figure of the difference, of the conflict (*Streit, eris*), between beings and non-beings, appearing and appearance, the true and the false, etcetera. The *polis* is not "worthy-of-question" for the pleasure of the question but because it opens the space of questioning, above all of this question: *Who are we?* Traitors or heroes, free beings or slaves, men or gods . . . ? Each time, a difference [*differend*] installs itself in the very place of Being, already opens itself in accordance with the *polis*. This is also why tragedy is the very display of "political" Being. Not because there would be "exceptional" destinies, but because already, beforehand, *Dasein*—or the exposure *to* Being (to the risk of Being: τόλμα)—is the exception to everything that is. Only *Dasein* can be what it is not and vice versa. It has no definition, no preassigned law. It must assign *itself*—in the name of Being, which it is not but which it takes the place of. Polarity is thus the trait or the "cut" (*Aufriss*) of all *polis* as such:

> Perhaps the *polis* is the place and the domain around which all that is worthy-of-question and strange (*Unheimliche*) in a worthy sense turns. The *polis* is πόλος, that is, the pole, the vertebra in and around which everything turns itself. In both words (*polis* and *polos*) *the* essential thing that the verb *pelein* says, in the second line of the chorus, finds itself named: the constant and change. The essential "polarity" of the *polis* concerns the being in entirety. The polar addresses the being in that it turns and concerns the being as manifest. Man in a worthy sense is referred to this pole, inasmuch as man, understanding Being, stands in the middle of beings and here each time necessarily takes a stand (*Stand*) with its circum-stances (*Zuständen und Umständen*). "Status" is the "State." Thus *polis* signifies as much as "State." We are thus already on a false path again when thinking *polis* as State, we knowingly or thoughtlessly confine ourselves to modern representations of the State [GA53 100].

Now, why does the discussion surrounding the "original" meaning of the *polis* intervene in the middle part of the course on "The Ister"? Let us recall the structure of the course: 1. The poetic language of the essence of rivers—the hymn "The Ister." 2. The Greek interpretation of man in Sophocles' *Antigone*. 3. Hölderlin's poetic language: the essence of the poet as demi-god. There is no obvious justification for the excursus on *Antigone*, and we could reconnect the first and third parts of the course without harming the interpretation of the poem, since the "essence of the river" and the "essence of the poet" are the Same (by means of the medium of the demi-god). If not direct, the connection is at least necessary, for *Dasein* is the being-between, the place-between, and as such is the very site of connection. At the same time, this place-between [*mi-lieu*], far from being a just milieu or a "measure" (Protagoras), is defined essentially as excess, immoderation, and thus asks the question of what the milieu, Being as hearth (as the second part puts it), is. The "between," as ex-istence, is ecstatic. From the first part of the course on it is a question of the place, but of the place as incapable of being situated in a space. It is not a fixed point but always a movement toward . . . : a direction [*sens*], an orientation. The river is the *Ortschaft der Wanderschaft und Wanderschaft der Ortschaft*, a chiasmus characteristic of the thinking of the Turn. It is the locality of mobility and the mobility of locality. About the form of such a phrase, Heidegger writes that the appearance of a pure play of language is not easily overcome. The words must be understood beyond the immediate, that is, logical, meaning of the type of pronouncement "x is y." Is it a question of speculative phrases (of the type "God is Being")? For that, there would have to be a subject. But if one term is reflected in the other, it is because their identity does not preexist the reflection of the one in the other. This is not even a reflection, since nothing is sent back. We cannot make an image of this for ourselves, because in passing from one term to the other the scene changes, making this a metaphor that is even more radical than a literary metaphor that supposes a stable point of comparison to which we return to relate one term to the other. This dis-placement (μεταφορά) does not spare the place itself, the place in which it intervenes. It is the displacement of displacement, the voyage of voyages, and thus the locality of the locale. Or better, none of these take place unless they are said at the same time, unless saying travels with he who speaks. This is what makes language the dwelling of Being, a nomadic dwelling that does not wander aimlessly, for the nomad is always governed by a *nomos*. This *economadism* is itself double, economy and nomadism. On the one hand, the dwelling comes from the spacing that bestows locality, and thus the river determines the here (*Dort*) and the there (*Da*) through which a coming-to-dwell is possible and begins. "The river not only grants the place in the sense of a simple position (*Platzes*) that living men occupy. The river itself retains the place. The river itself inhabits." It inhabits in the sense that it gives place, *bewohnt*, which is to be understood as *be-wohnt*, the capacity to inhabit (just as the thing, *das Ding* is described as *be-dingen*, the capacity to thing, be-thing, "condition"). This is a gift, a dowry: the river *behütet* this habitation, safeguards it precisely in giving place to an inhabiting (and "it is in huts that man lives . . . ").

But on the other hand, no place is fixed forever. "The essence of the place in which the coming-to-dwell finds its beginning and its access is that it travels. The essence of this voyage is the river. The place is here and there, not by chance, but according to the hidden law of a coming-and-going (*Wanderung*: migration)." But the here and the there are not points in a given space succeeding each other in different ways. There is no succession but an accession that is always also a de-cession. The preceding place is always kept or conserved in the following, to be sure, but, on the one hand, this apparent succession follows no necessary order (history is an unregulated succession), and, on the other, there is no result, no final point that totalizes the others. For the place always changes direction / meaning [*sens*] in that it "is" or gives direction / meaning: orientation. To be sure, the history of meaning always begins with the Orient (if not, where would the orientation be?), Indus, in Hölderlin's poem: from East to West, from the *Morgenland* (the "country of the morning," the Orient) to the *Abend-land* (the "country of the evening," the Occident). Nonetheless, a place-between must be introduced between East and West, and this will be Greece, turned in both directions, *bi-polar*. This also explains the median position in this course. However, this median is itself the place of the Turning in direction / meaning, the trope par excellence and thus the only beginning. (We see clearly here in what way Heidegger distances himself from Hegel, who saw in Greece the moment of "infancy," of abstract immediacy, to be passed over.) The crucial point is that the Ister (a Greek name; the archaic form for the Danube) runs against the current:

> But it seems to me to nearly
> Run backwards and
> I believed it must have come
> From the East.
>
> Der scheinet aber fast
> Rükwärts zu gehen und
> Ich mein, er müsse kommen
> Von Osten.
>
> *Sämtliche Werke* 2:1 191

At its source, the Ister seems to return upon its steps or to linger; it dwells. Then, after a bend, it withdraws and goes toward the East. But the essential point is this hesitant beginning. It makes the orientation appear other. The Occident is this very disorientation of meaning / direction [*sens*]. Or rather, the change in meaning / direction is essential to the Occident, so that meaning / direction appears only as this turning of meaning / direction upon itself. Its meaning / direction is the turning of meaning / direction. The same obsession governs modernity from the Copernican / Kantian revolution to the Heideggerian *Kehre*, passing by way of Hölderlin's "return to the homeland" and even the Nietzschean inversion of values. Even if it means changing the political translation of this obsession, we can say that Heidegger inscribes himself (despite himself, it is true) in this tradition of the rupture. Meaning / direction appears in and as turning, but this turning is itself one more turn, a re-turn in two senses, alteration and iteration— itin-erratic, again. This is the return to a beginning necessarily lost in that there is no beginning to the quest for meaning / direction, for the Occident, except in the experience of the loss of meaning /

direction. But by the same token this is also the (re)invention of this origin by means of a supplement of the origin, a hyperbole in the movement of radicalization.

To gain access to the *polis* as that locality that is "worthy-of-question" is just as much to gain access to the "poetic" inhabiting Hölderlin would open. Just as the community offers itself only as inoperative, out of order, so the poetic foundation of place will in no way be a production of the idea according to a hierarchizing principle. This will rather be an exposition at the limits of the unfoundable, a going to the foreign that alone makes the path a becoming-"native." But what is the foreign here? It is not, according to the evidence, *just any* foreign that could lead us there. "The foreign related to the return that is but one with it is the provenance of the return, the initial welcoming-coming of the proper and of the native. This foreign to the historial humanity of the Germans is Greece, for Hölderlin" (GA53 67). This return is not simply a loop that returns to the same in passing through the other. For this other is precisely nothing other than the "source" of the same, and that is what must be appropriated for the same to *become* properly the same. There is indeed a turn or a turning, but it does not turn *backwards*, precisely because what we are to turn ourselves toward does not *re-*present itself. It has not moved behind, but, in a sense, "in front" of us; it remains waiting for its own beginning. It is the welcoming in everything that demands appropriation because it is provenance (*Herkunft*) as promise (and promised land). The relation between the proper and the foreign is in no way simple or even dialectical. "The ordeal of the foreign" is not only a voyage (*Wanderschaft*) in a foreign and distant land, preparing for the return and thus appropriation. It is not a question of an indispensable education in life experiences in the mode of the *Bildungsroman*, but of the very experience of the proper, which is not completed upon the return but *starts* in the foreign, a beginning that is itself already and only appropriation. In the beginning, there is the foreign as this provenance of welcoming. Experience is this and nothing else: a going to the source, toward pro-venance, that is, the foreign. There is no return as *telos*; there is nothing but the turning that makes the experience of the foreign a remote source. Such is the "free use" of the proper that Hölderlin says is the most difficult to learn: *in the beginning, there is nothing but the Greek.* But the "Greek" is properly Greek only when it is shown as the *other pole.*

Wir lernen nichts schwerer als das Nationelle frei gebrauchen ("We learn nothing more difficult than freely to use the *Nationelle*") (*Sämtliche Werke* 6:1 425). "*Das Nationelle*" is a foreign word, even in German. It is not even certain that it exists. To be sure, "national" makes sense, but we must realize that in this first year of the nineteenth century, the nation is a new idea in Europe, and especially in Germany, where nothing corresponding to a national, united State exists, be this State monarchical or a Republic, one and indivisible. It is only as a consequence of the French invasion and in reaction against Napoleonic oppression that the concept of the "German nation" arises, notably in Fichte's famous *Addresses to the German Nation* (1809). Oddly, even though it is in reaction to a foreign invasion that German national sentiment is born, and even though the idea of the nation came directly from the French Revolution, the Revolution is given as an ideal of universal liberation. But this is indeed the history: it is made of appropriations (and of misappropriations) of foreign elements; it is an (and perhaps the) experience in which the proper always comes from the other, but also alienates itself in use.

To attempt to grasp what Hölderlin "meant" by *Nationelle* (and thus the "proper"), we must see what the word relates to, what other word it forms a couple with as its "foreign." This other is precisely what Heidegger would have named "Spirit": "culture," in opposition to "nature." Or rather, since "culture" is a Latin word that partakes of the bucolic and religious, the other of *Nationelle* is *Bildung*, what Heidegger evokes in his *Schelling* as the condition of the German "nation." Passing from "culture" to *Bildung*, we pass from one culture to another, if I can put it thus. But while a foreign language can be learned, one's "native" language cannot: it is given. The native language must be taken just the same, so that it quickly becomes apparent that the difference between the foreign and the proper, as soon as it is a question of language, as we have seen, is more than a matter of translation, is infinitely fragile and perhaps even indeterminable as such. But *Nationelle* indicates the proper in a determinate aspect, that of the "nation" or of a people. In this regard, it is a question of "provenance," of history, if you please, but a unique history. To put it bluntly, it is a question of "destiny," that is, of the suitability to provenance. In this history, "we" (we "Germans," Holderlin would say) must learn the proper, must learn to appropriate our provenance (Greece) for ourselves. I will not enter further into this extremely complicated relation designated under the name "return to the homeland," a relation that in many ways marks a stage that has been "passed over" in Hölderlin's progression. We would, in effect, have to untangle a tight interlacing of conceptual relations (and yet is it a matter of concepts?) forming a chiasmus, an asymmetrical one, moreover. Before all else, we would have to question the identity not only of these (given? forged?) "terms," but of the addressees. To put it bluntly, about which Greeks are we talking? Is there a Greek unity other than that of the Greek language? And as for the Germans, whose entire history is precisely a problem of identification, can we forget that in Hölderlin's eyes they did not exist, or that, inversely, those who "really" existed had nothing to do with the poet? Can we forget this statement from the letter written to Böhlendorf just before Hölderlin emigrated to France: "But it is at the price of bitter tears that I have resolved to leave my fatherland again now, perhaps forever. For what do I have in the world that is more dear to me? But they have no use for me" (*Sämtliche Werke* 6:1 427–28).

"They have no use for me" is the English translation of a German expression that in the first place speaks of usage or of employment, *brauchen*: Hölderlin is out of work because there is no need of poets. And there is no need of them because, since Plato, poets are perfectly useless; they are useless mouths because, excluded from the city, they have been reduced to silence, because the "nation" functions differently, according to another *poiesis*, because they believe they do not need to learn the proper, since it is given. But precisely because it is given, the proper is forgotten. It is a law of culture, Hölderlin says, that "with cultural progress, what is properly *Nationelle* will always have the least privilege" (*Sämtliche Werke* 6:1 426). To translate this better: culture's original trait, that one that at first comes as being ahead (principle), will become blurred, will retreat into a *retrait*. For with culture, what occupies the foreground is precisely what is put on stage or given form, fictioned. Form has features and draws everything toward itself, rejecting everything else in the shadows, the unformed. But everything else, the remainder, is precisely the given. Thus the foreign element, which must be learned, acquires a decisive (formative) hold over everything, quite simply because it is what gives form. For example, rational logical clarity, conquered by Greek philosophy after a long struggle, henceforth passes for the prerogative of the Greeks, their privilege, their gift proper, thus covering up the origin, all that is obscure, "terrible" (δεινόν), chaotic, or Dionysian in them, and that it will take Nietzsche to uncover. This vision is too simplistic, though. The proper risks appearing as the dark side of the moon, a bit like the repressed unconscious. But the fact that it has been forgotten is perhaps not the effect of an unhappy fate. It may be that there is something proper about forgetting, because the very status of the given is never to be able to appear, or not "as such," in the light of its form. Thus, far from being lost "with the progress of culture," it would preserve itself all the more profoundly in the Being-in-disappearing [*disparêtre*] that would mark its proper being.

~

Let us now enter into the course of the explication of Antigone. If polarity is the proper meaning of the *polis*, then the place in which this polarity is displayed will not be the political but tragedy, Greek tragedy, of course. More precisely, the exemplary place of this display, for Heidegger, but already in a sense for Hegel, will be Sophocles' *Antigone*. Although here and there, and notably in *An Introduction to Metaphysics*, Heidegger is interested in the figure Oedipus (it is on this occasion that he gestures, with reservations as to its "subjectivism," toward Reinhardt's "recent" interpretation of *King Oedipus* as the "tragedy of appearance"), the text he will comment upon the most often is the famous first chorus of *Antigone*. To what extent Heidegger up until this point identified with the figure of Antigone, we can only sketch out here. Oddly, the figure of Oedipus, of the "blinding" constitutive of a *Dasein* who wants to know too much and who, according to the phrase Heidegger takes from Hölderlin, has "perhaps one eye too many," could have better described the thinker's political "error," *on the condition that he recognized it*. There is no indication that would allow us to determine if this is so. But Oedipus could not have described that error unless we once again agree to situate the "tragedy" of the thinker on a strictly political level. According to Heidegger, however, we must take everything the wrong way round, or at least on another level of precedence. It is thus that I read the "historical" preliminary to *Schellings Abhandlung über das Wesen des Menschlichen Freiheit* (Schelling's Treatise on the Essence of Human Freedom): "1809: Napoleon reigns, that is to say, in this case, oppresses and outrages Germany" (1). Should we read, "1936: Hitler reigns, that is to say, in this case, oppresses and outrages Germany"? This would be tempting, all the more so since if we identify Hitler with Napoleon, we could imagine Heidegger at Erfurt in the place of Goethe, but this time in order to respond firmly to the politician for whom tragedies "are things of the past" (was Napoleon a Hegelian?) and who declared that the only destiny in the present age of the world was the political: "No, spirit is destiny, and destiny is spirit. But the essence of spirit is liberty" (*Schelling* 2). It would even be tempting, here, to replace Napoleon by Hitler, in whom two years earlier Heidegger also saw the "soul of the world" riding under his windows, and in the place of the "Come to Paris . . . there the conception of the world is grander," from Napoleon to Goethe, put "Come to Berlin . . . " from Hitler to Heidegger. . . . We could then dream about this scene that did not take place, about a Heidegger telling Hitler, attentive, for once, his four truths. But, besides the fact that neither Hitler nor Napoleon could stand contradiction, this dream is not only utopian and even the u-topia properly speaking (a spiritual politics or an enlightened dictator: the ancient philosophic tradition goes back to Plato, the founder of utopia as the politics of the Idea), it is a (bad) staging. For it is in the very name of "Spirit" that three years earlier, in his Rector's Address, Heidegger called upon his dumbfounded auditors to see in the Führer (or at least the National Socialist "revolution") the "destiny" of the German people. Destiny and liberty are confused and cancel each other out in the identification with the Absolute by which the subject determines itself, above all in producing itself as self in a sublime staging. What, after all, does this call to liberty mean? Nothing other than the philosophical, dictatorial definition, dictating the law of the Subject as total "reality": "give yourself your own law."

And yet, it is to Antigone, the same woman who stands facing Creon, another "dictator" for whom destiny is politics, the same woman who has always figured the spirit "just beyond the law," to cite Derrida (*Politiques de l'Amitié*), that is, the spirit of a beyond-justice, in accordance with the disproportions of the law itself, that the thinker addresses himself in 1943. It is to Antigone that Heidegger addresses himself, then, to bring out the question of the "Greek interpretation of man" as the height of δεινόν. An entire chapter is given to the translation of the word, which Hölderlin rendered as *Ungeheure* (monstrous, unheard of), although Heidegger proposes *Unheimliche*, precisely because it maintains an intimate relation with *Heim, Heimisch, Heimat*, what I will call Dwelling (*Herd*: the home explicitly assimilated to Being). But it is first of all a matter of emphasizing a multiplicity of meanings, this multiplicity itself being run through by a duality, or rather by an intimate adversity that constitutes the heart or home of Being-man. In his recapitulation, Heidegger clearly distinguishes the polar nature of the *Unheimliche*: the Terrifying can be what provokes terror, but also what, even while it is giving birth to terror, holds back permanently, suspended before that which permits no approach and so displays the dwelling in the distance that is reserve, respect, modesty. It is, then, the "venerable" (*Ehrwürdige*). Tearifying, it tears out of the beaten paths (*aporos*, in the chorus) but by the same token tears toward the "secret" (*Ge-heimnis*): the sacred as prohibited, limit, and thus place. The *Unheimliche* already names a power, a reign (*walten*) in the double sense of a violence (of which *An Introduction to Metaphysics* speaks more precisely) and of creative power. Finally, it is the inhabitual; but it is always inhabitual in the double sense of what contradicts habit and the familiar, of the in-habitual (thus disquieting), and of what bestows an inhabiting because, reserved in everything, it is what is addressed or, better, con-*sent*ed upon ([*con-venu*]; *das in allem Geschickte*). This duality is the very heart of the Being of man in that it announces his belonging to Being, that is to say, to the Differend that is Being itself in that Being is no being and yet gives place for all beings. That is also why it is important to understand that the proper is in no way a being either, that if Antigone represents the highest degree of *Unheimlichkeit*, it is precisely for representing nothing at all, if I can say so.

> Antigone is herself the supreme audacity inside the domain of δεινόν. Being this audacity is her nature / essence (*Wesen*). She undertakes as the ground of Being ἀρχή τἀμήχανα—that against which nothing is to be done, since it appears in itself (no one knows from where). Antigone undertakes as the con-sented what is sent to her, from that which deploys itself (*west*) beyond the gods above (Zeus) and below (Dike). But that is not even the dead, though it is also not her blood ties binding her to her brother. What determines Antigone is that which first gives foundation and necessity to the privileges of the dead and of blood. What that is, Antigone, and that means the poet as well, leaves without name. Death and Being-man, Being-man and bodily life (blood) in each instance belong together [GA53 146–47].

I jumped directly to this passage because, like a radical short-circuit, it explodes all interpretation relating to Antigone, especially that of Hegel, who saw in the Creon / Antigone conflict the conflict between two determined spheres: the universal State and familial Religion, public and private, masculine and feminine. These two terms are themselves structured hierarchically, according to an evident metaphysical principle, so that the feminine is immediately devalued. Hegel speaks of a process of "undermining" (*sape*) or of alteration: "Womankind—the everlasting irony [in the life] of community—changes by intrigue the universal end of the government into a private end, transforms its universal activity into a work of a some particular individual, and perverts the universal property of the State into a possession and ornament for the Family" (Hegel 288). The irony of this text is that Antigone, acting for the good of the family (or of her blood—what ties her to her *brother*) against the universal laws of the State, is the *unheimlichste*. Her "family" is of an *other genre / gender*. Thus, the conflict is not between the familiar (Creon) and the inhabitual (Antigone), for as Hölderlin had already remarked, Creon also exceeds all measure. The conflict is between two equal but opposed "reigns," as Karl Reinhardt puts it,[4] two modes of *Unheimischsein*, of being displaced: Creon, lost in the "bustling activity without opening into Being," and Antigone, lost in the without-name, but truly on the path toward dwelling, in the "coming-to-dwell through the belonging to Being." We must understand this: to belong to Being is to belong to nothing, not even to the dead or the gods below.

But we should not go about our chores too quickly. If we can reject the "usual concepts and categories with which there has been such a struggle since the time of Hegel to penetrate to the essence of the *Antigone*," as Reinhardt writes (64), first of all because these concepts and categories are either too general or too narrow for this single tragedy, it is especially because they are falsely dialectical. They impose from the outside dualistic schemas that, in opposing one other, do nothing but neutralize one another. If, as Reinhardt again says, "the need to think dialectically has not gone completely without finding satisfaction in this play" (Reinhardt 65) (but also something upon which to break itself), it is because the two reigns in opposition "carry so far in altitude, as in depth, that their dispute touches upon difference itself," less the difference of the "virile" and the "feminine," or of the "general" and the "particular," than that of Being *itself* (as difference). It would actually be easy to show that, even in Hegel, the "virile" does not correspond with the "general" or that, inversely, the feminine is not necessarily identifiable with insurgent particularity. Refusing to make the distinction between her brother the friend and her brother the enemy, Antigone transcends "political" law, refuses it the status of *human* universality. For her, every brother is all (completely) brother, or man is not "political" in the first place. Inversely, in taking the first initiative of the act, in repeating it, even *overtly*, she manifests more "virility" than Creon, who, as Hölderlin puts it, does nothing but follow in her footsteps. We must avoid simplifying Hegel's interpretation excessively and thus must not forget that if femininity is the "irony" of the community, it is *created by that community*, which makes femininity its own "interior enemy." There is no community except on the basis of a sublation of the family. If only one of the brothers was honored, it is because he was the only one to identify himself with the *polis*, to have made of it his "family." Without the very value of "familiarity" (proximity, presence), no "political" legitimacy can be assured. We still see the demonstration of that fact (which we call the "nation"). There is no nation without this (natural? cultural?) value of "fraternity" that culminates in dying for one's country. (Is this the privilege of men?)

The crux of Heidegger's interpretation is situated in a very peculiar reading of the famous Creon / Antigone dialogue. He is concerned with determining the reasons that pushed Antigone to break Creon's edict, *that is to say*, the edict of the "community." I emphasize, for it is precisely this identification of the prince with the community that Antigone begins by denouncing. She contests the legitimacy of the Prince, of the *Führer*, one might say, even though Creon is in no way a tyrant in the modern sense. At the very most, he would be a dictator in the literal sense: decreeing the law, but in the name of what principle? After all, was Creon not right, from a strictly political point of view, not to treat the usurping brother in the same way as the legitimate brother, even if, "below," among the dead, perhaps ("who knows," says Antigone) another custom reigns, a custom that nevertheless does not have the force of law on earth? When it is a matter of justifying herself, of saying why she has dared break the "political" prohibition, Antigone calls upon other laws, to be sure, the famous "unwritten" laws of the gods. But there is something almost sacrilegious in calling them "unwritten," as Hölderlin remarks. It is to act in the place of the god in order to recognize "the Spirit of the Most-High" as "outside the statute"—outside the law (*gesetzlos*). This is an absolute excessiveness, for if there is no divine law, or at least if this law is not written (which plainly comes down to the same thing, at least from the human point of view: what is a law that would not be *textually* formulated?), it is not only to conspire against the divine itself (which cannot know itself, humanly speaking, except in "rigorous mediateness," Hölderlin recalls in translating a fragment by Pindar). It seems first of all to be to deprive oneself and one's action, even if pious, of all legitimacy. That is why, in the logic of such an excess, Heidegger (like Reinhardt) translates Antigone's response in verse 450 thus:

> It is not in effect Zeus who ordered me to do that, nor the Dike either, living with the gods below, who set that law among men; and your edict did not appear so strong to me that, from its human spirit, it could extend beyond the unwritten and steadfast words of the gods. Essentially of neither today nor yesterday, but from always, that is. And no one knows from where it has appeared [GA53 145].

When we read *that* (ταῦτα), we cannot help being a bit lost: to what can "that" refer? If "that," as it was traditionally read until Reinhardt (Hölderlin included), no longer designates Creon's edict, what is "that" which comes from neither the present nor the past, but "from always," although no one knows from where "that" appeared? Antigone transgresses the written laws, but in the name of other laws, laws *without name* that she essentially cannot cite. If for her Creon is committing an infraction, is guilty of having legislated where no man has the right to do so, where "the action of justice is extinguished," René Char would say, that is to say, where there is no longer any law at all, at least no written law, we can ask ourselves precisely *where* she situates herself. She does not have the law on her side either, neither that above nor that below, neither heavenly Zeus nor subterranean Dike. She no longer has anything, and yet it is from this nothing stronger than anything, from this "is," *west dies*, that translates the Greek ζῇ ταῦτα ("it lives"—what life?), that she knows herself to be strong, living, dwelling on earth. In face of and against everything, she lives from "that." She lives from it but she dies from it as well (or first of all?), immured living in a tomb without hymen.

What is that? Without name (at least without a written name), according to Heidegger it is the only "it is," the most intimate hearth and home of Being, but a home that burns and consumes every being who attempts to make his dwelling of it, a hearth and home that dies in dwelling [*de-meurt*]. Only in Being toward death do beings come to dwell. Inversely, human beings are not at home except when outside dwelling, like he who can be outside all beings and permanently there: "in" this dwelling of the proximity of death as the "coffin of nothing." This nothing is not pure nothingness. On the contrary, a polar adversity exists in the nothing. It depends upon the side of the differend on which one places oneself. From the point of view of what is, of beings or of the real, Being is nothing. But from the side (which is not a side and certainly not a "point of view") of Being, those who confine themselves to beings everywhere and always achieve nothing. This is the meaning of the *pantoporos aporos*, but also of the statement in the *Sophist* speaking of the aporia in which the philosopher facing the meaning of the word "Being" finds himself. The place of the human being is this non-place in the middle [*mi-lieu*] of all (beings): Being. But because this non-place cannot be occupied like an ordinary place, because one cannot simply pass by there as one passes through a city or a country, one cannot thus bypass it. It is "lost" and man, in turn, is under the orders of (left by and over from) Being. He forgets Being because he can understand it, but because he does not understand except with it, he can never do anything, unlike with any being. Because of this fact, man is in his very being a catastrophe, and even the unique catastrophe at the heart of all that is. Man is a catastrophe in the literal sense of the Greek καταστροφή: not a fall out of the original paradise, for the origin is precisely the catastrophe, the irruption of the Differend at the very heart of Being, commanding simultaneously its retreat and the deployment of historial powers, that is to say, of wandering. We should no longer assimilate it to a negativity, Heidegger continues, even negativity that is dialectically sublated or transfigured in the Nietzschean affirmation of the totality of the will. Rather, if we must give an example of this catastrophe at any price, we must give the example of Greek tragedy as that representation of polarities that cannot install itself at the center except in de-centering themselves and each other. Nothing acts in the sense of a subjectivity; there is nothing but *pathos*: the παθεῖν is, for Heidegger, "the fundamental trait of all doing and all acting: τό δρᾶμα, that which constitutes the 'dramatic,' the 'action' of Greek tragedy" (GA53 128). It is on this occasion that Heidegger challenges the modern interpretation of tragedy: the heroes or heroines of Greek tragedies (supposing that they could be qualified in this way) are neither martyrs nor exceptional characters, pathological geniuses. The tragic must not measure itself except against the truth of Being and the simplicity in which it appears. "That is why almost nothing happens in Greek tragedy. It begins with the decline" (GA53 128). What declines the decline is "destiny."

Heidegger cites a statement by Aeschylus about destiny, which is also the central figure of tragedy in Hegel, a figure without face and that swallows up all faces and figures by the fact that they posit themselves, oppose and expose themselves, to perish one at the hands of the other or even at their own hands. It is not without importance that this statement be cited in the political "profession of faith" that is the "Self-Affirmation of the German University." For from the beginning it relativizes and makes fragile everything that this Address affirms, and affirms in the sense of a "self"-affirmation. Aeschylus' statement colors the entire *Rectorship Address* with a properly tragic tonality, as though Heidegger had known in advance that his taking a stand was doomed to failure and even disaster. Prometheus, that is to say, the mythic inventor of philosophy, of that knowledge that must come *before* everything as the original knowledge of Being, of statute and of Law, recognizes nonetheless that "knowledge has considerably less force than necessity," which alone has the force of law. Thus, tragedy not only precedes philosophy, which according to its proper concept and destination must nonetheless precede everything, but marks it like a branding iron. Not only every work, be it a work of art or of political institutions (this confusion can be fatal), cannot but fail before destiny's "over powerfulness," but this destiny also defines philosophy at its birth: "all philosophy fails; that responds and belongs to its concept," Heidegger will repeat in his *Schelling* of 1936 (*Schelling* 118). If philosophy is tragic, this is still in a sense other than that in Nietzsche (where it is a matter of a Dionysian *affirmation*—a self-affirmation—up to the point of affirming this breaking and failure). Philosophy is tragic first of all because the destiny of Being *calls* its own retreat [*retrait*], forgetting and decline. That signifies that there is still something *above* Being which destines it to appear (and to dis-appear).

But what destines? That remains "without name," "no one knows from where" it has appeared, Antigone says. But, bowing to this Nomos, to this Edict without name, adjoining herself to it as to the address of Being, of its proper Being, παθεῖν το δεινόν, being put to the test of the without-name, Antigone is immediately "exposed beyond all human possibilities," not only in an implacable antagonism vis-à-vis the common place (the *polis*) but also in the position of her proper "self," which is lacking all content. She is *apolis*, not as *upsipolis*, like Creon, who dominates (or believes he dominates) within the common place. She is absolutely without a proper place. "*Sie ist unheimisch schlechthin*," and that, Heidegger specifies, has nothing to do with her actual death, for it is something at least, which thus reattaches her to Being and gives access to the home back to her.

The figure of Antigone, such as Heidegger describes it, is perhaps not "historically" exact (what would a historical exactitude mean here?), but it is gripping. She seems to draw herself up purely and simply, and to a certain degree resembles the rose of Silesius, which "flowers without reason, flowers because it flowers." She is, and this being explodes Being, if we can say so. She destroys all appearance, all positions, true or false, at the same time that in a dream marriage such "nuptial" destruction accomplishes the essence of Being (at least, of Greek Being): appearing as such, with nothing else that appears (or then, with the "completely other," the *daimon*), the phenomenon in a pure state. In the end, Antigone has absolutely no reason to have "taken the *deinon* upon herself." Neither the cult of the dead nor "family ties" clearly suffices, in Heidegger's eyes, to found such a gesture. On the contrary, Karl Reinhardt writes more scrupulously: "What carries the appearance, the choice, the death of Antigone, what embraces them and supports them like the most profound and universal ground from which only the particular can draw its growth is no less radical than what was, for Deianire, Ajax, Hercules, the source of their being. Only that, however, this rootedness, in the present case, is still more removed from our modernity. It is a matter of funerary cult and myths of the classical epoch" (Reinhardt 118). Heidegger, however, writes: "But because the exegetes of this tragedy incessantly try to find an explication for Antigone's deed in her speech, that is, a statement about the being who causes her act, we arrive at nothing but a return to a being, be this the ancient cult of the dead or blood ties. We misjudge that Antigone speaks of neither. We still cannot see that she absolutely does not speak of a being" (GA53 144). It is thus that, looking to return beyond the cult of the dead or blood ties, thus beyond beings and toward Being, Heidegger comes to say of the cult of the dead and blood ties that it is Being as "home" that gives these two ontically and historically determined forms "foundation and necessity": "The belonging, proper to man *and to him alone*, to death and to blood is itself only determined by the relation of man to Being itself" (GA53 147). (I emphasize because that means that animals have no relation to either death or family!) But in all rigor, this extreme ontologism remains a humanism inasmuch as the relation to Being is that of a privileged being (man) and can even justify an arche-nationalism with a superior force. Even if I don't like these terms, it is an anthropo-phallocentrism. In the same way, if what Reinhardt calls "the voice of nature that is most proper to man" (Reinhardt 115) speaks through Antigone, each of these words remains to be investigated: "voice," "nature," "the most proper," and of course "man," it being a matter of a female figure, though invented by a man and for men.

If the "blood" and the dead, that is to say, the "ground," are rooted in the relation of man to Being, they can by all rights appear as "sacred," *still more* so than they could in a simple mysticism of "*Blut und Boden*" which would only be biologically and politically, that is to say, ontically, legitimated. To put it otherwise, if for Heidegger the conflict at work in Sophocles' tragedy is not between State and religion but at the very heart of Being, "that which constitutes its most interior adversity"; if the tragic "counter-play" plays between Being-*unheimisch* in Creon's sense ("bustling activity without opening into Being") and the other Being-*unheimisch* in Antigone's sense (becoming *heimisch* "from the belonging to Being"), then the stakes are simply displaced by a degree, returning toward the originary. For despite everything it is difficult not to identify Heidegger's Antigone with a form of "religion," be it a religion without gods, without rites or dictates, a religion without religion that could be called "poetic," though in a sense that is absolutely unheard of: *unheimlich*.

§ 7 On the Origin (of Art)

Why reread *The Origin of the Work of Art*? Heidegger himself tried to do so. He felt the need to add, first, an epilogue ("partially written later") and then an addendum ("written in 1956," twenty years later). This was certainly no exception to a long practice of rewriting. The essay "What is Metaphysics?" would be coupled with an afterword and a preface and was thus framed by strict limits that aimed precisely at situating and even containing it. But here, something else is at stake, the "truth" of writing, we might say. At the end of the addendum, Heidegger tries to imagine the trouble his reader will have reading his text "from the inside": "It is inevitably troubling that the reader who comes to the essay from the outside imagines and interprets, at first and for a long time, what is in question precisely not from the silent region of the source of what is to be thought" (*Poetry* 87).[1] The reader is not in the first place at the origin, at the source. He remains on the outside. Does this "troublesome" situation nonetheless define only the reader? The "author" is also not without "difficulties," different difficulties, especially that of knowing to speak, "each step of the path, . . . just the language that is suitable" (*Poetry* 87).

Heidegger emphasizes that he is in no way responding to the "enigma" of art; he is not going to say what that might be. In a sense, he too is on the outside. Yet the question of the origin, like that of the essence, is heard beginning with the first words of the text: "The origin of a thing is the source of its essence / nature" (*Poetry* 17). Immediately, the origin conceals itself. It does so, on the one hand, in a double referral from the artist to the work, and vice versa, that amounts to a troubling reflection, and, on the other hand, in this third (and first) origin that would be art but that can by no means be shown as such. There is no essence of art. The empirical method, like the transcendental method, does nothing but build illusions. Nothing but the circle remains, a going from the one to the other, from the other to the one, without ever being able to find an exit. This is a circle that we must not hasten to call hermeneutic, if by that we believe we are able to designate an honorable exit. Something like an essential limit, and not merely a limit of thought, is touched upon in this essay. Heidegger remarks upon it twice, when in the Supplement he returns to put his finger on the wound. He cites himself:

> For this reason there is the note of caution . . . "In referring to this self-establishing of openness in the Open, thinking touches on a sphere that cannot yet be explicated here" [*Poetry* 86].

This reference in effect touches upon the limit-question, that of the essence of Being, or of Difference. Let us say it openly, although, perhaps, from the outside: to say that truth institutes itself is to efface difference and thus to accomplish the gesture proper of metaphysics. Put differently, from the inside, this is to say exactly the opposite: to show an essential finitude of Being, of the identity that can never establish itself but by the effect of a difference that is strictly unspeakable as such, and that, therefore, must not be expressed as "simple" (if ontological) difference. Which of the two meanings is the true one? I'm afraid it might be impossible to respond to this question. We enter into an essentially undecidable area.

My hypothesis is first of all on the exterior level, since I do not see how one could get into a text, if it even has an interior (but since there is no exterior either, no "outside-text," we will not be able to leave the circle). But my hypothesis also finds itself contradicted by a generous internal movement: from the moment a text allows what will have been said only in disguised words to be heard, even in the form of pure eventuality, it must be read in this way, if not saved. (A text can never be saved. Like the origin, it escapes. In the same way, it can never save anyone.)

According to this text, art is determined as the putting (in)to work(s) of truth, which is perhaps no big deal inasmuch as truth gives the horizon of all occidental art. Even post-modernity, or what calls itself thus, is held entirely within this circle, whether or not it is committed to a different concept of truth. Conceptual art, for example, which has nearly banished every notion of the work but still speaks the language of the work insofar as it always envisages its work in the frame of an installation, cannot but produce the truth of what it represents in its own manner (by bricolage or some other whim). It serves no purpose to evacuate metaphysics if only to continue living in its shadow (that is to say, its light, its idea, its concept, only barely weakened, sanded down, impoverished: a "white conceptology"). If the Heideggerian determination of art as the putting (in)to work(s) of truth, the installation of truth into a stela, as Lacoue-Labarthe would say, gives the truth of art and its concept, it is perhaps not a question of opposing it with another conception, another truth. We must think what makes this conception of the work (as the installation of truth) possible and what will remain inconceivable as such, inconceivable but not *sticto sensu* unthinkable. Or if this is unthinkable, it is because the thinkable is not of the order of what is called "thinking," of the identity of Being and of thought, of presence and re-presentation. The unthought toward which we will be called is not so much what has escaped thought, a sort of beyond that would be graspable (with what hands?). It is what escapes thought, like the Being it thinks, what does not demand that it be . . . thought, but what gives Being to be thought. And here, that means the work, which only "is" (gives itself) under the figure of art.

In one, and even *the*, thesis (of art as thesis) in the essay, Heidegger posits the fundamentally *historical* character of art. This can be understood as a reductive ontologization, which it is in part. But we must also see what, in this very violence, opens an abyss under us, we who are accustomed to believing in the eternity of the concepts of art, truth, etcetera. There is perhaps no art, at least no art in its truth and carrying the name of art, except in the Occident. Philosophy has taken as its point of departure, its undisputed principle, its need to be rooted in the essence of the human being. To say that the essence derives from a philosophical origin, that it is the work or fiction of philosophy, is to show the clearly circular definition of the origin as begging the question [*pétition de principe*]. The more a principle wants to be originary, the more it is, as such, (re)petition. To speak of the origin when considering art is already to make art speak the language of the fundamental, of essence, of truth; it is to ontologize. Heidegger knows this. That is why he is not concerned with the origin of art, but with the origin of the *work* of art. The question is displaced. Must art, or what is named art, always and everywhere be the origin of something like a work? At the same time, without a work, art is, rigorously speaking, nothing. It is around this nothing that "The Origin of the Work of Art" turns, around "poetics."

The first thing Heidegger establishes concerning the work is that it *means nothing*. It means nothing else, and in this sense it is not an allegory, a symbol, or a sign that would refer to an external signified. Of course, it is always possible to make what Heidegger says with the names *world* and *earth* conform to the old difference between signifier and signified, form and content. This explains why, as a preliminary measure, he takes so much care to deconstruct the three dominant interpretations of thingness. Considering art from the point of view of poetics falls within the same strategy of *Destruktion*. It is precisely because poetics breaks the old difference, which was always hierarchized on the side of the signified, into pieces that it is elevated to this distinguished role. It remains to be seen if poetics does not, despite everything, correspond to the old theological function of meaning, especially if the new difference reintroduces the old division under other names (earth / world) that are more difficult to situate. Let us remember that "poetics" is not a question of allegory or metaphor, as, for example, when we say we find such or such a monument "poetic."

Thus, we might ask if the temple itself says everything Heidegger makes it say. Does it say anything at all? How could a temple (or a painting) speak if speech is refused to stone? If the temple speaks, it is not for having a mouth (even an oracular one) and a tongue. Besides, that is not what speaking is: the voice of Being is voiceless. If the temple speaks, it is in the same sense that language speaks. It says, shows, or rather lets itself be (re)said. To speak is to show, and if the temple shows, it is because it *is* this showing without intermediaries such as words. It shows before all speech, in the Open of this essentially voiceless milieu that is the disclosure of Being, before language as a means of expression and communication of a sense (through words). Language is this as well, of course; it would be stupid to deny that. Otherwise, Heidegger would not have needed to communicate the other ("correct") conception of language. Yet that is but an expedient, a derived and secondary supplement. What is essential is that. . . . But having arrived at this point, we should be stopped short:

> Language is thus that saying in which a world arises for a people, and in which the earth is preserved as closed, and thus properly begins to open itself; this saying, in the preparation of the sayable, at the same time brings the unsayable as such to the world [*Poetry* 74].

What is unsayable is nonetheless said, and said in the formulation "the unsayable *as such*." For we read that the essence of language consists "properly" in that "it carries beings *as* beings into the open for the first time." There are no beings as beings except through language, and thus, as sayable. The *as* (*als* and not *wie*) is the mark proper of language, the mark by which language makes it possible to say anything at all. Without the *as*, there are quite simply no longer either beings or language; there is not even the unsayable. The operation of the *as*, which *Being and Time* named hermeneutic, is that of the putting (in)to work(s) (into the open): the manifestation of saying itself. It is clear that this manifestation must go before every given language, for example, must pass into the temple *as* temple. If not, this would not be a temple but merely a heap of rocks.[2] This would not even be the earth, because it cannot appear as earth, or what refuses to appear, unless it enters into the space of the *as*, and, for example (but is it one?), into the space of the nameable.

Earth is a strange name that reappears often in Heidegger's work with very different meanings according to the context. I will not examine this polysemy because it is possible that the question of meaning has no object here, at least in the sense of an ultimate signified. *Earth* is a pseudonym for the without-name. It corresponds neither to the material, nor the sensible, nor even the elementary (or the a-historial), and resists all appropriation by meaning, so that wanting to say *earth* as such is properly to disfigure it. This is nonetheless what happens in the project of the world. Earth appears, then, as an inappropriable remainder. Earth wants to say / means the unsayable, which precisely cannot and does not want to say (or be said), and which nonetheless will be said, but *as* unsayable, in and through the work. The entire nearly unbearable tension of this struggle between world and earth lies in the fact that the earth, or the unsayable, always has the final word. It will never say itself entirely; it will never come into the full presence of the work. This means that the work is doomed to ruin from the start, but also that this ruin is its very fulfillment, for only the ruins manifest the final word as such, give the final word to the unsayable in that it ends (in the work breaking itself, and thus in the poetic word that is cut off) by manifesting itself as unsayable and thus being—said. All this comes down to saying the same thing Trakl says: "One can never communicate." As a result of the poem's saying the unsayable without communicating it, but in showing it to the work as what ruins the work, this incommunicability, far from being a simple deficiency in speech, is quite simply speech's chance, its most proper possibility. The unsayable, as Heidegger puts it clearly, is—Nothing, or is the Origin itself as the leap into what comes before everything, including every work. What founds the work "of" the origin and makes it original is this leap into what comes before everything.

We imagine the conflict between world and earth like that between two unequal instances, abstract or symbolic actors, and even like mythological powers in a philosophical version of artistic genesis. There is genesis there, but certainly not in the sense of a creation of the world. This is so, first of all, because there is neither creation nor creator, and also because what we call the world does not correspond to what Heidegger understands as the world. The world is, here, the very project of the There. But there is indeed genesis, that of the truth. We often pass blindly over the sentence that tranquilly pronounces, "The truth as opening *becomes* in the project of poetry." Becoming is not opposed to Being. Where this project is problematic is, as always, in its origin. Where does it come from? The question is inadmissible: it would be to question the origin of the Origin. The Origin has no origin. The Origin with a capital must be distinguished from the origin without one. We thus remark the process of propriation that marks the entire operation of the leap into an original language, the leap from a common to a proper noun. But the effect (even the origin?) of this leap is always a counterjump from the proper to the common. This cannot but affect all of Heidegger's language with a dangerous ambiguity, and this is why the only origin of the work "of" the origin is the immemorial, which cannot have an origin. This amounts to saying that the historical is without origin and thus is immemorial. If it could put up with a logic that is itself posited as an Origin without origin, the reading of Heidegger would push to such logical non-sense. But as with the unsayable, we must reverse the perspective and see that if we can only speak of the immemorial, it is because history reigns *everywhere*, even where it appears to be dissolved in the mists of time. According to Heidegger, however, history appeared all of a sudden, in a moment he can even situate in history under the name of the Greek beginning. Therein lies Heidegger's logocentrism. There is a questionable bias, here, even if it be philosophically justifiable, philosophy being, according to its very name, this bias.

Every beginning is essentially illegitimate, and yet we must start somewhere. To begin is to appear. The beginning is this sudden, unjustifiable manifestation that cuts and strikes like a flash of lightning. In the case of Heidegger's reading of history, the flash of lightning that sends Being in its brightness is identified as the absolute beginning, at least the absolute beginning of history. But from where does it take its leave, from where does it depart, and from what does it separate? From the before, which then and only then appears "as" the before, but which is no more before than after, since it simply *is* not, is not a matter of Being as having entered into presence. We must therefore say that the immemorial is fundamentally just as unsayable as the unsayable, but that it is said as such by the springing up of the historial, since the immemorial is the very point of the springing up. But this springing up is a point that cannot be situated, and it is here that Heidegger fails his own thought. When it is a question of two instances like world and earth, then, we must realize that it is not only a combat between unequal forces but a struggle in which defeat is the only possible outcome, at least the only one in order for the combat itself to appear. Earth, or rather reserve (itself double), will always have the final word; but since it is the word given by the other, the world, the earth sees its victory stolen from it. By the very fact that it will always appear victorious, it will appear, and thus will be defeated. This is not a simple dialectic in which the loser wins, for this would always suppose that the goal is to win, to aim accurately, to say the truth. To be sure, the truth is what is at stake, but as the *opening* of the combat. As soon as the combat is open, the games are done, since the open says the coming of truth and thus equally of the world. The world reigns, and therein lies the entire tragedy. Let us take Oedipus; as soon as he attains royalty, he is lost. But is he not lost in advance? If not, the tragedy (the putting [in]to work, knowledge) of this loss would not take place. It is the tragedy that wants Oedipus's ruin and wants it not out of sadism or even for *catharsis*, but because it is his destiny to be ruined,[3] to break himself against destiny. His proper destiny is to be a tragedy. Short of not being, tragedy can do nothing against this being. But as soon as tragedy *is*, it is *finished*. That is precisely what Sophocles says in *Oedipus at Colonus*: not being (not sprung up into Being: μὴ φῦναι) prevails over logos. But as soon as tragedy appears, it returns as quickly as possible to non-being. We unjustly call that pessimism and even nihilism. It is simply the tragic manner of Being (in tragedy). It is certainly not the only manner of being, but that is all we can say about it. Were we to say that this is not the best way to be, we would be blind to what commands (and begins) this Being, blind to what Heidegger calls its *Entschlossenheit*. Being decides "itself" as such or such (a being); but first it decides itself absolutely, in the sense that it decides to be. In tragic being, that means signing its loss in advance, from the beginning, in truth, as departure (or bias: taking Being's side against non-Being, such is the risk).[4] This is why Heidegger says that Being is *Abschied*, that its departure is its catastrophe. *The history of Being is the catastrophe of the origin coming into its own.* This accession, this act of absolute birth, signs its death certificate in advance. The proper will enter into presence only under the figure of the Figure, and even if it calls for the status of the proper, in the statue of the god, "for example," this figure will never be able to efface its improper origin, its proper status as figure. To enter into presence will always be to enter into the space of (re)presentation. To take on a figure will be to enter into (dis)figuration. But does Heidegger not write exactly the opposite when he says that the statue of the god in the temple "is not a representation of the god" but a "work that lets the god himself come into presence, and . . . is therefore the god himself"?

In a sense, Heidegger is right to distance the ordinary meaning of representation, external mimesis, making according to a model. According to what model does the sculptor operate? He can only represent the god in terms of human beings, according to what is called the anthropomorphism of the Greeks, which is accompanied by a divinization of the human *morphe*. What Heidegger does not determine is the ontological status of this statue that "is" the god himself. We cannot understand this as a pure and simple identification. The god is not stone, and yet he "is" the statue in the sense of an analogy with Being itself. Just as the god manifests himself, makes a remarkable modality of presence (visibility, *eidos*) that has entered into presence, so too the statue brings the truth of appearing into presence. In its brilliance, what appears effaces all difference between the present and presence, what appears and appearing. The work as bringing into the open of presence "is" presence, difference that has been effaced because returned *into* the work. But the effacement of difference takes place in the name of an analogy with Being, a metaphoricity, a transfer about which Heidegger does not speak. The work has the divine quality of bringing the god into presence, because presence itself is quasi-divine, or better, because Aletheia is a goddess. All this does not appear until the reading of *Parmenides*, the 1942–43 course we have already encountered on the occasion of the discussion of the privileging of sight. But it is indeed the sense of presence, of Being *as* presence, that is at issue. Heidegger simultaneously rejects anthropomorphism and theomorphism because both presuppose a person or subject as their basis. Nonetheless, he avoids explaining the whole question of figure, of *Gestalt*, by immediately positing that figure as conceived or experienced from the moment (I hesitate to say, in the image) of its entrance into presence, that is to say, as Aletheia. Aletheia procures visibility, is the source of every image, but is not itself an image. Therein lies the whole aporia. How is it that Aletheia could be a goddess and that Parmenides spends a great deal of time describing her palace to us? Heidegger denies that it is a question of allegory there, alleging that if truth (nonconcealment) is a goddess, it is because if we change the accent in the Greek word *thea*, it can also mean pure view, as in "theory." However, if the statue of the god is the god, then in all rigor we must then say that it not only gives itself to be seen (as a particular image) but that it is this very glance. The fact of deliberately choosing the temple because it is made "in the image of nothing" clearly indicates the rejection of a mimesis from the pure (sacred) domain of the Open. The temple, as its Greek name indicates, is the cut, the enclosure that is sacred because it is withdrawn from the profane. At the same time, the paradox of this delimitation is that it exposes nothing but pure facade, a pure in front of, before. The behind, the inside, remains empty. There is nothing but the purely phenomenal, nothing that would be behind and of which it would be but the appearance or representation. There again, we must acknowledge that Heidegger is right. The temple represents nothing at all, no more so than does the statue (in the temple). But it represents in an other sense, in a sense we must call theatrical in the sense that the theater and theory are representations conceived of as putting into presence, that is to say, by the same token, stagings. *Lichtung* is the theater of Being, its scene, and thus implies staging—the works that (re-)present it. Otherwise, there is no possibility whatsoever of understanding Greek tragedy as the ne plus ultra of the putting (in)to work(s) of truth. Truth is this open scene and nothing else, the exposition that is also a deposition, a written deposition, truth being unable to present itself as such except, for example, in Parmenides' *Poem.* The "as such," which is the essence of presence and thus of sight, implies the gap of a double that precedes it. But the double also takes its place as the figure, the *persona*, the mask of this entity essentially without figure, without face, without presence, and that would be called Aletheia. Since Parmenides, the philosophical theater of concepts is announced as a staging that cannot figure the blinding whiteness of *eidos* except in contrast to shadows or simulacra, phantoms or ventriloquist sophists, because these are the only (technical) means of presenting what, according to the evidence, can never present itself in person, or rather what will present itself only in person, that is to say, in a mask. Aletheia becomes an allegory, a double of itself, inasmuch as it cannot present itself except in dividing itself, splitting itself into truth and appearance, presence and absence—the whole series of binary concepts. The paradox of this philosophical theater is that the blinding whiteness of truth immediately turns into the sepulchral whiteness of specters.

What Aletheia figures is nothing other than the myth of the truth of Being, of a pure phenomenon, of the Sacred as the other name for difference, difference appearing by suppression of all content, of everything we would call reality as opposed to appearance, the inside in relation to the outside. We must admit that this is neither a simple myth nor a simple metaphor, all the less so since the metaphor always has a metaphysical origin and is thus derivative in relation to this Origin at the origin of every figure or trope, but also every concept, beginning with that of metaphor. Like Aletheia, truth is essentially a, or rather *the*, myth. At the end of *Parmenides*, after having spoken of the essential difficulty of seeing the Open, of how we cannot see truth come but how that inability is the sign that it has already come (or that Being itself is already assigned to us) and "for this reason always withdraws itself again," Heidegger writes:

> ... *aletheia* is the looking of Being into the open that is lighted by itself as it itself, the open for the unconcealedness of all appearance. Could what has such an essence be a mere "concept"? The endeavor of our entire foregoing reflection has been nothing else than to bring us to a thoughtful experience of this astonishing question.
>
> *Aletheia* is *thea*, goddess—but indeed only for the Greeks and even then only for a few of their thinkers . . . [*Parm.* 162–63].

Occidental myth expresses the beginning, that is, the still concealed essence of the truth of Being. The word of occidental myth preserves the belonging of occidental humanity in the home region of the goddess Alètheia [GA54 240].

As long as it thinks of Being, that is to say, as long as it thinks, it is impossible for an Occidental humanity to "demyth" such a myth. This is the myth of the Origin itself. We cannot climb back above it except in passing beyond Being and thought. What such a step [*pas*] beyond would be clearly would make no [*pas*] sense, and thus could not be said. Thus an unbreakable limit would mark itself, but in the conditional. As the reader will now be able to see, the limit is the place proper to thought, that from which it begins to think, what gives thought its identity as the thought of identity, and, first of all, of the identity of Being and thought. From the beginning, identity, unity, and totality trace the contours, in the archetypal figure of the circle, of this "eucyclism" of *aletheia* that Parmenides' *Poem* describes. However, what this figure can never think is the *cut* that gives its birth, the alpha of its proper name; or, it only thinks this cutting in the form of an originary negativity, and even a Nothing. In the same way, the erection of the temple is always preceded by the cut in the earth, in the unsayable, a cut that implies that the sacred or the saved (*Heilig*) is never at the beginning but must always be reinstituted, cleaned of all blemish in a mimetic repetition (of the sacrifice, for instance). This cut, which opens the possibility of the proper and the sacred, of the property that by definition is always private, remains, however, unsayable *as such*. It is even unsayable as unsayable, because it precedes the "as such," making it simultaneously sayable and unsayable—as such.

Let us now read the following three passages:

... great art is never "contemporary" (*zeitgemässe*). Great art is art that carries its essence to complete fulfillment, that is to say, puts into its work the truth that must become the measure (*Mass*) for a time (*Zeit*). But the work cannot conform (*gemäss*) to the times. To be sure, such artistic products exist. But they have not leaped-ahead (*Vorsprung*) because they are without origin (*Ursprung*), but always nothing but an after-effect. In the wake of all essential art, there is always epigonal art, "after-art" (*Nachkunst*). This art has the same air about it as essential art, can even have more beautiful effects than it, and yet differs from essential art by a jump (*Sprung*)—and not merely a degree.

But where art is, truth takes place, History is. This is why we can also say the following: where there is prehistory, there is no art, but only pre-art (*Vorkunst*). This means that the products of prehistory have no need of remaining simple tools (*Werkzeuge*) or a simple product in current use made by means of these tools, a utensil (*Zeugwerk*). They might very well be this means-to-an-end we can classify neither as utensil nor as a work of art (*Kunstwerk*).

But the work of art never (re)presents anything. And that is so for the simple reason that it has nothing to (re)present, being itself what in the first place creates what enters into the open for the first time thanks to it.[5]

Nothing appears to connect these three excerpts to one other, in particular the third to the first two, at least not immediately. The first two, which are separated by a page, can be articulated around the question of "great" art, which each excerpt delimits in its own way: the first, by excluding epigonal or "after-art" (*Nach-kunst*), the other by excluding, in just as categorical a manner, "pre-art" (*Vorkunst*) from this same field, which is the only art to merit the proper name of art. "In *great* art—and it is with it alone that we are concerned—the artist remains indifferent in relation to the work, almost like a transitory passage (*Durchgang*) that destroys itself in the creation." If we take it literally, this declaration resembles a declaration of war. We can understand why Heidegger holds to eliminating the personality, the lived experience, of the artist from his meditation on the origin of the work of art. But we cannot at all see how it is possible purely and simply to erase such names as those of Rimbaud, Trakl, van Gogh, etcetera, as though they were pseudonyms. We can of course say that "lived experience (*Erlebnis*) is the element at the heart of which art is in the process of dying" (*Poetry* 79). This conjunction of what is lived and death seems to be nothing but a paradox, which is without doubt why Heidegger felt obliged to add: "It is true that it [art] dies so slowly that it takes several centuries in order to die" (*Poetry* 79). Heidegger seems to repeat Hegel's lesson in the *Lessons on the Aesthetic*, to which the third excerpt alludes, taking up, in order to contest, the word *darstellen*, to present or represent.

Questioning "great" art, the art of the origin, Heidegger cannot avoid the topos of the death of art. The art of the origin, "great" art, is Greek in its essence, that is, *as* art. The *Anfang*, the beginning, in the sense of the original jump (*Ur-sprung*) that jumps out in front of everything that is going to come, that precedes everything and thus already contains it, this Beginning takes place, Heidegger writes, "when beings in their totality and as such want to be carried into the open." That is to say, it takes place "for the first time in the Occident with the Greek world" (*Poetry* 76). There might perhaps be other beginnings elsewhere than in the Occident, but in the Occident there is no other beginning except Greece: "what will subsequently be called Being was then decisively put to work" (*Poetry* 77). Even if it is repeatable, the Greek beginning remains irrecuperable. It is irrecuperable in the sense of being the beginning itself, the *anfängliche Anfang*, an overdetermination that seeks to carry the Greek *Anfang* to the absolute summit. It is the beginning of the beginning (of Being, quite simply), and not the beginning of an epoch: epochs cannot take place unless the possibility of epochs has been opened as such in the first place. Before Greece, there is no history; there is simply prehistory, and thus we can say that there is no art either, on the condition that we think art (and its history) as opened by and in the open of Being. But what if art was not in the first instance, not originally, a question of Being? Would it be possible to think art without Being, as one could and even should (according to Heidegger himself) think God without Being? Perhaps not, at least not philosophically. For if everything that has been said of the Greek beginning can be upheld, it is only as this regards the birth of philosophy. But this birth is belated, even with the Greeks. By the same token, is it possible to tack the history of Being onto that of art in order to read the history of art according to that of Being?

The beginning is what is greatest, and the art of the origin is great art. The logic is extreme and disconcerting. How are we to speak of an absolute beginning or of an absolute greatness? Is there a beginning without precedent? And is greatness not a relative notion? What is the measure of the great (or of the sublime)? Let us linger a moment over this strange notion of the beginning. The work is the work "of" the Origin, not in the sense of creating it, but rather in the sense of issuing from it. There is no art except initial or original art. But as the origin of the work, the Origin must also withdraw into the work and thus escape it as Origin. The Origin must escape the work exactly as the work escapes its author. It remains ahead but is no longer confused with a primitive state or a golden age; it is mythic in the sense that the origin of language is mythic and yet never ceases to spring forth in every child's words. It is unlocatable and nonetheless as though on the edge of every utterance. If there is no origin of language (other than as unsayable, as cry or unarticulated chant), it is because language is itself the Origin. Language is even more originally the Origin when considered as the *Ur-sprache* of a people—poetry, if we remove from poetry every historical form and even the word *poetry* itself, which is inappropriate, if we recall that the initial Poem "comes from nothing," and yet never from nothingness (*Poetry* 76). This is yet another apparently gratuitous difference of pure terminology, a play on words that nevertheless shows language to be the (original?) place of difference. It is thus that we should understand the Origin: there is nothing similar to it, nothing comparable. It irrupts suddenly, immediately, then, but not in the Hegelian sense of the immediate that has not yet been mediated (negated). For Hegel, the beginning is already in the end and is surmounted by the end as result, while for Heidegger it is the beginning that already contains the end in itself. It does not contain the end in the sense of an inherent necessity (everything that is born must die), but because it has already projected the end and thus passed it over. The singularity of the beginning is that, although immediate, it does not conceal itself from mediation, since it authorizes and founds that mediation. Henceforth, what follows will not cease to be in relation with this beginning that nonetheless has already arrived ahead of it. Thus, the Greek beginning determines the entire history of philosophy, even when it takes a new departure (with the Cartesian *cogito*). Every sending remains determined by the sending itself, its initial cutting that suddenly cuts out the country or the space in which the parts will be played. We will be able to play different roles; the nature of the game is already inscribed from the beginning without our being able to return upon it. It is in this way that history is a "free succession." But as succession, it can never be free as regards the beginning itself. We end up with this double bind: the beginning is liberation, ungrasping, but what begins is under the hold of this un-holding, prisoner of this original liberty.

Ein Rätsel ist Reinentsprungenes, "An enigma is pure springing forth," says Hölderlin in "The Rhine" (*Sämtliche Werke* 2:1 143). Such is the enigma of the source that even in springing up it conceals itself in itself and withdraws in what springs from it. The Origin "is" this scission with the self, what I call the *departure from belonging* [*départenance*], which is to be thought as the simultaneity of belonging and its distancing or departure, as a farewell (*Ab-*

schied). Being cannot spring up except in splitting as difference (from beings). In his commentary on Hölderlin's line (GA39 235), Heidegger speaks of the suffering of Being as the irruption of a counterwill at the very heart of the Pure. The river that most purely springs forth wants to return to its source. It is this counterwill that makes a "destiny," a *pathos*, of the river. Thus, the origin is itself "pathetic" (or rather, tragic), witnessing a conflict at the very heart of Being, a conflict similar to the one reigning in art between earth and world. It is the work of art (and here, Hölderlin's hymn) that carries this conflict to its *summit*, though never to its resolution. The work makes the conflict in breaking off there, this break repeating sending and the cut it occasions. The work of the origin breaks, and this is why we cannot have a relation with it except in breaking ourselves upon it in turn, in having the experience of the beginning as unheard (of).

There is a duplicity in the Origin itself, thus justifying the Greek determination of art as mimesis. But this is an imitation that would in each instance be original. The origin can never be present to itself except in the mode of repetition. It must reject what it allows to spring forth, a rejection that in its turn springs back upon the result (the work). It is thus that the Greek beginning sprang back upon itself in engulfing itself in its own originality. But this collapse, this initial catastrophe, also sprang back on what follows (on "us") to the point that all originality cannot be determined except in relation to the Greek beginning. There is nothing original about the Greek origin, at least not in the modern sense of the origin as that which seeks to distinguish itself. On the contrary, far from wanting to singularize itself, the origin effaces itself in itself, for "to the essence of Being as such belongs the fundamental rejection (throwing back) that springs back from itself to itself. Being lets poetry spring forth in all liberty in order to find itself originally in poetry, and thus finds itself in poetry in reconcealing itself as secret" (GA39 237). The original work does not want to emerge from the source but to return to it. This is why we do not distinguish it immediately and do not find it except at the end, when we have stopped looking for a point from which it would emerge like a reef from the bottom of the ocean. This is also why Heidegger says that the true beginning remains withdrawn and takes on the appearance of a "falling back" (*Ruckfall*). To return to the source is not to return to something, and especially not to a past model. On the contrary, it is continually to confront the absence of models and precedents, to confront the without-origin and without-sense at the origin of presence itself. It is to face the original lack of a foundation, this founding lack that is the secret of the purely springing-forth. It is to leap, but with a bound that can support itself on nothing or that must leap beyond itself: no one can leap who has not already leapt in projecting the space he has to cross as already passed over. *The leap precedes itself, has already passed over itself.* And this, so that every leap will only be its own repetition, but the repetition of what has already withdrawn in projecting itself into the future. This projection, this throwing in front, such is the initial *Ent-wurf* of the poetic, throwing itself into its own abyss, not to fall into it, but to re-source itself there [*ressourcer*].

But must we not also recognize that for Heidegger the Greek beginning remains the only reference for, and even the model of, every beginning? In relation to the beginnings (medieval, modern) that follow, it in fact has the exclusive privilege of being "absolutely" original, the very privilege in which Being sends itself for the first time, even if this is also to send itself to its end. It is the beginning of the History of Being, and thus is the beginning of destination as such. This is what emerges clearly from the second excerpt at least: where there is as yet no history (and that means no history of Being), there is no art (no "great art") but only pre-art (or pre-history). If we replace "art" by "Greek art," we get the same, almost tautological, formula. Does Greek art therefore provide the measure of what is and is not (not yet, or no longer) art? That the art of prehistory not yet be art appears a questionable prejudgment. In what way is Lascaux not already all of art? But that pre-Greek or simply non-Greek art be nothing but a prehistory of art transgresses the limits of even the most extreme biases, of the spirit of the temple, all the more so since in prehistoric (or prehistorial?) art, the anonymity of the creator has never been so pronounced: one thinks of the megaliths or of the statues of Easter Island. But is this effacement of the artist not a characteristic of "great art" in Heidegger's very eyes? Another question then arises. If art properly speaking only appears with the beginning of History, and if this beginning is given in the Greek beginning, how is the immemorial dimension that makes the whole "originality" of the work of art to be preserved? If "truth is essentially terrestrial," it is truth that is played out in the conflict between the double reserve of the (non-historial) ground and the manifestation of the work, which always projects a world. But can we say that there is no world except the historial, and thus occidental, world? Is there no American Indian world, for example? Do "world" and "historial" necessarily form a pair, including in the "pair of shoes" that manifests the "world" of the peasant (who is closer to the earth than to history, even the "history of Being")? One final question: what are we to do with an art without works? Must we qualify it as "post-art" out of a concern for symmetry? Heidegger obviously does not speak of this, and I have mentioned elsewhere his (feigned or willed) ignorance when he admits to knowing neither where modern art places itself nor even if it is looking for a place.[6] That he took a painting by van Gogh as an example, moreover, that he spoke of the "path" of Cézanne or even ventured as far as Klee (though to say nothing of him, to mark the limits of thought), is hardly convincing. In effect, even Cézanne, in whom we can see the beginning of modern art, produced a Greek oeuvre simply in the sense that he produced an oeuvre. (Is "copy nature" not the repetition of the guiding doctrine of mimesis, that is, of *good* mimesis, that mimesis that does not make itself seen as imitation, that effaces every trace of imitation and installs "itself" in Being, just like nature?) Cézanne puts truth into works, he installs the being open of beings in the rigorously limited space of his canvas, and in that sense remains in the cut of Greek beginning. The same would no longer be true of Duchamp. An art that would no longer respond to the principle of exposition, an art neither determined nor determining (and that thus would give no "historial mission" for any people), would risk not being art, in Heidegger's eyes. What truth, what historial assignation emerge from the readymade? None whatsoever, and this would not be art.

In linking history, especially in its essential meaning, and art so closely, we obtain a strange delimitation of the history of art. It is neither progression nor evolution, but a sudden and unique leap which would correspond, in the end, to a kind of swallowing up in the moving sands of the without-history, of that ahistoriality that characterized America for Heidegger in 1943. A post-history of post-art (the post-modern?) would logically correspond to the prehistory of pre-art. Before the beginning, there is not nothing but a muddle that is the prisoner of "matter" (which cannot appear as such), and after the beginning there is not nothing either, only the unbridled reign of just anything at all. In both cases, there is no truth because there is no work. But can we even speak of a before and after? Does the beginning not abolish precisely the conception of time as a succession measured according to before and after? Can this temporality that *Being and Time* described as "vulgar" qualify the history of art in the historial and non-scientific sense of the word? This is still not the strangest part. If we formalized Heideggerian discourse, we would obtain the following sequence: pre-art / great art / post-art. But the second moment, the central moment between the before (past?) and the after (future?), is precisely not the moment of the present, since it designates the Greek beginning. We must recall the moment when Heidegger writes in black and white that works "are no longer what they were," that they are ruins or vestiges, "has-beens" (*"die Gewesenen"*). Even if we could encounter them now in some museum, for example, they have been torn from their world, itself irrevocably swallowed up. They are, at present, but traces, half-effaced signs, vestiges. They are this in a different way, of course: because their mode of presence has been extinguished irrevocably by the modern alteration from presence into representation. Transformed in advance into (thrown) objects, the works can no longer be present in the sense of Greek presence, regardless of whatever concern their curators may have for the preservation of these works. (It remains to be determined if this original presence is not already a myth, the myth of self-presenting presence.) Does that mean that Greek presence is the only authentic one or that there is only a Greek present, that at present, and compared to the splendor of the Greek beginning (of Being), "there is no Present" (Mallarmé)? Indeed, and that is confirmed if we examine the status of the third moment in the series. True, Heidegger does not speak of this moment, and I have had to reconstruct it to complete the logic of the sequence. But this silence in itself speaks clearly. Where are we placed? And do we even take place? (As regards his own contemporaries, Mallarmé was not certain of this.) Do we have a present that would be something other than the vestiges of a disappeared (and irretrievable) world, or the premises of a world to come (and that perhaps would no longer be a world)? If the Greek temple has so much presence, it is not only that it retains the trace of the initial beginning (of that beginning, that sending, that destines the Present itself), but that it in advance opens the entire continuation that, in its way, will *still be Greek art*—but in which the properly Greek (the *divine*) will have withdrawn or completely obscured itself. In its departure, which is also its swallowing up in the Departure, the temple thus seems to carry everything along with it, stamping "presence" without temple (modernity) with non-presence. Such is the Heideggerian reading of what for Hölderlin was certainly less massively negative. But what is proper to the beginning is that it collapses into itself, returns to the nothing that is its "point" (not) of departure. The beginning in which the present destines itself for the first time can never be present to itself except in an infinite distance, a gap in which the Present then appears, and then only, as having-been.[7] In this sense, not only does the beginning contain the end, but it does not appear (*as such*) except at the end. That is why there is no possible return to the Greeks, not only because the return to the departing mail slot is impossible, but because for the Greeks, sending, beginning, the opening of Being, can*not* appear as such, precisely because they were entirely immersed, and even ruined themselves, in it. That is why we must think (be) more Greek than the Greeks, more "originally" (cf. GA53

100). We can achieve this only in thinking sending or the beginning itself in its finitude. It remains to be seen if such a passage to the limit can be accomplished without a certain return of speculative thought, that is to say, of the limitlessness of the limit.

I will leave the question open in order to return to the first moment in the sequence, that moment that is precisely never first, since the beginning has not yet begun there. The same indetermination that reigns in prehistory seems to reign afterwards (in post-art) as well. The things given as works of art cannot be works (since there is no putting [in]to work[s], into the open) but they are not simple utensils either. They float in an undetermined ontological system, halfway between the utensil and the work. That sort of psychedelic spoon, for example, is at once more than a simple spoon and less than a work of art. This obscurity is cleared up, however, as soon as we consider the status of those "things" that are displayed to us in museums of modern art and that we indeed often hesitate to qualify as works of art, so much do they resemble nothing at all. We could even find something that corresponds exactly to the psychedelic spoon in the ready-made signed by Duchamp. Moreover, is it not significant that modern art was born through its association with the "primitive" art that Heidegger so cordially ignores? Considered with a neutral eye, one indifferent to all aesthetic sense (and it is thus that it must be viewed), the ready-made is nothing other than a product in common use. The only difference is that it is an unusable utensil that almost approaches the status of Lichtenberg's knife. It is a work of art only because it is displayed in a place considered artistic (a gallery or museum). This exposition recalls the installation in the open at the same time that it neutralizes it. It is no doubt to this neutralization of meaning that the ready-made owes all of its ability to fascinate us. But neutralization or indetermination is by no means less taken up in the cutting of initial determination than is simple imitation. That is perhaps what escapes all post-modernity, a term that is like a catchall in that in it we at once embrace Romantic tendencies aiming at the suppression of historical difference in a medium of reflection and the final repetitions, representations, or installations of the ultra-modern avant-garde in the fulfillment without end of a self-destruction that is no less mimetological. All of this leads back to the metaphysical gestures of the anti-metaphysical reversal, that is to say, of a complete nihilism. It remains for us to think what an art without works, without sense, without truth, and, above all, what this "without" would be. For "without" might well mean a simple privation: the insignificant or absurd, just as so many "works" said to be modern present themselves as just anything at all, in which case there is nothing more to do but pull the rug out from under them. Another possibility for this "without" would be that it refer to sense or meaning in a manner that would be complex indeed. That would imply that sense or meaning would never be whole, present to itself in presence, but always self-affected with a "without sense." But it would also imply that the *without* is also not whole, put differently, that there is no pure non-sense, or that the without-sense is not non-sense, and thus that the *without* is not reduced to a negation or to a nihilism that is always the weapon sense uses to reduce the other to its mercy. This also means that at the same time the work is not the final instance *and* remains what cannot be passed over, not because there would be nothing else, but precisely because by its very breaking it testifies for the other to whom it refers, without, however, this reference making sense.

~

Let us return to "The Origin of the Work of Art" and to the "final" question of *Darstellung*. There is, first of all and as always, the problem of translation: we should translate *darstellen* as "to represent" rather than as "to present," on the condition, however, that we understand this representation in the sense of a theatrical representation and not a representation of the world. In the theater, it is not a question of ideas but of the scene. In the same way, to be successful a painting that would represent a battle scene must give the spectacle of the mêlée itself and not a representation of war. But in the metaphysical interpretation of art, *Darstellung* itself becomes a representation in the reflexive sense of the word (where the German prefers the word *Vorstellung*) as a result of the well-known aesthetic categories form and content. That is why, it seems, Heidegger rejects *Darstellung* just as categorically as *Vorstellung*. If representation is a matter of "carrying content into the form of art," as Hegel understands it, then art represents nothing. Instead of a putting (in)to work(s) or into the open, we have a simple putting into form that makes art appear secondary, a supplement. But art *must* be initial. If we understand *Darstellung* in the sense of the Kantian transcendental exposition, however, then art represents, though not a content (time and space being *a priori*). The Greek temple represents nothing, but it presents the scene. It does not spring up *ex nihilo*, it comes "from the Earth." It is not a question of knowing what that resembles, since it is the image of nothing, but rather of knowing how to think the image *when it is the image of nothing*. Perhaps the image does not let itself be thought without an image. And the image of the trait could enlighten us. He who draws a line [*tire le trait*] retraces the tearing, the *re-trait* [withdrawal], of the Earth that does not want to be exposed. That is why Heidegger cites Dürer: "For in truth art hides itself in nature, and he who can draw it out of there possesses it." But art does not hide itself literally, like a treasure hidden in a field. It hides itself as nature hides itself, or better, encrypts itself, according to Heraclitus. This analogy exposes the trait proper to the origin (its generative impropriety). The *retrait* [withdrawal] into nature cannot be extracted except in being *re*-traced [*re-trait*] in art, and as the art of the origin. That is why from the beginning every work cannot be but an extract, an excerpt of the origin in withdrawing [*retrait*], a trace that makes a sign toward its whiteness.

What does a work as a work of art sign? The origin, to be sure. The trait of this origin is that it does not mark itself except as *re-trait*, in the double sense of non-appearance (withdrawal) and repetition [*re-trait*]. This duplicity itself refers to the traits proper to what does not have the status of a work: the thing (because of non-appearance) and the product (because of repetition). The originality of the work therefore always already appears second, its propriety being to draw together two distinct heterogeneous, if not conflicting, proprieties / properties under a single face, a face that is itself bifacial, double, and perhaps not even a face, since it also partakes of invisibility (that of the thing). However, the work does not draw together distinct traits into a composite whole after the fact. As the work "of" the origin, its drawing together *must* be *a priori* like the synthesis of transcendental schematism with which, moreover, the work has a close affinity, schematism being the production of figurability *as such*. The complexity of this operation does not exclude an extraordinary simplicity, that of the putting into the fold, which cannot be represented as a *simple* duplication.[8]

I have already spoken of the duplicity in the origin, where the springing forth is always recovered or refolded into what springs forth, so that it withdraws in it. The work always appears at fault; its "beauty" even comes from its own brilliance in withdrawing its origin from view, and thus appears as natural as a tree. And yet does not Heidegger himself speak of "producing" (*Herstellen*) as one of the constitutive traits of the putting into works? Let us examine this moment that constitutes the second constitutive trait of art, alongside (and with the same originality as) the first, installation (*Aufstellung*). Initially, it is difficult to see in what way the two traits are different. *Herstellung*, Heidegger tells us, must be understood in a "corresponding" sense, in analogy with, and in such a manner as to respond to, *Aufstellung*. We translate *herstellen* as "to produce" and thus pass over the thing if we think of the fabrication of a product, be it the furniture made by a craftsman or an automobile on an assembly line. For if we see what the work is supposed to produce, we must admit that this is not producible, either by craftsmen, industrially, or artistically. The work would in fact produce . . . the "Earth." It would not produce a material, whatever it be, but the occluded, the closed in, the inaccessible, and, *a fortiori*, the unproducible. *Herstellen* is thus not to produce in the common sense of products in use, but aims at an ontological or onto-phenomenological mode, which the Latin *pro-ducere*, to put in front, as one produces a play, a document, would mean. In this sense, though, the difference between *Herstellen* and *Aufstellen* (not to mention *Darstellung*) is reduced still more to a thin film. The "production" of the *eidos* of the shoe by the shoemaker and that of the *eidolon* of the "same" shoe by the painter differ only by a degree, and it will not suffice to reverse the Platonic hierarchy to exit from the mimetological schema. Mimetologism is not only the devaluation of imitation in relation to the "thing itself," reputedly inimitable, as we too often believe. It lies first of all in the elevation of what has existence only in a pair to an un*pair*alleled status. If we take the "example" of the temple, we might naïvely believe that, since the temple apparently imitates nothing, Heidegger avoids "a renaissance of the opinion, luckily superseded, according to which art would be an imitation and a copy of the real." It is also not a question, Heidegger specifies, of a conceptual or eidetic imitation, that of an Idea of the temple. "And yet," he adds immediately after having rejected the claim of an ideal mimetism, "and yet, in such a work, if it is one, it is indeed the truth that is at work." Heidegger does not think of the case of a work that would imitate itself—but let us leave that aside. For what is essential is precisely this primacy of the essential or of the thing itself over everything else, and notably over products. Where does the originality of the work come from? It comes from the fact that this production produces nothing, at least nothing that would be useable, by which I mean, nothing that *refers to something else.* Artistic production would be an absolute production in the strict sense that it would no longer refer to (intraworldly) beings but would give place, purely, to Being (the "it is"). This is why Meyer's poem is then cited. It seems to copy an, even the, essence of the fountain; but in truth, it only puts the truth (in)to (a) work. The stream goes from basin to basin, each time overflowing the basin, this overflowing *figuring* the movement of Being: an overabundance, the gift that exceeds itself. This, then, is my interpretation, which should not be taken literally. The poem does not imitate the movement of Being, which would permit making a metaphor of Being (in the figure of springing forth, of the fountain, of the excessive gift). There again, metaphoricity passes by way of an analogy. Just as a fountain "gives and takes, pours and settles back again," so too does the poem. It is the poem that puts into a work, that is to say, figures, and does so because the poem issues from Being itself. The fountain figures the springing forth of water just as the poem figures the springing forth of Being. There is the same double movement of giving and taking. What remains unexplained is how the truth (the disclosure of Being concealing itself) can be put into a work without immediately being *in the image of the work*. The work is a putting into the open and the open a putting into works. It is this analogy that should be accounted for.

The example of the Roman fountain leads us back to the privilege of language, recognized and torturously demanded by Heidegger. It is a question of language playing on two different levels. Its duplicity is even its primary property, which makes it unique. It resonates, like music or birds, but it "installs" as well. What it installs is in fact something other than the earth; it is what must always remain something else, the transcendent, the world. But do we not therefore return to the metaphysics of the sign, that which is put (installed) in the place of something else? That this "thing" not be a thing, that we can call it, for example, Being, a god, or the world, changes nothing in relation to the sign. The temple is an allegory; it speaks for something else, not for itself, but for Being. It could certainly be noted that Being does not preexist the temple, of course, but that it is constituted by the temple's erection, constituted in the strict sense in which the temple joins and gathers together, in a certain way cements the world in the same manner that it is itself situated, materially, in the stature of its construction: an assembling of stones, certainly, but not in view of the stone itself as a mountainous mass that raises itself up only in assembling rocks according to their own folds and fractures. In the mountain, stone is living, physical. In Aristotelian terms, in contrast to the mountain the temple has its *telos* outside itself. In this it is a different being, a *techne* and not a *physis*. It imitates the physical mode of being, no doubt, but this imitation (in the assembling, the joint, the folding) also supposes a *gap*, that of the production of the *eidos as such*. It is precisely this "as such" that makes all the difference. For if we can say that the mountain constitutes itself as mountain, only we can say this, only we can read the geological formation of the earth. The earth will never read anything. It gives to be read, but does not know how to read, nor even what reading (or connecting, reconnecting, making a relation) is. It is a bit like Pythia of Delphi: an oracle, pure orality, but not signifying the slightest bit except from the moment in which the *a priori* schema of meaning is projected upon it. Illiterate, the earth nonetheless gives to be read, but by something else, and in another manner. It is in this sense that the "primary" (non-analogical) mimetic scheme is improper. In no case does the temple rise up in the manner of a mountain. Were it to resemble anything (natural) whatsoever, the temple would not be a temple, because the mountain resembles nothing, or resembles only when appearing as an *a priori* scheme that has been instituted or installed, on the one hand, and, on the other hand, which is only the other side of the same condition, because the temple must emerge from the earth, must make a violent exit, which is also a breaking and entering, even though what exits is *materially* nothing other than the earth (what else could there be on earth than the earth?) and yet is something radically other: the temple *as* temple. This "as" seems to add nothing and in effect creates nothing. Nevertheless, therein lies the whole operation called *Aufstellen*, installation, the installation of the There, which precisely is not there, not available, but which always *arrives*, suddenly, takes place in giving place. The There, first named *Dasein* then *aletheia*, is Heidegger's major, and perhaps even only, discovery. What remains to be discovered beyond the Open?

Presence, however, would not be a matter of being invented as one invents an expedient. It is historial and is in no way eternal since "with" its coming comes time. Time is therefore not eternal either. It is historial, and that means that it does not always come; it comes only at certain moments, decisive moments in which it decides "itself." But it never decides (itself) except in cutting itself, in cutting itself out—*for example*, in the figure of the temple. The ancient philosophers said that Nature makes no leaps. That remains true. Only History can leap. As long as it comes, History is this leap. Sometimes it even leaps so far that it is irretrievable. Thus it arrives with the Greek conception of presence. It names difference itself, the leap that nothing can equal and that resembles nothing, or that could not but have the semblance of an "original" work: a temple, for example! The "lesson" (in the sense of a reading) of "The Origin of the Work of Art" can thus be summarized by the following: presence is the poetic discovery. Being is a poem and even THE initial poem. It is the poem of which the Greek temple is an "example," always an inadequate one, it is true, since there can be no *Beispiel* (example) for this *Spiel* (game). But the inadequation of this example bears witness precisely to the non-presentability of presence as the law and origin of all presentation or exposition. That is why, in the end, the ruin of all exposition will testify for this very deposition. Being will have said its final word in forbidding itself to appear as such, in entrusting itself to what will never have appeared except in its absence or by proxy, the earth. If truth is terrestrial, it will have been all the more guarded since the earth always keeps its secret. We will always be able to make it speak, since it has never had speech except through a mouthpiece, except by way of an example, or better through the archetype of what will have been a work, the *extemple*.

§ 8 Step (Not) Beyond

Under the title of a point (not) of departure, let's stop at the title—*pas au-delà* [step (not) beyond].[1] We should probably renounce *trans*-lating, passing beyond. For if nothing is more dangerous than language, then this is indeed a dangerous passage. What does it mean to pass not only from one language to another, but across language *itself*, to pass through the word *pas*, for example? In that word we do not simply pass, as from one bank of a river to another, from what would be called "signifier" to what would be its unique and *trans*cendent signified. This passage itself, the effacement of the signifier for the benefit of the only signified that could "properly" signify, does *not* come to pass: for example (but is it a simple example?), what do we signify in uttering the word (and it is first of all a word inscribed in *a* specific language, Greek) "Being"? If the signifier "Being" is incapable of signifying anything (this is the original a-poria, the stop in stepping), even though at the same time the signified seems to "be" self-evident (and thus empty), then all of metaphysics rests upon a deceptive passage [*tour de passe-passe*].

Before taking this step and passing to the signified of this "step (not) beyond," therefore, we must question the meaning of the passage itself, a regressive question that does not, however, return to anything already there, such as a simple past. All of Heidegger's steps could be read in this step backwards (*Schritt zurück*). But (walking always being a passage from one foot to the other) we must also go beyond, beyond overstepping (including the overstepping that is meta-physics) and wrong-foot the title, hear it with another ear, as an injunction imposing a limit: not [*pas*] beyond!

To be or not to be, to step or not to step? That would be the question—of aesthetics. But what is aesthetics? Recently invented (at the end of the eighteenth century), the word is first of all a scholarly term translated literally from Greek. From the beginning, *mimesis*, the imitation of nature, but here of a dead language, presides over its destiny. A *Fremdwort*, a foreign word: nothing is original in it, so that it is difficult to know to whom it could be traced back. It cannot be returned to the original Greek, where *aisthetikos* (an adjective first, not a noun) has nothing to do with Baudelaire's *Aesthetic Curiosities* or with plastic surgery [*chirurgie esthétique*]. For the word *aesthetic* does not particularly relate to beauty but refers rather to meaning or sense: the "aesthete" understands, has a feel for the situation, is astute and finds the right word for things. Discerning, sifting, like a sieve that separates the wheat [*le froment*] from the chaff, he is, in short, a critic—or a philosopher, which comes down to the same thing, depending on one's point of view (and theory makes *a point*[2]—a decisive argument—on viewing).

But as a *noun* designating the "aesthetic science" (just as logic is the *logike episteme*), aesthetics is a metaphysical invention. If the word is modern, the thing itself that the name "aptly" denominates is, Heidegger writes, "as old as the consideration on art and the beautiful in Western thought" (*Nietzsche* 79). In order to avoid any ambiguity concerning this antiquity (which for him is the condition sine qua non of authenticity), Heidegger adds that "philosophical consideration of the essence of art and the beautiful even *begins* as aesthetics" (*Nietzsche* 79). Even if the word did not exist, the thing was there; what is more, it was there *as such*: I emphasize because it is not obvious that a thing could be "as such" without the name that gives it being, at least if the "as such" is considered the primordial process(or) of logos, that is, of (philosophical) language.

This is one of the curiosities of aesthetics. Before taking up the other, let us ask why aesthetics is the way in which "science" (philosophy, the foremost knowledge of the thing itself) conceptualizes what is named, improperly, "art" (*techne*). With simple recourse to a Greek word, we could have imagined a "technical" science. Oddly, the word *technical*, which also first appeared as an adjective in the eighteenth century, is exactly opposed to the aesthetic: "That which, in the domain of art, concerns the processes of work and expression more than inspiration."[3] This definition reflects a division as ancient as the aesthetic as "thing." Not only is the division a divorce, it is a violent hierarchy, for such has always been the properly metaphysical trait: below, process (technique); above, inspiration. The sensible and material are the support for the ladder leading beyond (and above) toward the super-sensible (idea, concept, and today, value); inversely, "the processes of work and expression" are systematically reduced to the level of the *basely* material, just as the artist will be elevated above the artisan, the simple craftsman [*facteur*]. It may be needless to point out that such an evaluation only appeared with the elevation of art to the Absolute, corresponding to the absolutizing of subjectivity. In Greek, a *technites* (or "poet") is neither a simple worker nor an immaterial genius, and what we translate as "art" was also called *mechane*: could art, then, be the *deus ex machina* of philosophy at its end?

Aesthetics as a theory of art thus appeared before the word, and essentially as the ontological point of view on a phenomenon that never claimed for itself the pure contemplation or *theoria* of Being. If the *aistheton* names the sensible not for itself but already in opposition *and* subordination to what gives sense to the sensible—*namely* the idea, which is never sensible—then the name "aesthetics" reveals its metaphysical origin. The beautiful has the privilege of making the non-visible of pure sight seen, of therefore being the postman [*facteur*] of Being, he who carries the letter of Being [*la lettre de l'être*] to the right destination. The beautiful produces Being, not in the sense of fabricating it (Being is neither made nor engendered), but in the sense that it displays or exposes it. Hence, art has always been thought according to what I call the "principle

Step (Not) Beyond 181

of exposition." Commenting on the sentence from *Phaedrus* affirming that in the hierarchy of beings, "to beauty alone has the role been allotted to be the most radiant, but also the most ravishing," Heidegger writes: "The Beautiful is that which, by a double movement into and out of itself, delivers itself to our senses from the first appearance, and by the same stroke carries us into Being, that is, what at once subjugates and ravishes. The Beautiful is thus that which tears us from the oblivion of Being and opens up the view on Being" (*Nietzsche* 196). The beautiful, as appearance, but an appearance that must allow Being to appear through itself, must therefore efface itself as appearance, must become *transparent*. The beautiful has no value in itself but only on behalf of what it allows to appear through and beyond (μετα, *trans, über*) itself: *transcendens* pure and simple, Being. Transparency equals transcendence equals metaphysics. Every concept of art, including that of modern art, rests upon this trans-parency or this trans-appearance of Being, the disappearance of that which appears (simple medium) for the benefit of the appearing itself (the end in *view*). If art "is rooted in the sensible" and is thus the source of the conflict (*Zwiespalt*), this is also in order immediately to leave its place there, to move beyond and outside itself, to "elevate us beyond the sensible" (*Nietzsche* 198). Even Nietzsche's aesthetics, presenting itself as anti-metaphysical, but above all as a reversal of the hierarchy that governs the relation of the sensible to what exceeds it, remains (for Heidegger) the height of metaphysics: to make the ecstasy of the senses the essence of aesthetic emotion or of the sentiment of surpassing "oneself" is to fall back once again upon transcendence or metaphysics, even though, transported to the "physiology" of sentiment, of "artistic" subjectivity, this metaphysics may be unrecognizable.

In the Greek tradition phenomenality has been thought in terms of light (φῶς), inasmuch as light makes everything appear. But in turn, everything makes light itself appear insofar as light op-poses itself to the obscurity of the impenetrable. Consequently, thingness, "matter," has always been determined *negatively*, as obstruction, re-covering, *lethe* in relation to *aletheia*, truth as nonconcealment, diaphanousness, "transparency." The imbalance evident in this conception has been translated by the privilege given to the spiritual as immaterial. The sensible that shines and resonates displays itself as *that* work of art which must *not* stop there; on the contrary, it must permit a passing beyond toward the "there" of pure Being or of the Idea. But what comes to pass, with art, is precisely that this does *not* come to pass: an interruption, a caesura takes place in the movement of passing beyond toward "true" presence (that of Being); instead of being a mere figure of transition in the movement giving access to (the) self, presence is distanced from itself by a death-in-speaking (dis*cès*). As Jean-Luc Nancy writes, showing (ex-posing, saying, figuring: all these words express the same thing—the *poietique-technique* of art) "is nothing other than placing apart, at a distance from presentation, going out of pure presence, making absent and thus absolute" (Nancy, *Muses* 122).

As a poetic example (examples always being necessary), or rather two, for like hands, two examples are always better than one, take Valéry and Ponge. Both speak, though quite differently, of transparency, one in order to pass immediately to the source, to the truth that shows through in language: "We say we are THIRSTY FOR TRUTH. We speak of the TRANSPARENCY of a discourse."[4] These expressions are only figures of speech, tropes, metaphors, truth not being, *properly speaking*, potable, not water. With Ponge, on the contrary, the metaphor, if it does not disappear, changes meaning, because at issue is no longer a one-way passage from a material base (water) to a "superior" truth; this time, the glass of water figures language inasmuch as by means of language transparency shows through the glass of water: "Allegory (here) inhabits a diaphanous palace" (Ponge 98).

The metaphysical division can be translated by the traditional conceptual couple of form / content. But while in science and philosophy form is only a manner of speaking or an inessential clothing for "true" content (the signified), in the arts, inversely, it is form that prevails. However, with "Ponge's" glass of water, it is impossible to establish a similar precedence. Form and content are in effect equally transparent; the glass allows the water to appear and the water, being itself transparent, returns to itself as it*self,* a glass of water. This is why the glass is best suited for the water: it *presents* the water in the best possible way, without adding anything of itself; but "in addition, the best way to present a glass (in the execution of its duties) is to present it full of water" (Ponge 103). This double reference annuls precisely the movement of transcendence, without, however, remaining a pure immanence. All this does not take place without recalling the *double* movement Heidegger spoke of concerning Beauty as *ekphanestaton*. The difference is that, far from being a simple moment destined to be passed by in the passage (toward Being or truth), the thing does not efface itself as signifying material for the benefit of an immaterial signified, nor is it the reflection or representation of that signified returning to the source of production, the *ego*. Transparency is not the fact of the Idea but comes from the thing. Form and content, glass and water, remain absolutely heterogeneous, even if they display the same transparency in their indissoluble unity, the glass of water. The relation between them should be described in strict analogy to the analogy of the thing and word, "glass of water." "Beginning with V, ending with U, the only two letters in the form of a vase or a glass, the word VERRE D'EAU [glass of water] would in some way be adequate to the object it designates" (Ponge 106–7). I will not try to give a "scientific" justification for this literal correspondence between what we call the signifier and what we call the signified. Such a justification would not only be impossible but would run against the current of (S)Ponge's intentions: every justification demands a reason for being, a foundation, and there is no foundation (or reason) to language by the very fact that it is through language and language alone that something like a foundation can be furnished or a reason given.

Were I to say GLASS OF WATER now, I would be obliged to represent things (the word *and* the thing) differently. We would perhaps hear the sound, the toll [*glas*], of another bell. Is language not the constant promise of a glass of water from all faucets? That is the least one can demand of a *potable* language. "But *potable* only means hardly passable. Oh! there is something rotten in the French language" (Ponge 113). Not only in French: every language is rotten from the inside in that it is never more than *a* language and not "the" language, *die reine Sprache*. We translate this as "pure" language, and I note that (no doubt erroneously) Ponge derives the verb "to rinse" [*rincer*] from the German *rein*, pure. Further, through what is probably an unintentional anagrammatical transposition, *rein* is in my edition written "rien" ["nothing"]. Despite everything, there is perhaps a kinship between all languages if only nothingness is "pure" (but the pure nothing does not exist). Every language has "something rotten" about it. As witness, I need only the French word *pur* [pure], which has given us "purée" as well as "liquid manure" [*purin*]. The word comes from the Old French *purer*, signifying "to pass through a sieve" (it is thus, in fact, that one makes a purée or produces literary criticism). Ponge sees the rotten in the example of "potable," which, instead of meaning capable (of being drunk), in conformity with its *proper* meaning, means *just barely* sufficient, just enough not to be entirely incapable.... In short, "adequate" [*passable*]. Every student knows that the grade "adequate" [*passable*] is practically shameful[5].... But the word itself says nothing of the sort. It expresses only the capacity, the capability (thus, potentially the excellence) of passing. Perhaps this is because language, more than a house of *Being*, is a sort of brothel [*maison de passe*] in which words and things, meaning and usages, are exchanged and are always more or less on good terms [*en bonne passe*] and always in good (clean) hands. I call *languaging* [*langagement*] this game of language with itself. But that also means the game with the use of language, its passage, thus, with *us* who pass through it and can, in order to have access to things, only pass through it. Purity is the most common fantasm concerning the property / propriety[6] of a language, but it is just as impossible literally as it is "spiritually" (in the sense that philosophy desperately seeks to avoid any metaphor, image, or ambiguity). If language opens up a play *between* words and things, if sometimes this mi-lieu, this place-in-between, is a "pure" transparency between them, it is on the basis of that impossibility which, at the same time, makes possible a *relative* transparency or propriety. What is at stake there could also be called (improperly, that is, according to the condition of general or generative impropriety of *any* language) *la passance*. At once less than a concept and more than a word, this term, by no means a *terminus ad quem*, but in these conditions not a *terminus a quo* either, unless we understand it as an invitation to pass, that is, as with the "to say"—this term, then, by its inflection which is neither negative nor positive, but rather neutral, would translate the passage of sense, the passage that *is* already the whole sense. There is no sense without passing; meaning or sense does not exist for itself. Sense occurs (or does not occur) only through what takes place between itself and the Other (which is *non*-sense only from the point of view of the positivist theory of sense, logic).

And what takes place? Nothing but *this*: the glass of water, nothing else—or the thing itself. But this is just as much the glass of water I drink as the one I read: "Let this book be a glass of water!" In this passing out of difference in which the signifier is valid as a signified, but in which the signified is, in turn, in the position of signifier, the entire system of metaphysical subordination collapses. Put differently, showing *itself*, art (transparency in both senses, from the sensible to the intelligible and vice versa) displays nothing, at least nothing that would be beyond: there is no-thing beyond art as ex-position, production, process, and so on. But if technique is already the whole of art, there is no sense in opposing it to aesthetics, for aesthetics always comes too late, and remains excessive(ly figurative)—a metaphysical supplement.

This brings me to the second curiosity of aesthetics.

The thing was there, not named (not properly) and yet already as such. This is somewhat surprising: Plato wrote no "Aesthetics," for example. We must wait until Hegel for the appearance of the title "Aesthetics," that is, also its *end*, an end, if not of the name, then of the thing, of its object: art, the beautiful. Art enters into the aesthetic the day it is declared, if not dead, then at least a thing of the past, surpassed as regards the Absolute (philosophy), as though this baptism were also a death certificate. The name is always the name of the dead, the name of the Father in the name of whom the Son would sacrifice himself only to be reborn in the Holy Spirit, his specter or spectator: the Concept. But is there a concept of art? And why *not*? Has not a new form of modern art been baptized *conceptual*? If this art really exists, one should conclude that there must be a concept of art. However, the very fact that there is a conceptual art might also mean exactly the opposite: as only a species of the genre "art," the other species thus being necessarily non-conceptual, the concept of art that would synthesize both in its unity (dialectical or not) threatens to be simultaneously conceptual and non-conceptual, or of an other conceptuality, heterogeneous to itself, and thus non-absolute, non-conceptual.

Art (the concept, to begin with the name "art" itself) always threatens to be without concept, or is rather the threat of the concept (and of the name, of the name as the substantive of the subject-concept). According to the necessity of phenomenology, the concept *must* be capable of presenting itself, of figuring itself. But as such any conceptuality finds itself threatened, exposed precisely to the "exposition" that, for want of a proper concept, could very well be the work in which, for want of a proper name, what is called "art" is at play. In place of the concept, this would be the *de-cept* [de-position] of art—to begin with its name, which has never been a proper name, or has never been anything but a proper name, that is, a name without signification.[7]

In the Epilogue to "The Origin of the Work of Art," Heidegger begins by returning to what he had crudely asserted in 1936. Then, despite everything, a concept of art was put to work, unconcealed, art as a "bringing into work of truth," itself understood as the play of unconcealing concealing itself: "Far from pretending to solve this enigma [art], the task is to see it" (*Poetry* 79). How one sees an enigma is yet another enigma, for in principle an enigma can only be heard. According to an ancient philosophical tradition that triumphs right into the arts, where everything culminates in figuration or representation, Heidegger systematically privileges sight. I will insist upon this precedence of theory (*theoria*), which is the precedence of sense as pre-sense and presence presenting itself to itself, only to remark, again, that it flows from the metaphysical project and that it prescribes *mimesis* as the founding concept of aesthetics. If theory (the pure sight of Being) precedes all *poiesis*, all technique [*facture*] and production will come later, will be a making-after. Art is never original in relation to Being nor in relation to the theory in which Being gives, presents, itself *as such* and not through (*trans*) the sensible or the work of art. The immediacy and transparency of art are at the same time its most impenetrable veil; the very reason why art does not reach the absolute is precisely because it makes means (that is, art itself) absolute in relation to the "end" (truth), or because it interrupts the end or sense.

The enigma is "art," art as such and not art as it is "felt" or "lived": "Everything is lived experience [*Erlebnis*]. But perhaps lived experience is that element in which art is dying. This death progresses so slowly that it requires several centuries" (*Poetry* 79). Following this, Heidegger quotes Hegel's famous statements about the "end" of art *in view* of the Absolute (which only philosophy can present, *being it* in its process of exposing itself outside itself to its proper Self). If Heidegger says that "the final word on this statement of Hegel's has not yet been spoken," he at the same time keeps himself from saying it. This final word, this decision (*Entscheidung*), will not fall until the end of History, like the Last Judgment. But "until then Hegel's pronouncement remains valid" (*Poetry* 80): it is the final word. Before the end, it is already the end, though not yet properly *spoken*; for that, we must await the final word. But since this will be the word of the end (of History, that is to say, of Saying), it will not be able to be spoken except as the end of the word, of itself, will never be able to say *itself* except as the *so-called* / *self-calling* [*soi-disant*] final word. As long as art is a historical figure, it is necessarily finished, since it has been passed by in the movement that is the history of its coming-to-its-end, a movement analogous to that in which the work of art comes to be as completed, fully executed. To take this a bit further, as long as art puts itself (in)to work(s), it is finished, in the double sense of perfection and of death (or of "becoming-immortal"). So true is this that now the only finality for art is to enter into a museum.

There, as Hegel predicted once again, the Muses are transformed into statues: "Statues are now the cadavers from which the living soul has fled" (Hegel 455). But we must note the strange status of these statues animated, if not with life, at least with a becoming-cadaver. How does something that has never lived die? Let us recall that *Erlebnis* ("lived experience") would be the element at the heart of which art would be in the process of dying—slowly, like a Greek statue damaged by the centuries. If there is a concept of art, it constitutes itself by demarcating itself from what it is *not*: "life," for example (and it will be necessary to return to the "example"). But how can art die if it has never been alive? Of course, we can speak of "living" art in opposition to a "dead" art frozen in the rooms of a museum-freezer. Yet even to the extent that, strictly speaking, only the artist is living and the work is a work only when detached from its "producer," when it "is" (lives?) for itself, autonomous, the distinction between living and dead art is reduced to a simple point of view, an image, a metaphor. Statues resemble cadavers and *always* have. They neither speak nor move; they look only with an absent glance, like Baudelaire's Venus: "But the implacable Venus looks at some unknown thing in the distance with her marble eyes" ("Le fou et Venus," in *Le Spleen de Paris*). This explains why the statue is surpassed by the gesture of the young girl who offers the fruits of art, that is, art as *signum* or vestiges, and who, in opposition to the statue, *looks* (at us): "the painting of the eye is itself the quintessence of painting, the painting of painting, and the painting of art in general," writes Nancy (*Muses* 95). Just as "I would be hard put to say *where* the painting I am looking at is," I would be equally hard put to say where the young girl is looking who is in the painting that itself is—nowhere—or (is) "the inside of the outside and the outside of the inside" (Merleau-Ponty 21). If painting, far from only "representing" already present things in another place (or way), "only" renders them present or "visible" (Klee), this visibility is never simple: it doubles itself with a veil of invisibility that, however, is nothing other than visibility itself: "What is proper to the visible is to have a lining [*doublure*] of invisibility, in the strict sense, that it makes present as a certain absence" (Merleau-Ponty 85). Visibility is itself traversed by a (minimal, invisible, but understood as *in* the visible) difference: and it is *in* this difference that art lives (in English, art *inhabits* this difference). Referring to exteriority, art (here, painting) does not refer to anything other than itself, and this is why Merleau-Ponty writes that painting can be figurative "only on the condition of being 'self-figurative'" (Merleau-Ponty 69).

Speaking of the statue of the god in the temple, Heidegger writes: "It is not a portrait whose purpose is to make it easier to realize how the god looks, for no one knows this; rather, it is a work that lets the god himself come into presence and thus *is* the god himself" (*Poetry* 43). The statue "is" the god. How is one to understand this: as an identification, a fetishism? But if statues have become cadavers, so too have the gods. (Were the gods ever alive?) This is why Heidegger can affirm that "great art"—the Greek art Hegel described under the title of "art-*religion*"—is, at present, nothing but a vestige, a has-been[8] (though in German *gewesen* is also a recollection or remembrance—*Er-innerung*—of *Wesen*, a living being or essence). From the beginning, art is finished, if only through its vocation, its determination (*Bestimmung*): the putting (in)to work(s) (*Ins-Werk-setzen*) is the bringing to an end.

The statue, dead before it is alive (it precedes what Hegel calls the "living work of art"), thus represents the first *manifestation* of the "artistic spirit" precisely in that it manifests itself as pure exposition or figuration, although in such an exposition spirit does *not* manifest itself, not primarily as Self but a-part or exteriorized as pure exteriority or figure. This figure "exists," is "there," is placed there (is already *Dar-Stellung*), and its being-there, its *Dasein*, is "as a thing." And yet it is not a simple thing, not a stone. Even if the "indwelling god *is* the black stone," is the statue, this thing is already penetrated, crossed through, trans-figured as figure or appearance by the "light of consciousness" (Hegel 428). In the same way, for Heidegger "the stone has no world" (*Poetry* 45). The end or finality of art already shows through; it effaces itself as thing or obscure stone to make room for pure Being. A statue, however complete, remains incomplete inasmuch as it must still be animated, inhabited by a living eye: "a nascent eye" must appear from "under the skin of the stones" (Nerval, *Vers dorés*). This eye, which *looks* like it is growing from the interior of the stone like a "pure spirit," does not, however, belong to the stone; it comes from elsewhere. The work is not a simple thing, but is first of all *produced* (shown). And it is precisely this characteristic (of being produced) that wants to appear and that art produces in its own way. But just as the thingness of the statue is not the thingness of a blind stone, its being-produced is fundamentally different from that of a simple product. What differentiates a work of art from a common product does not reside, however, in technique [*facture*]. Duchamp demonstrated this by exhibiting a thoroughly common product, *ready-made, as* a work of art. The difference is precisely this *as*, the operator of ex-position. Both product and work are manufactured products, artifacts, and there is no point in looking for a difference in their technique: the work of art may be technically more complex, or, on the contrary, more rudimentary. We pass over what marks a work as such if we insist upon remaining on the level of technique(s). The difference has nothing to do with appearance, so that a product can look more beautiful than a work of art. Similarly, the example of van Gogh's shoes is in no way chosen by Heidegger for its so-called "aesthetic" value, as if the painting as painting (and all the more so for being signed by van Gogh) were more beautiful than the *same* shoes on a farm (or in an urban setting). The difference does not even lie in the fact that the painting would merely represent real shoes or even the essence of the shoes, shoeness, or that one cannot take a step in the painted shoes. The difference is much more unapparent, but, as unapparent as it is, it passes by (through) appearance, traverses it to bring it out as such, that is, as the trans-appearance of the "that it is," the appearance of Being [*apparêtre*].[9]

Thus, Heidegger writes: "To be sure, 'that' it has been produced belongs equally to any product in use. But this 'that,' far from being prominent in the product, disappears in it" (*Poetry* 65). Whereas the product makes its being-produced disappear, the work produces it, exposes it as such, that is to say . . . *says* it. Thus, the difference between product and work of art is first of all the appearance of Saying, and of Saying as the space or clearing in which the appearing appears manifestly and as this being-manifest. Once again, an example: the only difference between any old urinal that comes to hand, *so to speak*, and the one we encounter in a museum in the form of the same urinal "exposed" is not so much that one cannot admire the first or relieve oneself in the second (one can always do so, though at one's own risk!), but that the urinal in the museum is not shown as a *urinal* but as (under the *name of*) "Fountain," that is to say: "Attention, this is art!" In the same way, Duchamp's window looks in every way like any other window, except that it is called "Fresh Widow," that is, to translate: "Attention, Fresh Paint." The painting is fresh and widowed of a letter in order better to espouse Being, to nearly *literally* espouse itself (another Virgin disrobed by the image of writing [*Schriftbild*]): the missing "n" is also that letter that is added—the Name, the proper name that signifies nothing but "shows." It thus functions as the supplement of Being or that "higher element" that the statue remaining in "exteriority, . . . the determination of *thing* without self-consciousness" lacked: "This higher element is *language*," that is, the supplement of the soul ("language is the soul existing as soul" [Hegel 430]) without which statues are but corpses, and not even "exquisite corpses," since, as live as they might have appeared, to the point of *being* the god himself, they, as we say of dogs, lack (but) one thing: speech (even more than sight).

Difference passes by way of language. Language marks the work as work of art. This precedence of language, which Hegel repeats at each moment of the "art-religion," from oracle to epic and tragedy passing by way of hymn, of language as the "perfect element in which interiority is just as exterior as exteriority is interior" (Hegel 439), marks the discourse of Heidegger as well when he defines *all* art as being "essentially *Dichtung*." Even if he distinguishes *Dichtung* from *Poetry*, he nonetheless adds that "the work of language (*das Sprachwerk*), poetry (*Dichtung*) in the strict sense, has a privileged position in the domain of the arts" (*Poetry* 73).

This privilege of language (or rather of *logos*) flows from the function attributed to art: *Ins-Werk-setzen, aufstellen*, Being-open, exposed as such. The statue, for Hegel, or the temple, for Heidegger, are already speaking works, even if they speak *without saying a word*, which is perhaps the "purest" way of speaking. They speak in the sense that they say what art does: putting into works is putting in the Open, ex-posing into the there that the work installs inasmuch as it is the there: "is there," Hegel also says, is the exteriority of the interior (laid bare). When Heidegger says that "this" painting (by van Gogh) "has spoken" (*Dieses hat gesprochen*), this is in no way because this "thing" would have attained speech through the intermediary of Herr Professor but because the painting has *openly* shown the Being-manifest of the (produced) being. But it is indeed the painting itself that gives sight—of what? This, at the very least: that it is a painting. Here, Derrida goes one step further, saying what Heidegger does: see "truth in painting." That is to say, on the one hand, that Heidegger saw what can be seen *nowhere*—"in" painting there is nothing such as "truth," which always lies beyond painting as a simple exposition. In this sense, the painting will have been only a pretext, quickly passed over to get to the thing itself: meaning. On the other hand, and with all the complexity of a deconstructive reading, Derrida does not content himself with saying that Heidegger had visions (or, in this case, voices: "this has spoken"), nor does he want to bring the metaphysician who always sees something other than what is there back to reason (or what passes itself off under this name: the evidence so dear to objective art criticism). Derrida's extra step is to say what no one has ever seen there, namely the painting as shoe, and, if I dare (say), as *thingness* [*chosure*]. With what Derrida calls the "remark in painting," it is not a question of making the shoes speak again, even to make them recite the "ancient" language of allegory or the *mise-en-abyme*: "This (what you believe to be shoes) is, *in truth*, a painting." On the contrary, if there is a placing into abyss, and *not* into truth, it is in a double interlacing of thingness [*chosure*] into painting and of painting into shoeness [*chossure*]. It is a double interlacing in the way of a double mark or re-mark: (1)

this is a painting, but this is "the" shoes—"the painting is *in* the shoes that we are" and that consequently overflows the frame; (2) "conversely the framing painting, that which gives itself as painting at a first glimpse [. . .] remarks itself [it is thus not a simple remark] as a (more or less shifty) pair of shoes. [. . .] If the painting could speak in its turn (it has spoken, Heidegger said) [. . .] would it not say [it would indeed]: I, like all painting, am a shoe" (Derrida, *The Truth in Painting*, 434). The painting is in the shoe which is (in) the painting. Everything overflows the borders; the part is bigger than the whole which is in the part, etcetera. There is no way to *say* what, of the shoe as thing or of the shoe as shown, "is" (shown, exposed). In taking as his "example" a pair of shoes "in painting," Heidegger seemed to have set loose a time bomb that, in an exemplary way, tears all of aesthetic discourse to pieces. The example explodes the frame as being already the *(w)hole* of art. The "this," far from disappearing in the universal "truth" that is its negation, resists the law of generalization (that is, of truth and of language) in interrupting its well-regulated play by not merely playing alongside (*Bei-spiel*) as an illustration of the main text, but as this text's only means of presenting "itself," which will also mean that it will never present it*self*, never as such. Still, it *must* present itself: in this necessity lies its defect, presenting itself for lack of the thing itself, which will never have been presented (especially if it is presence itself) except *in its absence.*

It is here that one could ask if what Heidegger presents as an example, a simple *Darstellung* (presentation), not of painting (since the example of painting is useless and could be replaced by any representation), and certainly not of the shoe, but of the "activity," of the *poietique* proper to "this" painting, is not already the *final word* on that in regard to which, in his *Lectures on Aesthetics*, Hegel says: "We no longer have an absolute need to bring content to presentation in the form of art"? If Heidegger's principal thesis is in agreement with this assertion, it is because, for him, art precisely never *presents* or exposes anything, for the simple reason that there is nothing it *could* present. And if art cannot present anything, it is because it is itself this nothing, this absence of content or message. It is this absence in the sense that it openly exposes it as the very place of art: the truth. Heidegger puts an end to art in another way, not in declaring it finished as regards its "supreme destination" (that of presenting the Absolute by "exposing" it in a sensible figure), but in accomplishing it as absolute exposition. This is also why language for him acquires its primordial dimension: in language, Hegel already said, and as Wittgenstein will repeat in a different way, there is never anything but language, nothing but Self, pure autology. In withdrawing the being of language from subjectivity, in making language absolute, does Heidegger not accomplish the secret vow of metaphysics, the disappearance of the "thing" *in* the "thing itself"? Thus, this disappearance repeats the scheme of self-transparency or the myth of presence—of art as well (of art as *divine*). As for the rest, it is precisely the *rest*, the remainder, that which remains of art when the myth of self-presence has been interrupted, when the "without" [*sans*] has cut off sense, when it *passes* (out of) sense [*fait passance*] and does not simply make no sense [*pas sens*]. To think art without sense, without presence, and without Being would be to take that step beyond which precisely does *not* go beyond, does not conclude a movement from art to Being, that is to say, always, to the end (of art).

§ 9 The Different Step: From Heidegger to Derrida

"Picasso is said to have told this story about his visit to an artist's studio. The artist showed him one of his paintings and asked Picasso to be lenient with it: 'I'm still working on it; it's not yet fully executed [*achevée*].' Picasso savagely replied, 'Executing it would be humane.'"[1]

It is with this anecdote that J.-B. Pontalis opens his final contribution to the final issue of the *Nouvelle Revue de Psychanalyse*, an issue that is also a deliverance, with the *Revue* ending, finishing (itself off [*s'achevant*]), as in a suicide, but a "beautiful" suicide, committed beautifully, like death in antiquity or the voluntary death that Nietzsche praises, with the title *Incompletion* [*L'inachèvement*]. A bit later in his text, which is also a meditation on the art of the fragment, Pontalis evokes Chekhov's death, Chekhov who is supposed to have said, "*Ich sterbe*," in German "in the text," if I can put it thus. He says "I am dying" in German, then, not only because one cannot say (although this is what every fully executed [*achevée*] work of art says) "I am dead," but because one cannot say it in one's own language. If there is no proper word for one's *own* / proper death, it is because there is no death "proper." That is so even though Heidegger tells us, from beyond the grave, that on the contrary there is nothing but that, or that death is the most proper thing in the "world." It's not that I particularly prefer incomplete works, like romantic ruins, like the "Temple of Philosophy" Gérard de Nerval speaks of in *Sylvie*: "This unfinished building is already nothing but a ruin, . . . and its steps, out of joint, are overgrown with brambles." Thinking is always, as Jean-Luc Nancy says, *a finite thought*, and in this very respect for finitude is never complete. Thinking is *not* a work, not even a work of art, since a work is only a work when complete, fully executed, when the last word has been spoken, when it has reached its end, been brought to term or to its *telos* (for Aristotle *energeia* is synonymous with *entelecheia*, having oneself as end). The "end" of thinking is not a telos, but rather something like an inner limit that forbids any closure on itself. Maybe the steps of this edifice that is philosophy are disjointed, out of joint. The steps are uneven, they are shattered joints. But here it would be a question of whether philosophy can still be shaped into a system, transformed into a work (even a work of art or of archetectonics), whether there is *one* unified philosophy or tradition that could be identified as such, as "Western Metaphysics."

Has philosophy come to its end, and if so what are we supposed to do? What task remains for us—to bury it? This question should be reminiscent of the title of a lecture given by Heidegger in 1964, "The End of Philosophy and the Task [*die Aufgabe*] of Thought." Heidegger claims that philosophy has exhausted all of its possibilities, since, metaphysics being the same as Platonism, and Nietzsche having characterized his philosophy as a reversal of Platonism, "with this reversal [*Umkehrung*] of Metaphysics, the extreme possibility of philosophy has been reached." However, the end of philosophy would mean that it has "entered its final stage" (like that of cancer) only on the condition that we do not understand what an end is, properly speaking: "The old signification of our word 'end' means the same as 'place.' 'From one end to the other' means from one place to an other. The end of philosophy is that place in which the totality of its history in its extreme possibility gathers itself. End as completion means this gathering."[2] From this point (this end), a pathway must be able to lead to the other end, by which I mean what Heidegger called *der andere Anfang*, "the other Beginning."

Now all of this is already well-known, and I don't want to comment once again on Heidegger's "philosophy," if only because we should not, according to Heidegger himself, be able to speak of "Heidegger's philosophy." This does not mean that I would blindly follow Heidegger on his way or take for granted that he did, in fact, achieve this "step back," returning from metaphysics to its hidden essence (also perhaps a specter returning from the beyond) that is the "unthought" of philosophy and that would therefore require an other kind of thinking. We must ask, first, whether such a step is possible, and then (although it is the same question) if this step [*pas*] does *not* [*pas*] repeat the philosophical mode of thinking, that is, return to an "essence" or to a "more fundamental" ground that is hidden and that, because it runs aground, becomes an abyss. But when I speak of a repetition, a re-petition of (the) principle, I should also insist that every repetition *as* repetition is an alteration, a different step. This leads me to the "thing itself" and to repeat my title: "The Different Step: From Heidegger to Derrida." Beyond the undecidable ambiguity of the "step" ("step" or "not," name or syncategorem), I must translate or, if that is impossible, refer what you, in English, call the "issue" (and that word, in French, means "exit") to what I have just said about the "end" of philosophy. If metaphysics is *declared* closed (in a kind of performative) with Heidegger, is this in fact the case (*casus*) or should we *not* [*pas*] understand the step [*pas*] passing metaphysics by differently? For this different step, we must step over into another thinking of difference itself, a thinking of différance.

Before taking another step, I will first summarize what is at stake in the question of "difference." In this preliminary step, I will take as a guideline Rodolphe Gasché's recent book, *Inventions of Difference*. The title is quite paradoxical, since the book begins with the affirmation that in a certain branch of literary criticism "'difference' has become the key term." "A quick glance at recent book titles reveals the term not only apposed to everything, but in everything" (82). Gasché argues that difference, in metaphysics, stems from identity, and that "what takes place from Parmenides to Hegel, and beyond, is a relative liberation in which difference, rather than being effaced in the face of identity, is shown to have its only meaningful place within identity" (Gasché 85). For example, when Hegel spoke of the "identity of identity and non-identity" (thus of the identity of identity and difference), this shows how restricted the function of difference is at the heart of the dialectical process. It has a "relative freedom," relative with respect to identity. Difference is allowed only to the extent that it in turn allows identity the possibility of having a content, of not being identical to pure Being, that is, of not being an abstract identity or the void of nothingness. Identity, therefore, is not only at the starting point but at the end of the process; or it is at the end because it was already posited speculatively from the beginning.

If we understand metaphysics as the unity of a single history going from one end to the other, then metaphysics is born of the violence that consists in reducing the other simply by naming it "the Other." From Plato, who reduced the Other to the law of the Same (the Idea), to Hegelian dialectics, in which the Other is no less excluded, precisely by being included, becoming a simple moment that *is* not yet and yet that is already mediated in advance, difference is always already recuperated, digested, incorporated (*Unlimited, Inc.*). It has always been kept at a distance, as if it constituted an essential threat to the integrity and wholeness of self-identity, that is, of Being (and thought, since identity is first of all the identity of Being and thought). Since unity, even if it is not the same, not homogeneous, presides over the relationship, the One will always express what the Other is or should be, even if it is in its name. Consequently, the One still re-presents the Other, even or especially *as such*, on the common ground of Being, presence. I simplify here, but it should nonetheless be stressed that the Other of presence is *not* simply an absence, which is an "other" presence, a transformed presence; nor is the Other a "not" in the sense of a negative. For this reason, the thinking of difference must not be thought as a negative ontology. For negation has always been a powerful means by which to reduce difference in dualistic schemes: contradictions and oppositions are the very means by which identity comes into its own (its self) as the totality controlling differences that have been reduced to homogeneous binary oppositions. Even calling what cannot be conceived of "inconceivable" because it never returns to itself in the identity of presence and the presence of identity is still a speculative tour de force. To leave the inconceivable without a name would already be a first step, provided that one does *not* stop there, as if it were enough to float in the empty blue sky of the ineffable. There is nothing ineffable there, even if there is nothing immediately comprehensible there either.

Identity is the philosophical name for difference, but in such a way that difference, once it is posited, exposed, (re)presented, expressed, is already forgotten. In Heidegger's terms, metaphysics is nothing other than the history of such a forgetting, the forgetting of Being as *this* difference. The question I will ask is whether such an oblivion is effaced or surpassed by a thinking that endeavors to think difference *as such*, or whether the very fact of speaking of difference "as such" does not once again come down to falling back under the domination of identity, whereas identity cannot *be* identity without passing by way of the Other (the "internal" difference by means of which something can be self-identical).

But first, what is "ontological difference"? In fact, it is not a difference at all—at least not between two kinds of things, two kinds of "beings." Not only is it not a distinction posited by "understanding" and so a difference that could be understood in the traditional way, where one compares two different things against a common ground, ontological difference is not a distinction at all. Gasché puts this well when he defines difference as a difference between "dissimilars" that have nothing in common but that are ultimately the Same (Gasché 91). (Heidegger always insists on the irreducible difference separating the Same and the similar.) Being and beings do not differ one from the other as a chair differs from a table. For such (ontic) differences are subject to the unity of a genus, and Being is clearly not a genus. It is the *schlechthin transcendens*, the "absolutely transcendent," and is not commensurable or homogeneous with beings. "Being" *is* not, only beings (chairs, forks, and even God) are. This "not" [*pas*], whose "first name" or "fore-name" (before the name) in *What Is Metaphysics?* was "nothingness," qualifies Being as different from any being. With regard to beings, then, Being is nothing. It is not a thing, a being among others. But that does not mean that Being is absolutely *nothing at all*. On the contrary, as everything, Being has always been thought by metaphysics as supreme Being, which allowed theology to seize upon it. But Being is the supreme being only insofar as it is the Being *of* beings, the most being part in beings. That implies putting aside ontic difference, for, with regard to the supremacy of Being, any particular being is disregarded as being only *a* being (not *the* Being). The supremacy of Being does not result from a particularity or from a specific quality that would differentiate Being from all other beings. On the contrary, the difference in Being results from its in-difference to any ontic difference, that is, comes from its absolute generality. This means that metaphysics is only a theology because it is first an ontology, and not the reverse. In *Identity and Difference*, Heidegger cites an "example" with a restriction that plays on the German word for "example," *Beispiel*: "nowhere in beings can we find a correct example for the essence of Being, probably because the essence of Being is Play (*Spiel*) itself" (58). The example (and the play on the word "example" in which the game is played out) comes from Hegel. Someone enters a shop to buy fruit. He is offered apples, pears, cherries, and grapes. But he refuses them all. What he wants is fruit—not apples or pears, but simply fruit. . . . Likewise, it is even more impossible to find anything like Being in its universality. At the same time, without Being and its generality, no single thing, for example a fruit, would ever be. Being a fruit is not itself fruit, but without this Being, no fruit can ever be, so that, in the end, not only is Being not nothing, it alone *is* properly, beings being only what are not, properly speaking, *me on*.

Now, what can we say about ontological difference? Could we say that this difference "is" something? No. That is why difference has never been properly thought as such in metaphysics. Heidegger writes that forgetting belongs to difference, for difference was destined to be forgotten: how can one *not* forget "nothing," or, at least, that which is not a thing, not an umbrella, for instance? Heidegger tried to step back from "Being" (as the Being *of* beings, as the "proper" identity giving ground and legitimacy to any being) in order to think difference for itself, as such, or, as he puts it in *Time and Being*, in order to think Being without any concern for beings. But is it possible to think difference *for itself*? Does difference have a "self," that is, ultimately, an identity? Or does it not rather differ from and in itself? If this is the case, we can understand the necessity of thinking "difference" differently, the necessity of that different difference called "différance." This other name for difference corresponds to the necessity of re-thinking the relation of difference to identity, and, first of all, of questioning the possibility of an identity of difference as such. The "as" of the "as such" is no longer self-evident. As Gasché puts it, "difference as such lacks the quality not only of Being, but of propriety as well, and to such an extent that no as such is *appropriate* to it. To think it remains therefore an infinite task" (Gasché 103). Further investigation would show that, in Heidegger's attempt to free difference (and Being) from its forgetting (that is, from its link with ontotheology), a repetition of the metaphysical gesture that I would very roughly qualify as "identification" is performed. Heidegger himself was conscious of this danger when, at the end of *Identity and Difference*, he wrote that the "step would remain incomplete" because "our Western languages are all in their own way languages of metaphysical thinking" (*Identity* 66). We already have a simple example of this in the "as" (*als*). To think difference *as* difference is already to think it in terms of logos, of gathering, of identity, or of unity.

If it is true that ontological difference is not a distinction stemming from understanding in the restricted sense of the German *Verstand*, does it therefore have absolutely nothing to do with the comprehension (*Verstehen*) of meaning, especially with the self-understanding of the meaning of Being as it has been determined in *Being and Time*? If *Dasein* has been chosen as the only being to have access to Being, it is because *Dasein* has the sense or meaning of Being, can in advance and always already understand Being by relating and acting not only to its own Being, but toward other beings. For *Dasein* only is there an other, and this is so because *Dasein* has the sense or meaning of difference (that is, of Being). *Dasein* is different from other beings, animals, objects. (This is clear inasmuch as *Dasein* is marked by negation and exists for death.) How, in this respect, could difference be something absolutely incomprehensible, but likewise, and symmetrically, how is a self-understanding, an understanding of inner difference that constitutes identity proper, the ipseity of *Dasein*, possible?

Self-understanding is not self-evident. Let us recall the last words attributed to Hegel on his deathbed. His was a brutal, senseless death, like all deaths: cholera has no dialectical meaning. There are two versions of the same story, if it is one. The first version is told by Heine, the second by Kierkegaard: "I touch here upon the comical side of our philosophers. They constantly complain about not being understood. As Hegel was lying on his deathbed, he said discontented, 'Only one person understood me'; but he immediately added, 'And he did not understand me either.'" In his *Concluding Unscientific Postscript to Philosophical Fragments*, Kierkegaard writes: "Hegel must have died upon saying these words, saying that no one but the person who misunderstood him understood him—and if Hegel was speaking of himself . . . ?"[3]

Is it possible to understand oneself? Isn't an other always necessary for that? Likewise, can one give oneself, this giving being understood in all senses of the word, including that in which giving leads to physical, sexual possession? Can one give, offer, oneself, as a witness, as a witness of one's "own" death or of one's survival? Who understands whom? A part should be more than the totality in order to grasp itself *as such*, as self *and* other. These are questions that should be answered (for), questions that bind us to an infinite responsibility toward our self *as* (toward) the Other, toward our self as *including* [*comprenant*] the Other in our self. Thus, what I am saying is understood or should be understood as included and understood in a language, my "own" language. My "own" language, and yet it belongs to me less than I belong to it. (To speak French, I must already be in a generality common to all those who understand French.) Before even being able to say or write a word, I would always already be taken (caught like a prisoner) in what comprehends (or takes) me (and others who share this understanding) without, for all that, being sure of understanding myself in it. Thinking takes place in language, but this "place" is anything but indifferent to what takes place in it. There is at least a passage from one to the other, and vice versa, so that neither could be isolated or taken for itself without including the other in this self. The same is true of *Dasein*'s understanding of the meaning of Being. But then, how can they be at the same time different from one another and the same in regards to difference itself, which puts them at an equal distance from beings? This question leads to Derrida's critique of the privilege accorded to *Dasein* (that is, ultimately, to human beings, even if not conceived of in terms of subjectivity). I will return to that later.

For the moment, I only want to pass from Heidegger's conception of difference to the "other" one, Derrida's. First, we have to know whether such a passage is possible, and then, whether it constitutes a (linear, homogeneous) progression, or whether it is rather an abrupt disconnection, something like a *gap*—a difference that could not be thought without thinking difference differently, to the point that meaning could no longer pass through it. And yet we must make meaning pass through it, for a difference whose meaning we do not understand would no longer be difference. To pass from Heidegger to Derrida there will not be the same "striking gap" to pass over as there is, for example, on the way from Rimbaud to Heidegger, since what difference there is, is not that between two worlds as incommensurate as poetry and philosophy. Heidegger and Derrida do indeed belong to the same world, if it can be called a "world": they are both philosophers. Of course, they are rather peculiar philosophers, since neither of them completely understands himself as being only a philosopher. It is even this non-understanding that brings them together, puts them on the "same wavelength," that of a certain discrepancy with regard to discourse, conceptual language, and the philosophical tradition from its beginning. Neither can any longer recognize or identify "himself" in a figure or code constituted by a corpus that reflects back to him something essentially troubling. To dismantle the representations or "covers" that block access to the "thing itself" is the task explicitly required of *Destruktion* in *Being and Time*. In this sense, it is almost *too* obvious that deconstruction (at least as a word or concept) comes from Heideggerian *Destruktion*. For example, I cite this passage from *Toward the Question of Being*: " . . . the lack of reflection began already in 1927 with the superficial misunderstanding of *Destruktion* such as it is discussed in *Being and Time*, a notion that has no other intention, as a de-construction (*Abbau*) of representations that have become banal and void, than to win back the experiences of Being that are at the very origin of those of Metaphysics" (36). In *Politiques de l'amitié*, Derrida cites a passage from *What is Philosophy?*, where Heidegger repeats that *Destruktion* "does not signify the demolition [*Zerstören*] but the deconstruction [*Abbauen*], the clearing [*Abtragen*], the putting-aside, of historical statements . . . " Deconstruction is no more a simple undertaking to demolish than is *Destruktion*. If it takes an extra step in this direction, it is not to add to the radicalism of *Destruktion* but, on the contrary, to cast doubt upon this very radicalism. Is there beneath the representations that have become banal and used up something else, something more fundamental to which we should *return*: an origin? It could be said that the deconstruction of the supplementary turn of the origin, the deconstruction of the re-turn to a one and single origin, sharply checked *Destruktion*.[4] This sharp check shows an *absolute limit* in the movement of going-to-the-ground (and running aground there). If the word "deconstruction" indeed comes from *Destruktion*, just as the word "différance" is a simple modification (one that cannot be *heard*, moreover) of "différence," this does not then mean that the "thing" is the same. Is there in fact any sense in establishing an origin for a movement that tends to deconstruct the very notion of origin?

If there is indeed some sense in passing "from" Heidegger "to" Derrida, it is more difficult to assert if this passage would constitute a progression, and in what sense or direction. Here the bond that is tradition (even in the disruption of tradition, which can itself become tradition) is not enough to explain everything, and especially cannot bring back the passage to the comforting scheme of filiation and genealogy. Derrida has never stopped insisting upon the distance "in relation to the Heideggerian problematics" that he has marked "in all the essays" he has published, a distance that is marked in both content and form, so that in reading only one of his texts we can see that "it does not *look* like a text with a 'Heideggerian filiation'" (*Positions* 71). In this sense, I agree with Gasché when he discusses an argument by John Caputo, according to whom Derrida, in his reading of Heidegger, produces confusion, so that not only does Derrida appear Heideggerian, but a certain "dissemination . . . has already taken place in Heidegger's text." Consequently, "it becomes impossible to establish strictly what is properly Heidegger's or what is Derrida's own" (Gasché 79). But I would first be tempted to reply: what does it really matter? Is it of any essential concern for us to delimit what is the property of each, his copyright, when difference does not issue from the Proper and when deconstruction does not belong to anyone, not even itself? However, this argument is erroneous insofar as the very word "différance" was invented in order to make it differ, in a strictly unheard-of manner, from simple difference. Not only is it different by the alteration of a simple letter (a silent letter, moreover, so that this is an unheard [of] difference); it refers to a double root in the Latin word (itself different from the Greek word *diaphora* to which Heidegger refers most often) *differe*, so that a temporalizing effect is added ("to differ" as "to defer") to the dimension of space. This multiplication of different meanings in the same word is not the most important point; what is crucial is that all these meanings (including others that I cannot evoke here) are different from each other to the extent that they cannot be united in a single, simple root, even if this root were hidden. When Derrida speaks of a cluster of various heterogeneous meanings, he does not presuppose their possible unification or synthesis. Not only does différance not have a *single* meaning, but, since it has several meanings that are irreducibly heterogeneous to one another, the "word" ultimately deconstructs the entire system of meaning in language, a system that is grounded in unity and self-identity. This does not mean that it has no meaning at all, but that it is not a word and not a concept either. For this reason as well, différance does not belong to the horizon of Being, meaning, logos. But I insist: that does not imply nonsense, which ultimately is submitted to the same law of the unity of sense, if only for the simple reason that nonsense is nonsense only in opposition and contradiction to sense, and because contradiction or negation is another branch of the binary logic of identity (the principle of identity as the principle of *non*-contradiction). As the condition of possibility of sense (meaning), différance is also its condition of impossibility as a single sense that would be identical to itself. Différance is the strict limit of what it lets be. It cannot present itself, or "is" present only in the way a ghost or a trace is, a trace that can only be effaced in order to allow any present difference to present itself. Such is the "arche-trace," which no archeo-logical (because logical in the first place) search could ever discover, and which can *never* be discovered, to return to the example of Hegel.

In this sense, one could object that différance is really nothing but an illusion stemming from the impossibility of complying with the minimal law of any coherent, that is, logical, discourse, an ancient law already formulated by Plato and Aristotle. According to this law, a discourse, a logos, must at least be a discourse on something, must speak of something, must be a *logos tinos*. Phenomenology complies with this minimal law, even when this "something" is not a thing, is not an apparent phenomenon. The Introduction to *Being and Time* already tells us that: what must absolutely be shown, the "true" phenomenon, is "obviously what at first and most of the time does *not* show itself," that is, "that which proximally and for the most part does not show itself; but at the same time it is something that belongs to what shows itself, and belongs to it so essentially as to constitute its meaning and its ground" (BT 59, 35). In the language of fundamental ontology, phenomenological showing must unconceal the Being of beings. Being withdraws in beings; it belongs to the being in giving it sense and foundation without ever showing itself in the way the being

The Different Step

appears. Even when scientific demonstration is not possible, some sort of "showing" is required in order to present the "thing" to be thought, the "theme." And even if, for the Heidegger of *Time and Being*, the main point is not to attend to a logical series of arguments but to "follow in the steps of Showing" (*dem Gang des Zeigens zu folgen*), even if it is not a matter of taking this different step (*zeigen*, to show, is not a demonstration, and there is nothing to be demonstrated in either Being or time since neither is a being or a matter of a statement), a *presentation* is still required in order that thinking be a thinking *of*. . . . On the contrary, différance being not only not a being but unable to present itself (and, therefore, to be presented), and residing within the horizon of Being, and therefore of logos, not being a question of the principle of exposition, it seems that to think this unheard-of différance is to think nothing at all, would not be a thinking. At least not a philosophical thinking, laying claim to truth.

As far as thought and truth are concerned, différance would mark out a radical difference from the philosophical scene / stage. This is indeed a familial scene, taking the classical turn of a parricide (which, since Plato, is inscribed in and as the philosophical scene par excellence). But parricide is not truly parricide unless there is incest too. The philosophical competition in which "the" truth is disputed bears witness to what is at stake. But Derridean suspicion concerns precisely these stakes; they are what he puts in jeopardy. Truth is at stake, and this is why Derrida, like Heidegger, remains above all a philosopher. Only, contrary to Heidegger, Derrida no longer maintains any claim to truth, at least not in the same way. He gives his attention to truth [*y tient*] without giving himself over [*s'y tenir*] to it. And he makes no pretension to detaining [*détenir*] it, to having or possessing it ("in a soul and in a body," as Rimbaud says). Pretension is first of all the demand, the claim to a title, a privilege, a right. To pretend to something is to aspire to it, to desire what by rights should be *returned* to us. Pretension is a firm and affirmed intention to return what is pretended to the self. But as it must affirm itself and, therefore, must pass through language, the original intention, resulting from a pure intentionality or unfissured wanting-to-say [*vouloir-dire*], risks getting taken in within the game of language (and languaging), risks being taken in, misled, there, and thus risks missing the intended object in taking it for the word (which also has pretensions to Being). The final truth does not always show up for the appointment, or if it does show up, surrenders, disappointed.[5] *Truth* barely missed being truth in missing Being. And on account of this always possible and thus necessary failing, those who make pretensions to truth also return with their hands empty, become pretentious. In different terms, the conception is always a deception,[6] just as the concept always risks being a *decept*, a theft of meaning and therefore of a heritage.

To take up the title of a recent book by Derrida, it is a question of this right "to" philosophy, of the right to the truth that is the philosophical pretension par excellence. Without having recourse to etymology as a universal pass-word, I will, however, recall that *to pretend* comes from the Latin verb *praetendere*, to hold near to, to present, therefore. Any immediate presentation is a pretension, a claim with a presumption to immediate presence. To pretend is to hold in the "near," an intentionality inscribed in the beginning of phenomenology, which fosters the privilege of presence. In a sense, the pretension to immediacy is *by right* always founded in philosophy. Radical and generalized Cartesian doubt is the most patent example. Naïveté (the state of nature, natural consciousness, etcetera) must be submitted to this suspicion that at bottom is *skepsis*. But the philosophical approach only suspects naturalness in order better to base its own pretensions. Philosophy "pretends" in the sense that it acts as if it knew, while it knows that it does not know, and thus already knows. . . . As though knowing that one does not know were *already* knowing something. Everything in Heidegger's approach is reminiscent of philosophical suspicion; we could even say that he carried this suspicion to the extreme, the point of no return, to the point of being suspicious about truth itself. But this is still a quest and a request for truth, a question and questioning of "the essence of truth." Yet when Derrida questions Heidegger, it is precisely to suspect him of privileging the question itself, of the quest for a *more original* truth, one truer than "nature" (that is, than this philosophical meta-nature). For example, *Of Spirit* is subtitled *Heidegger and the Question*, since what is really in question, as Derrida puts it, "is the subtitle of my book, the question of the question, which is almost constantly privileged by Heidegger as 'the piety of thinking'" (*Points . . .* 183). If the question is "almost" always privileged by Heidegger, it is because he "almost" goes back on this in taking hearing / understanding—listening to, understanding the other and thus oneself in the other—as preceding the privilege of *Fragen*, questioning. The whole question turns upon the precedence of the question, which is also that of *Dasein*, that being privileged in the quest for the meaning of Being because it and it alone can question. The question therefore turns upon the return of humanism in the thinking that pretended to dethrone the human being of his pretensions (to being a subject, a reasonable animal endowed with logos, etcetera). However, in a reverse and complementary gesture, Derrida constantly insists on the necessity of the question as a prerequisite for deconstruction, including the deconstruction of the precedence of the question. I will cite, for example, this passage from the beginning of *Of Grammatology*: "[I]t is indeed the *question* of Being that Heidegger poses to metaphysics. And with it the question of the truth, of sense, of the logos. The incessant meditation upon that question does not restore confidence. On the contrary, it dislodges the confidence at its own depth, which, being a matter of the meaning of Being, is more difficult than is often believed" (22).

In order to hear / understand the other, one must begin by no longer hearing / understanding *oneself*. We must remain silent, efface the "self" and thus *return* speech, give it back, to itself—here, the Logos that has been confiscated by the tradition and become logocentrism. The whole difficulty of this "restitution" is contained in this silent voice, these dead letters. . . . An immense, infinite task of deciphering, of translating (trans-lating), in short, of what we might call Heideggerian hermeneutics, is thus opened, engaging, quite simply, the meaning of reading, the reading of meaning, its very meaning as a necessary dis-orientation. This happens in such a way that we can understand Derrida's uneasiness, even his anxiety, when, after some summary and by no means clear investigations, it is suggested that we conclude with a "Do not read Heidegger!" It is *forbidden*. Is it dangerous? This command is all the more peremptory in that it stems from ignorance. We must not read Heidegger because he has been declared unreadable, which comes down to wanting to *do away* with him. As a single counter-example, I take the following declaration by Derrida: "Briefly: 1. to think (speak, write) the *logos* 'before' these oppositions, 'before' voice and meaning (*phone, semainein*)—another 'history of philosophy,' let's read Heidegger, for example . . . " (*Points . . .* 179). Derrida, like Heidegger, tries to think "logos" or difference before conceptual and metaphysical oppositions (in which logos, the source of all oppositions, itself becomes the single master term of the opposition). If Derrida put quotation marks around "before," it is because he reads the word in another way, does not relate it to a historial before, to this *Anfang* that would be the origin of the History (of Being), identified by Heidegger as that of the Occident. This is another "before," and another fore-word, before-saying, as well; but if the place of this before cannot be situated in either time (even in a more original temporality) or space (an archaic Greece), it is no less a before, a kind of *arche*. Otherwise, why call the trace of the Other "arche-trace"? I refer to another passage from *Of Grammatology*, where we can read: "For example, the value of a transcendental arche [*archie*] must make its necessity felt *before* [my emphasis] letting itself be erased. The concept of arche-trace must comply with both that necessity and that erasure" (61). There is a double right here: the right to philosophical necessity and to its erasure, which does not efface the philosophical but displaces it, deposes it to give right [*droit*] to what the Law [*Droit*] has *excluded*. It is in this way that Derrida's "double science" can be read.

If there is no way leading out of the enclosure of metaphysics, however, no language other than that of metaphysics; if there is no difference except as the forgetting of difference, precisely because arche-difference is not and can never be, can never be present as such; if one cannot pass from one side (the metaphysical) to the

The Different Step

other (which is not simply *non*-metaphysical), it is precisely in this point (of no) passage, this threshold or step (not taken—the impossibility of passing from one to the other without taking a leap), that something takes place [*se passe*]. This something I name with an untranslatable word, since I invented it (an invention of the other in the proper): *passance*. This invention would like to translate the (non-)passage in which sense is suspended—not annihilated, but interrupted, opened to its very opening. There is no sense without *passance* [*pas de sens sans passance*]. There is no sense (or difference) existing by itself, no sense of sense. But again, that does not mean that there is no sense at all, or that difference, which opens the possibility of sense but does not constitute sense as its metaphysical ground or even as its transcendental condition, would be nothing but an empty word. Différance precisely cannot be reduced to a word, whether it be proper or figurative. As regards language, the possibility of a difference between a proper and an improper (metaphorical) sense, the possibility of a passage or translation from one to the other, rests on the *impossibility* of a clear-cut difference, the impossibility of making any decision in favor of one or the other.

The passage is also that across "the line." I refer here to Heidegger's "Über 'die Linie'" ("About 'the Line'"), which is itself a sort of "suspensive" citation, adding quotation marks similar to those put around the word "spirit" to Ernst Jünger's title, in which the *über* clearly has the value of a *trans-*, beyond. In his title, then, Heidegger himself would have returned upon his "overcoming of Metaphysics" (that is, of nihilism) inscribing a warning there: do not step beyond [*pas au-delà*] this "zero" line, but only about, "on," concerning, up against it. To pass beyond this line would be to pass beyond the desert, which essentially has "*no* [*pas*] measure." It would be to pass beyond the "There is no present" that opens all the *Solitudes*[7] precisely because they refuse to pass over this unique step (not taken) and take this refusal of the (heroic?) gesture of getting ahead of ourselves (of trying to be absolutely modern), refuse the temptation to move on to something else too quickly, refuse the temptation to pass over to the other side and thus to fall into the abyss. It is a matter of casting doubt on the possibility of a reversal that would take place through the abyss, at least that reversal Heidegger, from a reading of these lines from "Mnemosyne," named Turning: "Yes, before them [the gods] / Mortals reached the abyss. And so, that turns / With them" ("Nemlich es reichen / Die Sterblichen eh' an den Abgrund. Also wendet es sich / Mit diesen") (*Sämtliche Werke* 2:1 193). That "turns," yes, but in what direction? Is it in the "right" direction, the direction Heidegger wanted, that of a *return into presence*, true presence, the true meaning (that has been forgotten) of Being as having come into presence? Or rather, has there ever been presence that was not fissured, ruined in the abyss? And is true presence not the founding myth, the myth of a full, undamaged origin that is self-present? To reverse, therefore, would not be to return to the origin, to pass into it, but simply to remain or resist. From a "fundamentalist" Heideggerian point of view, this resistance will appear "retarded," not having taken the leap, deferring the moment of the True. But what if every instant, even the "flash" (*Augen-blick*) of the event (*Ereignis*), must defer "itself" and differ from "itself" and pass into an *Ent-eignis*? We must insist upon this: such is the different / differing step, the step deferring and differing from *presence* (proper, presence to and of the True).

In the "explanatory" exposition of the seminar devoted to his lecture "Time and Being," Heidegger distinguishes two features of thought. Thought is understanding (*verstehende Denken*) and explication (*auslegende Denken*). Heidegger then immediately asks if, in general, explication (or interpretation: *hermeneia*) can characterize that thought in which taking up the question of Being once and for all is at issue. "Understanding" and "explic(it)ation" are structures of *Dasein* that are clearly exposed in *Being and Time*. The distinction is inherited from Dilthey and as such is only suitable up to a certain point. The structure of understanding and of interpretation is prerequisite for meaning or sense, is its pre-sense. It is anticipation as the donation of sense; but there is no sense without Being-there, and, consequently, there is no Being without *Dasein*.[8] That is why thought, in that it takes what is *given* to it into care and establishes itself in a relation of receptivity and thus of finitude, remains preparatory. It is preparatory in the double sense that it can never do anything but pre-dict [come before] what is already coming upon it, always taking it by surprise, and in that it comes from this very coming; that is, in the end, thought can never appear to itself, never think itself [*se penser*], but always spends itself in thinking itself [*se dé-penser*] because it is dispensed with [*dis-pensée*] by the very thing in view of which it is thought. The anteriority of understanding as the anticipating project of meaning is nothing but the result of the *a priori* of the donation itself. We thus understand Heidegger's insistence, his defense against expositions. Exposition is a secondary mode of explic(it)ation. It has to do with words and not with the thing itself. What is more, it is only interested in already disclosed beings. Even when apophantic, exposition remains derived. That is clear when I stand before a Klee painting or even when I hear a poem by Trakl. Neither one nor the other (re)presents anything that has already been disclosed. As concerns them, it is as though we were in the middle of New York City—we don't understand a thing. But at the same time, we are no less on the look-out for or concerned by what is happening. On the contrary, we are taken by something that understands *us* in advance, even though this thing is almost nothing at all, the "little piece of yellow wall" in front of which Bergotte died in Proust's *Remembrance of Things Past*. To be taken thus, dispossessed of self in order to attain a more proper Self than one's self, such is the movement Heidegger has in view under the name *Ereignis*.

If only we could understand this word, a common word still in use in everyday German: event. Of course, Heidegger says that *Ereignis* is not an event in the sense that we speak of historical events, like the "European market" (which, I fear, for him did not constitute an event worthy of the name). But can one withdraw entirely from common language? If *Ereignis* is a hapax that is entirely incommensurate to all common dwelling, is language not the "house of Being"? Or have we landed upon an intransmissible idiom, be it that of the proper itself? Things become even more complicated when we consider the peculiar way in which Heidegger de-composes the word (*Er-eignis*) and discovers in it the "proper" (*eigen*). Does this "proper" name therefore name what is most proper, the making come into the proper? But we must not forget that all making-come [*faire-venir*] is also an origin or provenance [*pro-venir*]: *Er-eignis* "comes into its own," as word, through everyday language. This appropriation of language presupposed that in the beginning language is not proper. It is this very impropriety that makes all appropriation possible. In the same way, if we say that the *Ereignis* is a reciprocal connection of appropriation between Being and human beings, we say nothing at all inasmuch as neither (if we can even think them separately, in themselves) properly has a proper (or own) *before* this appropriation, and inasmuch as this appropriation is the event for Being as for human beings, the event that makes language itself "proper." Let us read the following passage from *Zur Sache des Denkens*, where Heidegger comments upon "himself," seeking to make "himself" understood.

> We understand this step at first as an "a-way from . . . " (*weg von*) and as a "toward" (*hin zu*). Thus, Heidegger's thinking would be the movement away from the unconcealment of beings to go toward unconcealment as such, which remains hidden in unconcealed beings. Yet something completely different is thought in the title "Step back" (*Schritt zurück*). The step back draws back before, gains distance from that which wants to come close. The gaining of distance is a de-distancing (*Ent-Fernung*), the liberation allowing what is to be thought to approach [ZSD 32].

The *Schritt zurück* is by no means a "retrocession" toward a more proper ground, toward Being as "meaning and foundation." It is not a question of disclosing what is withdrawing in what is approaching, Being in beings. It is rather a question of drawing back before this proximity, of gaining some distance, of liberating oneself not only from beings, but from Being as the Being of (or in) beings. *Ent-Fernung* is to be understood in a different way from in *Being and Time*, since it is not related to intraworldly be-

The Different Step 215

ings. In *Identity and Difference*, Heidegger uses the same word to explain the meaning of the step back. By *Ent-Fernung*, we free "the matter of thinking, Being as difference, and we let it present itself to us in a face-to-face that can remain without an object" (*Identity* 55–56). Being as difference is not an object to be contemplated or re-presented by a subject; but it still presents itself anyway, coming close (*prope*), and for this reason, coming into its own / proper (*proprius*): into presence. However, *Ent-Fernung* can also be thought as a distancing (that is, of beings or of Being as the Being *of* beings), for the *Ereignis*, the event, is that there is no Being or time except inasmuch as both are *not*, that is, inasmuch as they are dispossessed of all propriety / property. This formulation is still misleading, for in order to be dispossessed of what one has, one must first of all have that. Yet what is peculiar about the dispossession proper to the *Ereignis* is that it takes nothing away, but on the contrary gives. To understand the event of propriation, we must begin no longer to understand anything about it. We must be expropriated, though an expropriation in the sense of the *Enteignis* or *Ent-fernung* that liberates the distance *in* propriation itself, opens a spacing there. This is not a simple alienation or even the process of a negativity. On the one hand, there is no result; and on the other hand, nothing is properly lost, or this loss announces what is proper to the gift—that it abandons itself entirely and without reservation, abandons itself in the gift and as gift. It is in this sense that we must understand the forgetting of Being as its proper sending, its generosity: Being forgets itself in what is, and thus Being does not itself appear, or disappears in being [*disparest*]. Being outdistances appearing, leaving it behind with a leap—with an origin, but an origin that ultimately cannot be exposed as such and in the light of the "as such."

> Insofar as the destination of Being now lies in the offering of time and insofar as both [Being and time] lie in the *Ereignis*, the proper feature is announced in the propriating: namely, that it withdraws its most proper feature from endless unconcealment. If we think from the standpoint of propriation, this means that it ex-propriates itself from itself in the aforementioned sense. Ex-propriation belongs to appro-

priation as such. By it [expropriation] appropriation does not renounce itself, but keeps its propriety / property.⁹

The "as" itself becomes indeterminable *as such*. It was first said to be "specious" (*verfänglich*). In other words, one could get caught there several times and in several senses, in several senses of being "caught," as well (to be caught in a trap, or caught up in a text). Being as (*als*) *Ereignis* could signify, first, a new thesis on Being, a continuation of metaphysics, then. But if we take a step back, returning from Being as the Being of beings to Being as difference, then Being (as the Being of beings) is part of the *Ereignis* and would even be a "genus of *Ereignis*" rather than *Ereignis* being a "genus of Being" (ZSD 22). Why the conditional *would be*? Because, first of all, Being is not, properly speaking, and is not a genus; and most of all, because it could not be said properly, at least not with the verb *to be*. *Ereignis* "would be" perhaps . . . but cannot be (anything whatsoever) in the first place because it "may be" (gives) Being . . . as such. But by the same token, does it make sense to speak of the "as such" concerning what gives it being? Does it make sense to speak of *Ereignis* "*as such*," properly speaking (and the "as such" is the mark of propriation "taking place" in and as language, as it is put in *On the Way to Language*)?

> Being disappears in the *Ereignis*. In the expression "Being as *Ereignis*," the "as" now signifies: Being, letting come into presence destined in the propriation [event], Time held in the propriation [event]. Time and Being are evented in the *Ereignis*. And *Ereignis* itself? Can we still say something about the *Ereignis*? [ZSD 22–23]

No, not really, not "as such." Propriation immediately turns into expropriation. But how does it happen that, turning into expropriation, propriation *keeps* its propriety? Why do we say that "expropriation belongs to propriation (as such)," if there is no propriation "as such"? And why not say the reverse: "propriation belongs to expropriation"? Is it because there is even *less* an expropriation "as such"? But is this not to recognize that propriation "is" more than the expropriation that belongs to it, as the whole is bigger than the part? And does the movement of propriation not recall the appropriation by sublation, *Aufhebung*? In alienating itself in the Other (not an other absolutely, but already *its* other), propriation could keep (*bewahren*) its Self, its Proper, so that in the end there is in fact no loss: the *Ereignis* saves "itself" through "its" *Enteignis*, its "most proper," as the Absolute is saved by the negativity at the heart of its procedure of self-manifestation and self-production. And the property owner always reigns over the whole transaction (what is yours is already mine . . .). The property owner is not the same, to be sure; he is not an absolute subject, not a human being. Nonetheless, if there is *Ereignis* and if it gives Being, it is only on the condition that there is "someone" to receive this gift. Thus a human being, if we call him *Dasein* or not, takes the place of Being in taking the place of its event. The place-holder remains there like the only one who could "accept" this present, that is to say, let it be *spoken*.

In a note at the end of the essay "Différance," Derrida writes: "Différance is not a 'species' of the 'genus' *ontological difference*. . . . Différance is not a process of appropriation in any sense whatsoever. It is neither its position (appropriation), nor its negation (expropriation), but the Other. Consequently, . . . no more so than Being is it a species of the genus *Ereignis*" (*Margins* 27). The reason why différance, this difference that is "older" than ontological difference and thus Being, older because it does not belong to the age or to the "epoch" of the history of Being, cannot be sublated in Appropriation (a sublation Heidegger represents in the form of an *Austrag*, at once difference and conciliation) is simply that not only is différance (like its homonym) not, but it is not even an appropriate word, not a *name*.

> "Older" than Being itself, such a *différance* has no name in our language. But we "already know" that if it is unnameable, it is not provisionally so, not because our language has not yet found or received this *name*, or because we would have to seek it in another language, outside the finite system of our own. It is rather because there is no *name* for it at all, not even the name of essence or of Being, not even that of *"différance,"* which is not a name . . .

What we know, or what we would know if it were simply a question here of something to know, is that there has never been, never will be, a unique word, a master-name [*Margins* 26–27].

Before concluding, a conclusion that must remain open, and therefore will not conclude properly speaking, I want to give a final example of the name of difference. As we know, the late Heidegger preferred the word *Unter-Schied* to *Differenz*. The difference between these two names for difference is not really important, since *Unter-Schied* names the same thing as *Differenz*, a "foreign" word in German that could be retranslated literally as *Austrag*.[10] In the last text of *On the Way to Language*, Heidegger tries to think *Unterschied* beyond ontological difference, as a difference between two "terms" that cannot be identified separately or, *a fortiori*, reduced to one another. *Unterschied* is, first, what carries (*trägt*), but in a double way. It carries to full-term (*austrägt*): *ein Kind austragen* means to give birth to a child, carry a pregnancy full-term. *Post austragen* means to deliver the mail, and the *Austräger* is the postman who delivers what belongs to x or y. *Austrag* is a delivery and a deliverance; but we can also take the verb literally: to carry away, out of . . . (to its term or terminus). Thus, in carrying the letter [*lettre*] or Being [*l'être*] *from* Heidegger *to* Derrida, for example, something gets lost, a letter, at least, though a silent letter, true enough: the *e* in difference. But something is gained as well: this very mutism, or the step (not) gained [*pas gagné*].

> *Der Unter-Schied trägt Welt in ihr Welten, trägt die Dinge in ihr Dingen aus. Also sie austragend, trägt sie einander zu.*
>
> Difference carries (delivers) world in its worlding, carries (delivers) things in their thinging. Carrying]them (distancing them from each other), it carries them toward one another [*Poetry* 202].

In delivering each, posted in the distance from the other, world (in its worlding) and things (in their thinging), difference brings them together, brings them into relation, carries them home, safe and sound, so that they correspond to each other, are appropriate

The Different Step 219

and appropriated. They are appropriated by this very placing apart, and are not only appropriated but reconciled, reunited *in* difference itself, whose proper name is pain.

But what is pain? Pain tears. It is the tear. But it does not tear apart into pieces. Pain does tear apart, divide, but so that it at the same time draws everything upon itself, gathers it to itself. Its tearing, as separating that gathers, is at once the pulling that draws and joins together that which is kept apart in division, like the lines that cut forward and up in a perspective drawing [UZS 27; *Poetry* 204–5].

I will limit myself to emphasizing the double movement that is itself structured into a single, uniting movement. First, *scheiden*, to cut or separate (since *Scheide* is a case, a sheath, and also a vagina, we must not forget), is to gather together by the very fact of separating. Then, and at the same time, tearing (it is also a tracing, a design—*Aufriss*) is a drawing *toward* the self, toward this very feature in which the differents are united (making it perhaps a sexual attraction of opposites), united not as likenesses (they are maintained at an extreme distance from one another), but jointed, folded into a single fold that *is* the very difference that, like a threshold or a between, keeps the differents at once separated and reunited. The possibility of a single support comes from "pain," which acts as a pulling (*Zug*) and a relation (*Bezug*) but first of all is *one* and has the very oneness of a support, and therefore a sort of subject. Of course, this is not a human subject, although, even if Heidegger refuses to consider it psychologically, by the fact that it is substantialized or nominalized, pain would be open only to the beings that are capable of experiencing Being as such (animals have a "poor" experience of world). More important than this possibility of a subject hidden behind the name "pain," more important even than the oneness of difference, is the final movement of reconciliation of the differents *in* difference itself. In the end, if difference expropriates (*Poetry* 206; UZS 29) the thing by delivering it to its other (the world), this expropriation, writes Heidegger in a way that recalls what he said about *Ereignis* in *Time and Being*, removes, steals nothing from the thing: "It removes the thing into its Proper: that a world remains." The essential word is "removes" (*enthebt*), in which we can hear an echo of *aufheben*.[11] We could translate it as "to depose." But this time it is a question of a deposition as a deposit one makes at the bank. The thing is delivered, placed in its Proper; from now on, you can count on it. Nothing will be lost of it, so we can sleep tight.

The question remains: where does the central place given to man stem from in such a game? Does not the cohabitation of Being and the human, even if it is not ontic, furnish the possible foundation of metaphysics? The human is close to Being, and vice versa, since it is to the human alone that the event (of presence) addresses itself. And if it already addresses itself in utterances, and even *as* speech, are we not back at the privilege that gives that definition, the *proper* name of the human: the being who "has" the gift of speech? Is not proximity, drawing near, the reign of language? Is it not what the metaphor of the "near" as "proper" betrays in turn? But is this really a metaphor, and what is a metaphor *properly speaking*? It could be said that the privilege of the human being does *not* reside in the fact that, among animals, humans are closer to what is. On the contrary, Heidegger has shown since 1929 that *Dasein* is a "Being of the far away," marked by distance. It is precisely in the opening of such a distance (of which death is the "proper," that is to say, *also* the metaphorical, figure) that presence and proximity can concern humans, approach them more than any other being that is *caught* in the circle of the world-of-life. We might well ask what an experience of death as death signifies for a being that is never *in the first place* defined by its belonging to life. We must also recognize that it is only by way of this de-positioning of the "proper" name of the human into that necessarily more metaphorical or poetic name "mortals" that the co-habitation of the human and death can be understood. It can be understood thus, even though "death" escapes all comprehension, escapes all meaning, and thus, contrary to what Heidegger posited in *Being and Time*, escapes all more or less hermeneutic "approaches." That "death" makes no sense, does not adhere to common sense, at least, opens the possibility for an other sense, but only *as* possibility, eventuality. And at bottom (but there is no bottom, no foundation here, nothing for us to take hold of and to stem from), possibility is greater than reality, even though possibility *possesses* nothing either by right or in reality. Possibility is richer than reality in that the less it is realized, the bigger it grows, bearing a child in a certain way, but without a womb. Such *is*, maybe (for we *may* no longer say anything but *maybe*), the extent [*portée*] that tends [*porte*] toward these parts of the near / distant, when wanting-to-say is suspended in order to *want* only that: "maybe" may be said, may be (said)—without Being (being said).

Farewell

> That which is the most difficult to find is, as the proper and the near, what we must look for the longest. And as long as it is being looked for, it is never lost. Any hasty and hurried search is not a search but a wild wandering about from one thing to another. The constant suspense of meditation belongs to the search. Meditation is like the withheld breath of modesty facing the awaited marvel. The search properly speaking is a constant hesitation, not the hesitation of someone who is simply perplexed and indecisive, but the hesitating of someone who dwells a long time, takes his time, looks in front of and behind himself, because he is seeking and dwelling in experience. The discovery and the appropriation of the proper are one with the dwelling of the step. Heidegger, *Hölderlins Hymne "Andenken"* 123–24

Heidegger brought back a testimony from his brief stay in Greece that has recently been published under the title *Aufenthalte*, "Sojourns."[1] It is an atypical text in which from the very first page descriptions that are reduced to the essential alternate with reflections guided by an idée fixe. Heidegger cites four lines from Hölderlin's elegy "Bread and Wine" and asks "why Hölderlin did not need such an experience," a "real" experience of the "world of the islands," that is, of Greece. Hölderlin, who began with *Hyperion* (subtitled *The Hermit of Greece*), nonetheless writes clearly in the foreword to the novel, "As for the theater of action, it is not new, and I admit to having once had the naïveté to think of displacing it" (*Sämtliche Werke* 3 5). If he did not do so, it is because he was persuaded that Greece was still the only *theater* "that was suitable for the elegiac character of Hyperion," in short, for "technical" reasons, literary conventions (*Sämtliche Werke* 3 5). The "law of genre" imposed the Greek "canon," which was certainly not new, but for this very reason was proven and appropriate.

This is as much as to say that for the poet Greece is a *fiction*. This fiction serves principally to make "reality"—*German* reality—seen in its true light, that is to say, "as" someone Greek landed in modern times might see it (somewhat as Hölderlin asked, "How can one *be* German?"). The result is catastrophic indeed: "[They have been] barbarians for a long time, rendered more barbarian by their zeal, their science, and even their religion, which is profoundly incapable of *feeling* the Divine, . . . empty and discordant like the debris of a discarded vase" (*Sämtliche Werke* 3 153). Hölderlin did not need to see Greece, though not at all for the reasons invoked by Heidegger: he had already "seen" Greece, recalled it through the coming of the "approaching god." No, what Hölderlin knew was that Greece—such as it *determines* our whole world in its advance—*does not* exist, has never been anything other than *our* invention. And he knew that it is from this fiction that *we* must be liberated in order to learn to make free use of the "proper," that is to say, of the *Greek in us.*

From the beginning, we are kindly reminded that "Heidegger was never a tourist." And yet it is indeed a *tour*—an organized cruise—of Greece that the thinker finds himself offered in the guise of a present by his faithful companion. It is a question of going "to see" and of going on a "tour" in Greece, that is to say, in advance, of a *return* [*retour*], a return to the sources of the "thought of being." Heidegger did not decide to go and see this without reticence. He was afraid of being disappointed. Not that he expected a revelation, an exotic, foreign, world. He did not go there to "disorient" himself. On the contrary, he went principally to verify his own experience, to encounter "ancient" Greece such as he imagined it but which he refused to believe was only pure invention, for then the "path of thinking" (*Denkweg*) would have been but a "path of mistakes" (*Irrweg*).[2]

We can be reassured that after a deceptive and even alarming beginning illumination will come. In Venice, the cultural and touristic place that remains "quite incapable of showing a path," "everything was aged but not ancient."[3] Everything was past, but there was no *Gewesenes*, nothing that remains for an expectation, a future. For if despite the fleeing of the gods and the devouring of its world Greece can still shine through its ruins with an incomparable brilliance, it is in accordance with that expectation, the glance thrown in front (*Vorblick*) that for Hölderlin metamorphosed what had been in a present, or, in his language as it is understood by Heidegger, in a tending-toward (*Gegen-wart*). Expectation thus reigns over this voyage from the beginning. But expectation has its own roads. Here, it is not directed toward a future but toward a past, which is in itself already strange enough. What is sought is not situated in front of us but behind us. A glance that directs itself backward (*Rückblick*) is thus necessary, even though it is nothing other than the anticipatory glance. How is that possible? It is only possible if what the glance is drawn toward and what is thus expected always already remains "in" view because it is at the very origin of the sight. Sight calls what is to be seen and makes it come, all the while giving it seat and foundation. The glance is drawn toward pre-sense, the already-seen [*déjà-vu*]: "We can, at any rate, only look for what we already know, be this in a veiled manner" (*Sojourns* 2). This experience is in no way an adventure: we have come here only to seek confirmation of what we already know. And as a result, knowledge (since the Greeks) has always expressed itself as a having-seen, in advance, a re-cognition. Sight constitutes much more than a simple medium. It is rather the horizon at the heart of which Greece will be able to appear as what it was, this having-been that addresses itself at once as origin (but veiled, deformed by what has come after: technology) and the recourse to a possible "turning," when the glance makes itself memory (*Andenken*) and not forgetting. In fact, what expectation is directed toward is not only already in view, but resides entirely *in* the view, or rather in what makes it possible, what bestows it. This is an essential nuance, for it makes the distinction between pure and simple description and experience, properly speaking. The whole question is thus *to see*—what seeing is.

Corfu, the first island "in sight," offers nothing worthy of being seen: the first glance (*Anblick*) did not "want to coincide with what the poet figured in book VI of *The Odyssey*": what had been felt and expected did not appear (*Sojourns* 5). The landscape seems more Italian than Greek. The same disappointment returns at

Ithaca: is *that* Ulysses' home? Once again, what shows itself does not stick to the "image" (*Bild*) that the reader of Homer had "before his eyes" (*vor dem Blick*) for a half century. But is it not therefore time to revise this image, to start seeing the thing itself directly, forgetting all presuppositions? Is that not the condition of all phenomenological experience? It is not a question of an "ideal landscape" or a "historical painting" (*Geschichtsbild*) that is just as ideal or bookish, but of a "world," of a specific *Dasein*. As the phenomenological "principle of principles" puts it, then, in order to grasp the phenomenon, we must not only suspend all presuppositions but put the observer between brackets, even if this is never totally possible. This is necessary, however, on the condition that we think in terms of observation. But that is what Heidegger refuses to do from the start. There is no question of being an observer, even a faithful, competent, and cultivated one; sometimes he refuses to get out in order to "go and see." In a certain way, he does not need to, since he has already seen or already has in view what he is going to see. But he does not need to, first of all, because we are not dealing with the same vision. To observe is in advance to take what is going to appear in the field of vision as object, placed there-before for the subject. Thus, the observer sees nothing of what is op-posed to him except what he has pro-posed to himself. He sees nothing of the thing itself, sees nothing but pre-formed views-of-the-world. There is but a step from the observer (even the scrupulous, "objective" viewer) to the tourist, who sees nothing other than what is placed at his disposition by the (technical) device of putting-in-place. Heidegger is not a tourist and does not want to be one. There is certainly a fair bit of pride in this will to be separate from the herd. But Heidegger does not remain blind to tourism, which appears to him not only a plague of the era of masses, but first of all a sign of the technical transformation of our world. Still, it is through such a world that he himself sized up that he intends to encounter the properly Greek world and *Dasein*. Far from putting himself at a distance from modern desolation, Heidegger consecrates long meditations to that desolation, meditations that appear displaced in such a framework, especially for an aesthete who would rather deal with nothing but the authentically Greek. From the point of view of a recollecting thought, of all its distance, which alone permits the proximity to what has departed but remains no less present in its own way, the aesthete and the tourist are but the two opposite and complementary faces of a single phenomenon, a bit like subject and object. Neither tourist nor aesthete, Heidegger intends to see Greece it*self,* such as it first was for itself and not for us, even though, by the same token, an "us" becomes accessible only through it. Ithaca still disappoints expectation, since instead of the Greek, "there we are in the presence of a piece of the Orient, of Byzantine" (*Sojourns* 7) in the figure of the priest. Will Olympia, that magic place of celebrations "gathering all of Greece together," be the site in which the encounter takes place? "But we have stumbled upon a completely ordinary village that new, half-finished buildings, American tourist hotels, disfigured still more" (*Sojourns* 8).[4] This is a regrettable entry into matter, all the more so since almost nothing remains of the site, only a few "powerful columns overturned by a superhuman force" (*Sojourns* 8). This is an occasion to send the archaeologists back to their excavations: they cannot reach what was built there because, for the Greek world, building in no way signified constructing, piling even gigantic stone blocks one upon the other, but first of all meant blessing, consecrating. But the Sacred is not a matter of archeology, or, at least, is a matter of another archeology, that of a *logos* attentive to the *arche*, the initial *Anfang*, the "great beginning."

A first flash of the awaited apparition shows itself not in the place itself but in the museum. But we know that the museum destroys presence through the (re)presentation that transforms it into a simple spectacle. Heidegger gives a precise example of this alienation: the pediments of temples were not meant to be seen face to face and at the height of humans but "from below and at a great height." Thus, they were not for men in the first place, but "their appearing in a flood of calm addressed itself as an offering to the glance of the invisible god" (*Sojourns* 10). Or is this glance of the invisible rather that of thought, a thought that chooses what it pleases to consider as properly Greek? It will disdain the Hermes of Praxitele, which is, however, of the highest quality, because it is no longer archaic but already close to the decline. Moreover, it is thought and thought alone that opens not only the glance but, first, the "horizon" (literally the circle-of-view, *Gesichtskreis*) within which the works and gestures of the Greek people must appear. Thus, even if he was not a sculptor, Parmenides makes the appearance of the temple possible. . . . Why? That will become clear soon. The glance is guided by thought, and thought is bestowed by the glance, but an other glance. Theater is one aspect of it, the theater of Epidaurus, which is nonetheless reduced to silence. Moving back in time, the voyage arrives at the island of Crete. But there again, it is not the Greek that appears, but the "Oriental-Egyptian way of being" (*Sojourns* 14). Ornamentation is associated with the enigma, so that Heidegger says, disconcerted, "perhaps there is a direct relationship between the labyrinth and luxury." He responds with one of his constant resources, the recourse to the origins of words. "As adjective *luxus* means that something is disturbed from its place, displaced and disconnected": dislocated [*luxé*], we say in French. This dis-placement also presides in the "maze" (in German, *Irrgarten*—literally, a garden of mistakes in which one becomes lost). Cretan luxury, which we could reproach for its baroque spirit, though in removing the tormented character from the Baroque, wants to shine for itself: it is a pure brightness that has nothing to disclose or conceal.

At Rhodes, Heidegger straight out refuses to disembark. He wants to meditate, above all, on the proximity of the "Asian" and what it brought to the Greek world—an "obscure fire" "of which the flame was placed in clarity and measure" by the couple *Dichten-Denken*. This fire, for Heraclitus, animates the *kosmos*, which Heidegger, conforming to the origin of the word, thinks first of all as "finery," "the brightness that leads something to appear" (*Sojourns* 17). This brightness is the gold of presence, of Being. But it itself, and with it what was waited for, the "great beginning," does not appear except at the moment in which the voyager disembarks on the island of Delos. Is it this island that instigates this "flash of (en)light(e)ning"? But Delos is desolated, nothing but ruins.[5] However, this abandonment is not a pure decline (*Verfall*). For a word, a demand (*Anspruch*), rises up, a statement that addresses—the awaited destiny. A promise. This statement is nothing other (we read with a certain astonishment) than the very name of the island that reveals itself as doubly proper, as the proper name of the Proper itself: "The island is named Delos (Δῆλος): the Manifest, the Appearing, that which gathers everything together in its Open, that by its appearing conceals everything again in one present (*Gegenwart*)" (*Sojourns* 19). It is not without use to recall the paragraph of *Being and Time* in which the pre-concept of phenomenology is determined: *legein ta phainomena*, "speak the phenomenon," is first of all, according to Aristotle, *deloun* (δηλοῦν), formed from the word *delos*, "manifest." To say is to manifest (ἀποφαίνεσθαι). And this is what the island of Delos, in that it "is" what it says (in its proper name), manifests to the highest degree, on the condition, obviously, that we accept the etymology of the island at face value. But an ill-humored spirit who would once again denounce the recourse to false etymologies (as with the name of truth, ἀλήθεια) in order to make a bid for philosophical power would only demonstrate his own blindness in view of the blinding evidence manifested by the proper name, in its accordance with thought's preliminary view. The awaited encounter took place because for once the name is *suitable*, is in accordance with what manifests "itself." Olympia was no longer in any way Olympian, all the less so since the name had been misused and obscured by the modern "Olympic Games" that for Heidegger no longer had anything to do with the pan-Hellenic celebrations gathering the people together around their gods and not simply their athletes. Crete remained pre-Hellenic. Rhodes was the "island of roses," but the roses are in no way specifically Greek or onto-logical. Ithaca was indeed the name of Ulysses' island, but that was only a bookish reference. In order to be a proper name, the name cannot simply designate in the manner of a signpost, remaining external to its signified; it must first of all *be* the designated phenomenon. And it is all the more convincing or manifest that the name Delos is given as the name of phenomenon itself (the name of the Manifest). That this be a sleight of hand, even that of a counterfeiter, is of little importance: does not the homonymy suffice to sanction the discovery? This is not, however, pure and simple nominalism. It is not because the noun means "manifest" that it manifests the "thing" as the manifest. There is neither cause nor effect here, but an encounter, an affinity that for a long time has been the very sign of truth. But is adequation (of the thing with the name or representation) not a concept derivative of truth and, as such, rejected as inessential in relation to the original truth, *aletheia*, which manifests precisely the onomo-logical manifestation of Delos? Or rather, have we forced the trait too much in accusing the name, and it alone, of being an opening-sign, of making a sign toward and thus disclosing the thing itself? Is it not Heidegger himself who writes that we are "barely" able to think "what conceals itself in the names of the island"? Is it not as sacred name that the island is the "sacred island," the "Milieu of Greece"? What withdraws itself is a duality, a duplicity that nonetheless comes to crown itself in a single Fold, that of disclosing and of concealing, in the image of the double birth of Apollo and Artemis: brother and sister, in the adverse unity of a single, divided origin. Both the clairvoyant god, who all at once sends off his luminous trait, and his sister, who on the contrary is at home, dwelling in obscure wildness, but no less lets her trait fly against whoever would attempt to see her naked, both have a unique way of being present: "powerful approach and sudden disappearance in the distance" (*Sojourns* 19). Their common *Heimat* (home) is that of the trait, of the arrow that signs and shows (*Zeigende*). Shows what? In order to say that, we would need a "glance thrown in front," beyond even what is given, present. This glance, which only poets and thinkers will have deployed, is accomplished as nomination: *Aletheia*. For it is first of all *Aletheia* that looks, addresses the glance and gives sight and thus the capability to name to all thought or poetry.

All poeticizing (*Dichten*) and thinking (*Denken*) is looked at (*angeblickt*) by it in advance. In this it is itself included in the looking ahead (*Vorblick*) of the mortal. *Aletheia* is glanced at (*erblickt*) but not properly thought in its Properness. Consequently, *Aletheia* remains unthought, unquestioned as to its provenance [*Sojourns* 20].

What were the Greeks lacking to think *Aletheia* in its properness? They indeed named it, and this name is itself the "authentic name" of Greek *Dasein*, the word properly speaking, since it is at the same time the word for saying, be it *mythos* (here translated by *Sage*), first, then *logos*, which is itself concealing, "keeping the fundamental trait of *aletheuein*" (*Sojourns* 20). But this trait is itself not truly thought; it remains out of the field . . . of sight, or of speech? After having identified *Aletheia* with the "hearth of the world," after having linked this hearth to the Heraclitean "fire" that shines as a *kosmos* (the brightness and order of appearing)—which comes down to concentrating everything, what will later be called "truth," beauty," and being, in the same horizon (that of the Same)—Heidegger, who has just found confirmation of his "long meditations" at Delos and thus can return satisfied, nonetheless feels the need to linger longer. His long preparation is finally going to open the glance and thus accord dwelling properly speaking: not in such or such a place (even though this is in its way a locality, a place-name: the very place of naming), but in the locality par excellence of all place, the "dwelling in *aletheia*." And this experience holds a big surprise in store for us.

> To make the experience of dwelling in *Aletheia* and of this latter as that which accords dwelling means the disclosing of the glance as the invisible in all things, which liberates every present in simply placing it in visibility and perceptibility and maintaining it there, in that invisibleness that, like un-concealing concealing, abstains from all sensible-materialization. [*Sojourns* 22]

The dwelling of dwelling, the place of place, *Aletheia* is also the sense of sense, and of that sense par excellence that is sight. As such, it is indeed the invisible in all beings, but also what makes all beings visible. But then, we do not see what the difference between it and the Platonic *idea*, it too invisible in that it is the source of all seeing, might be. In what would it differ from what modern philosophers call the *a priori*, and what I call pre-sense: what is in advance present in everything present, in that it gives sense and, here, visibility and perceptibility to everything? Does it not lead back to the metaphysical distinction par excellence of the sensible and the non-sensible (the "intelligible," which means perceptible only by the meta-phor of the eye of the *nous*, of thought)? In what way would even the translation of *idea* as "idea" be unfaithful if such perception "abstains from all sensible-materialization [*Versinnlichung*]"?

Do these questions concern the "secret" of *Aletheia* or do they only show why this secret must escape even the Greeks, that is, that people that nevertheless had openly made its dwelling in the Open? What remains unthought in the Open? Its "provenance," Heidegger says. But how can one ask "where" the "from where" of everything that comes (into presence) comes from? Can this retrocession toward the origin of the Origin only be envisaged, and from what point of *view*? In what seeing does the invisible show itself? We get a first response in the oracular speech that has already been cited many times, that of the god of Delphi through the "mouth" of Heraclitus (fragment 93). Heidegger translates it thus: "it neither reveals nor conceals but shows." "Showing," *Zeigen*, is the key to the enigma because it is a "making seen that, as such, veils and keeps what is veiled." The important thing is this "as such": to make seen is not to reveal the thing itself. It is to veil it in the given "view," but at the same time this is not hiding either, since what is given to be seen is indeed the thing itself and no-thing else. The thing hides itself and shows itself at the same time, just as it itself is, like its open view, manifest. To hide would be the "Egyptian" mode in which everything refers to something else and in which sense finally always remains withdrawn, incapable of being found, like the exit from the labyrinth (which precisely has no outside: everything is labyrinthine). On the contrary, for the Greek mode of existence everything is outside, exposed in an "open-view" (*Aussehen*), which at the same time permits the inside to be purely sheltered, invisible because *in* the visible, and nowhere else, the in-visible in everything (visible), and that is nothing other than the being-manifest of the manifest (the "as such"). But where the in-visible is most manifest (and thus most guarded) is in speech, precisely because it is in speech that exposed sense comes to *re-g(u)ard* itself without ever going elsewhere. Speech (re-)g(u)ards precisely in that it indicates in its very saying what has already come out, manifest. The place of manifestation, speech nevertheless manifests nothing, since everything is already manifest. But if everything is manifest, it is *as such* (as manifest) that it remains veiled. Speech, and more precisely nomination, carries out this veiling, preserving the secret of unveiling. A name does not reveal what it names, but does not dissimulate it either. Rather, it "shows." A name installs and *retains* what has come into Being in the light of the "as such" in which it can sojourn, stay, shine.

In Heidegger's "sojourns,"[6] this mysterious power of the name again finds a notable place, when upon leaving Athens the boat draws alongside the island of Egine. The name of the temple will be a guide:

> Already the name of the arche-ancient divinity *A-phaia*—the non-appearing, withdrawing herself from appearance, the Disappearing—names what *Aletheia* says. Thus the goddess *Aphaia* keeps / guards the enigma of *Aletheia* [*Sojourns* 29].

The name keeps the secret. Aphaia is probably a terrestrial divinity, and the earth itself is thought by Heidegger as what refuses to appear, the Concealed. In "The Origin of the Work of Art," the "truth" is said to be essentially terrestrial. A bit later, Heidegger cites a line from the poem "Greece," where Hölderlin evokes Delphi in the figure of the "navel of the earth." Nothing but ruins of Delphi, of its site, remain, Heidegger says: "The region itself discovered itself under the high heavens . . . as *the* temple of this place" (*Sojourns* 31). The region opens the space in which mortals can institute their works because it keeps the secret: it is that a-part that makes sharing possible (*chora*).

Heidegger does not content himself with calling Greece the "world of islands." Even though attached to the continent, Greece is entirely a single island. It is the magic moment of the departure that metamorphoses it thus: *Der Abschied von ihm wurde zu seinem Ankunft*, "the departure (the separation that takes leave of Greece) becomes its coming (its arrival)" (*Sojourns* 33). Greece comes to dwell, that is, to situate itself in a delimited figure. Greece is an island in that it is separated from the rest of the world not by mountains but by the *departure* or sending of a destiny, the first destiny "as such" and therefore the only "great beginning." This sharing has been assigned, that is to say, properly, marked by the Sign, the sign of the sign, marked "as such." And it dwells and remains a sign even though the gods have departed. Greece opens the secret of a dwelling beyond the realm of technical equipment because the secret is *dwelling* [*de-meure*], our future by the very fact that the glance remained [*demeuré*] suspended and thus kept there. *Aletheia* is suspended forgetting: stopped, held in a stance, a stature or a statue, an erection. If we compare *A-phaia* and *A-letheia*, it appears that appearance is at the same time a theft, a disappearance. The presence of the most present, the Greek gods, is that of the ephemeral Greek "miracle," of what is departed, of the deceased who precisely cannot come except in his departure, *Abschied*. Inversely, if *Aletheia* holds itself back from appearing, it is thus that it maintains itself: but for what destiny? That is nowhere said. And it must not be said, if saying signifies making-appear. Thus saying is a reserve in a double sense: a prohibition (to unveil the "secret" of disclosing) and at the same time the resource that keeps the same secret in its a-phasic purity, a secret for which there is no place to be said and whose saying will not take place. The secret must [*faut*] not be said because this saying fails [*faut*], if I may say so. But we will only be able to fail the word and thus betray the word's lack, like its already exposed secret, as the most manifest, manifestness itself, Being. *Being is the name of the secret, as the name is the Being of the secret.* And the secret is nothing other than the name of Being, a name all the more secret for saying nothing, nothing other than what must be (secret) and fails Being (the Secret).

Reference Matter

Notes

Foreword

1. [The reference is to the customary transcription, *c'est-à-dire*, which is translated as "that is to say" or simply "that is." In asking if the title can be understood as a question, the author refers to the habit of saying "*C'est-à-dire?*" (roughly, "What do you mean?") when the intent of a statement is unclear. As will become clear in the following sentences, leaving the expression without hyphens makes the verb a copula and creates the intimation that something is still or about to be said.—Trans.]
2. Marc Froment-Meurice, *La chose même* (Paris: Galilée, 1992).
3. Mallarmé, letter to Vielé-Griffin, August 8, 1891.
4. [The reference to Hermes' stone is elaborated in the opening pages of Chapter 1.—Trans.]
5. [The word for "toward," *vers*, is also the French word for "verse" or poetry, so that the movement "toward" is also the movement toward verse, or a certain poetics.—Trans.]
6. Heidegger, "Hölderlins Erde und Himmel" (GA4 165). This is an *open* secret—and even an open casket—since it is also spoken, written there, in black and white. The fact of an empty casket means that there will be nothing but such writing.
7. Let us consider the sentence from a course given in 1942, in the middle of the blind belief in nationality according to blood ties and being born in the country in question: "Das Sein aber ist kein Boden, sondern das Boden-lose" ("Being is not a ground but the ground-less")

(GA54 223). With this sentence, the whole thinking of Being is "founded" upon the absence of a foundation or of a ground. Only Being can be solid and take the place of a ground.

8. For Trakl, I will refer to my *Tombeau de Trakl* (Paris: Belin, 1992). As for Rilke, we must read the passage from the course on Parmenides (*Parm.* 151–61; GA54 225–40), where, with an unheard-of violence, Heidegger throws the poet of the "Open" into the hell of the jumble: the metaphysics of subjectivity, psychoanalysis, secularized Christianity, irrationalism, simple-minded Nietzscheism, etcetera. Why this obvious injustice? It is, Heidegger would say, because it was necessary to preserve the purity of the Open as the heart of *aletheia* from all contamination by the virus of "creatures." But in reserving the path of truth for *Dasein* alone and thus forbidding all access to Being to the living and to the world of life, does Heidegger not, despite everything, reintroduce the privileging of the human being at the heart of creation? Isn't he more "metaphysical" than Rilke?

9. See Rimbaud, "L'Eternité," in *Œuvres complètes*, 79:

> Elle est retrouvée
> Quoi? L'Eternité
> C'est la mer allée
> Avec le soleil.

10. [Each time the English translation uses the words *hearing* and *understanding* in this paragraph, the French repeats the word *entendre*, which can mean both.—Trans.]

11. [The word *passance* does not exist in French and will remain untranslated. The word plays upon the two words that it is apparently composed of, *pas* ("step" and "not") and *sens* ("sense," "meaning"). But it also alludes to a *passant(e)*, a passerby, as in Baudelaire's "A une passante." Perhaps most prevalent in the word, however, is *passer*, with all the implications of passing, passing by, passing over, passing from one place to another, and so forth. Though the word would have to be translated in a number of ways, according to the context, it most strongly refers to this sense of passing.—Trans.]

12. René Char, "A la santé du serpent" (To the serpent's health), in *Œuvres complètes*, 267.

13. [The word *é-venant* does not exist in French and here suggests that the eventing, or the event, is what escapes Being, what does not arrive at Being.—Trans.]

14. This is George Steiner's thesis in his *Martin Heidegger*, p. 16, a thesis that rests upon the unquestioned evidence of common sense, whose universal claim is maintained only by the fiction of a "natural language." From another point of view, this fiction also feeds Richard Rorty's considerations on the "final Heidegger" (Derrida), who is said to propose only fantasies for "private use."

15. The indifference as regards the distinction *general / particular* or *subject / object* (and even the deconstruction of that difference) is equally a "Chinese" characteristic in Heidegger. However, can we say that Lao-Tzu was "already" familiar with ontological difference, especially since ontological difference can only be said in the language of ontology?

Chapter 1

1. [There have been at least two such programs called *Hermes*. The first involved a satellite, used by Canada and the United States, that was put into service in 1976 and taken out of service in 1979. The more immediate reference, however, is to what in France was called Programme Hermès (1989), a network of transmissions sending strategic information from the Elysée (the seat of the president) to a number of air force sites. The author would also seem to be alluding, if only indirectly, to the work of Michel Serres on communications.—Trans.]

2. Cf. Heidegger, *Way* 29–30, 121–22, where he relates the "hermeneut" to the god Hermes but also recalls Plato's statement in the *Ion* (534) describing the poets as the "messengers (ἑρμηνής) of the gods."

3. GA54, 103; *Parm.* 69. French is the language in which *language* and *tongue* (as physical organ) are both designated without there being any distinguishing between them. Does that make the French "barbarians"? And what about the universality of the French language?

4. "Just as the Greek word *ousia* is used in everyday language and means there 'capital,' 'possessions,' 'goods and chattels,' 'estates' (*Anwesen*), and just as at the same time the everyday *ousia* is elevated to a word of thoughtful speech and then comes to mean the presence of everything present . . . " (*Parm.* 95; GA54 95). Heidegger is hardly talkative about the "everyday" meaning of "capital."

5. This would be the place to introduce the engagement with things (see Francis Ponge, *Le parti pris des choses*). But I intentionally prefer the singular, *the* thing. Elsewhere, I hope to be able to demonstrate that Hei-

degger ventured quite far in a thinking of the thing that was not limited to the "simple" thing (of the type of the jug) and that surpasses even the (to my mind very formal and still ontotheological) structure of the *Geviert*. The thing is a party to the fold, to difference, so that it is in no way simply a question of either Being or "more than Being."

6. *Translation* here signifies a transport or transfer: "The transfer [*translation*] of Napoleon's remains is an offense against his renown" (Chateaubriand). The translation of the word from one language to another (in English, *translation* cannot be translated as "translation") performatively illustrates the process of the generation of languages from one another. But the "original" word originally appeared in the twelfth century and signified "translation," so that here the foreign language (English) is more "proper."

7. See Antoine Berman, *L'épreuve de l'étranger*.

8. Pindaris's seventh *Olympic*, 1:45 λάθας ἀτέκμαρτα νέφος, which Heidegger translated as *der Verbergung zeichenlose Wolke*, "the signless cloud of concealment." (GA54 110). Pindar, Homer, and others indeed experienced forgetting as what conceals everything and forbids appearance, but they never related *aletheia* to this forgetting, not even as its "opposite." This is Heidegger's whole difficulty; in the beginning, he finds only pseudo-essences as counter-essences to *aletheia*.

9. He refers to the Indo-European root *ver-* that appears in numerous German words: to begin with, *wahr* (true), but also *wehren, die Wehr, das Wehr*, all of which indicate guarding, as in the French word *verrou* [bolt].

10. " . . . a total word, new, foreign to language," wrote Mallarmé. I have already described this attempt to absolutize; see "Solitude of the Word," in *Solitudes*.

11. [See Jacques Derrida, *Mal d'archive*.—Trans.]

12. The analogy between Benjamin and Heidegger stops there. For Heidegger, it would be impossible to postulate a unity of *all languages*, since Greek is immediately marked by an original difference in that it is not *one* language among others but is already the announcement of the language of Being. It would without doubt be appropriate to note the nuances of this privilege. When Heidegger proposes translating *Tao* as *Weg* ("path"), he thinks of climbing back to a source that is even more original than "meaning" or even "logos." "Perhaps the secret of secrets of thoughtful saying conceals itself in the word *Weg, Tao*, if only we will let

these names return to what they leave unspoken" (*Way* 92, 198). The arche-word does not truly become that unless it is silenced or, better, unless it is sent back to its silent source, the *non-word*.

Chapter 2

1. [The author is no doubt referring to battlefields and concentration camps.—Trans.]
2. [" . . . *l'une y est restée, honteuse*": The "part" referred to is the second part of *Being and Time*, as the following note by the author makes clear, but there is also an allusion to *parties honteuses* ("private parts," in colloquial English).—Trans.] In the preface to the seventh edition, we read: "While the previous editions have borne the designation 'First Half,' this has now been deleted. After a quarter of a century, the second half could no longer be added unless the first were to be presented anew. Yet the road it has taken remains even today a necessary one if our *Dasein* is to be moved by the question of Being." I annex this note: this final sentence finds itself nearly re-cited in the "letter to Richardson," although all mention of the "first half" has been abandoned, which explains the insistence upon completion: " . . . cannot be completed but by him alone who takes completion *into account*." I would like to know who is speaking here, the *first* or the *second* Heidegger? This distinction, we recall, is justified inasmuch as (1) we have access to H1 through H2 and (2) H1 is *possible* only if he was *already* contained (implicitly, like a preformed seed) in H2. For a "hermeneutic circle," we can do no better than this. I nonetheless deduce from this that if "even today" one must pass by way of H1 (that is, by way of *Being and Time*), it is because, as full of holes as the kettle "was," it communicated with a second one placed "under" (or "in") it. In short, there was a *double foundation*.

Let us return to "even today": this today is not dated. We can suppose that it is a matter of the moment when these lines were written; but, by contrast with the first edition, which was *dated* (the birthday of the assassinated Father, Husserl), there is no date for the preface. It is simply "after a quarter of a century"—in fact, 33 years later, if we trust the editor. But it is just as well *even today*, since from the moment a text is *written*, it enters into eternity. Let us suppose that we are given half an orange. Thirty years later, can we be given the "other" half? Let's be reasonable. Mourn this missing half. Say, finally, that you have eaten it *all*.

Forget, efface, all mention of the "first half." Don't even think about it [in English in the original]! But how are we to arrive at that point? And why would we renounce the "first half"? Because, if we were to "annex" it, we would have to begin over again. Worse, it is the idea of the whole that is broached. The second half cannot be added, like one piece of an orange to another piece. In effect, it is not made of the same "substance," is not an orange, but something else, irreducibly *heterogeneous*. What takes place between the two is—time: breaking the unity of the title, the closure of the book, the very meaning of Being, or the conjunction *and* that should play the role of a *that is to say*, of an "is." But what *would have been* the second half (in fact, the third section of the first part) will explain to us that time *is not*. This "not" *turns everything around* from *Being and Time* to *Time and Being*, a turning that is not a simple inversion, for one plus one never makes simply two, but an additional one, one too many—the one of the second half that is other than the two halves. *Being and time will never be one.* There is one word too many in the title, *and* this word is "and," which forbids having the final word, forbids the One (as the Other) from constituting itself as a whole. In the same way, "death" will never be the realized *totality* of *Dasein*; its account is left forever open and *overdrawn*. *Dasein* is not complete when it is "finished" (for then it quite simply is no longer); it is complete only when it *exists*, that is to say, is *to* its end, promised [*pro-mis*, put before] its end, in an alliance that is at once always already *entered into* and *consummated*: a pure hymen of "now or never"—now, *that is*, never . . .

I will not insist upon this. It is, however, impossible not to evoke here the sentence deleted in the note on the "privilege of the now" at the end of the second section of the "first volume," a sentence that called for a return to this thorny question in a future considered to be near: "We shall come back to this in the first and third divisions of Part Two" (cited in Derrida, "Ousia and Grammè," in *Margins of Philosophy*, 37). Of this deletion, Derrida says that it gives the note all the force of its meaning. In effect, it is not now that we are going to illuminate the privilege of the "now."

3. [See Plato's *Sophist*. Socrates indeed fishes for the fisherman in that he tries to give an accurate definition of the sophist and—to do so in a methodical way, moving from the general to the specific—demonstrates how one might arrive at or fish out a definition of the fisherman.—Trans.]

4. " . . . [*il a à l'être*": *Dasein* is not currently Being but *has yet* to be

it, in the future. This is why the future is the primary dimension of time in *Being and Time*, and this also begins to explain the importance of "being toward death."—Trans.]

5. I will not enter into the incredible history of *Being and Time*'s translation into French. Almost an entire book would be necessary to do so. Let us note only this: for a long time there circulated a book titled *L'être et le temps*, which presented only the first section (of the "first half") but *without saying so*. It is true that the author himself had begun by furnishing only this section for his tenure, and that it was returned by the ministry with the grade "Insufficient," as if it were the destiny of this book to arouse halves that pass themselves off as wholes, and wholes that double themselves. "In time," the French editor took it upon himself to make up for this incompletion. But, as the result of complicated quarrels over the inheritance (as in all self-respecting families), the appointed translator, invested with the legitimacy of the "universal" legatee (Jean Beaufret), was also somewhat late, so that he ended up being passed, trimmed at the chopping block, by another translator eager to deliver the thing in its *totality* and, if possible, in its integrity. The result of this difference, or deferral, is that today there are actually *two* "complete" translations of *Being and Time*, one by François Vezin (Gallimard, 1987), authorized and circulating on the market (even though it is difficult to read because of a desire *not* to translate), and the other by Emmanuel Marineau (Authentica, 1985), "under cover," almost pirated, and thus just as difficult to read, though in a different way.

6. ["*Mannigfaltigkeit von Tondaten*": I (re)translate the more "liberal" translation of the French, for it will resurface throughout the chapter.—Trans.]

7. The verb *causer*, preferable to "to hold a discourse" [*discourir*], defines the everyday use of speech very well. We find a good example of it in Raymond Queneau's novel *Zazie dans le métro*, in a speech from the mouth of the parrot Laverdure: "You chatter, you chatter, that's all you know how to do." To be sure, Heidegger would say that a parrot that chatters, even if this were only to say "you chatter" (etcetera), is not very "profound". . . . That remains *to be seen* ("must see a psittacoanalist," p. 147 of the folio text): is not *mimesis* the first step of articulate speech, a step that always manifests itself as a jump, a tearing of the "sonorous babbling" of the *infans* who does not yet have speech?

8. This gives the lie to the proverb "He who says nothing consents,"

at least if we understand the word *consent* literally.... What is more, for the word *mot* [word], the dictionary or "book of words" (*Wörterbuch*) gives an "obscure" origin: "to say *mu*." Is this an original mutism? The motif [*mot(if)*, motive word] of silence as the origin of the word is omnipresent in Heidegger. Take this passage from the *Beiträge zur Philosophie*, which I translate as best I can: "Language founds itself in silence. Silence is to take measure, to keep it in the most profound" (GA65 510). Silence, the seal of language, seals language in its most profound interior and in the extreme generosity of a "measure" that is nothing other than the *Ereignis*. On the "voice of the friend," I refer to what Derrida has to say in *Politiques de l'amitié*.

9. There are no "pure" sounds: "We hear the column on the march, the north wind, the woodpecker tapping, the fire crackling" (BT 207, 163). What, then, do we hear when we go to a concert? Distractions?

10. Charles Baudelaire, "Correspondances."

11. "Schopenhauer's 'world eye'—pure cognition" (EM 63, 48). The blinding of the Cyclops by Ulysses can be read as the triumph of sense over pure animality. It is Ulysses' ruse that allows him to leave the cave a few centuries before Plato, above all through the invention of the *ideal* proper name, "Nobody," the absolute pseudonym that Polyphemus, in his pre-phenomenological naïveté, takes absolutely literally. In contrast to the single eye of the Cyclops is Ulysses' duplicity, that is, the eye of the word, always more and less than it, its trans-parence as the difference of the letter from Being. Logically speaking, it is Ulysses, as the being who "speaks (of) himself in multiple ways," who should have called himself poly-phemus (even before being polymorphous). I dedicate this note to Christine Irizarry.

12. Cf. Jacques Derrida, *Writing and Difference*, where the same citation from *An Introduction to Metaphysics* is found, with the following commentary: "This does not contradict but confirms, paradoxically, the disdain of writing which ... saves metaphorical writing as the initial inscription of truth upon the soul" (184).

Chapter 3

1. *Der Zirke ist ein besonderer Fall des genannten Geflechtes* (The circle is a special case of our web of language) (*Way* 113, 243). In a note in the *Gesamtausgabe* (GA12 230), Heidegger indicates that the name *Geflecht* is "bad," while "circle" is good. Nonetheless, he continues as follows:

flechten: *plectere*, συμπλοκή, and we remember that *symploke* is the art of a royal weaving, or dialectics, for Plato. From that, we have *falten* ("to fold") and *das Gefalt*, a word "invented" to express the unity of the Fold [*Pli*] gathered upon itself, en-folded, made its own accomplice [*complice*].

2. It is on this point that Heideggerian thought stumbles. It does not seem to give sonority and the vocal their due and aggravates the semantic domination prevalent in the philosophical determination of language even further inasmuch as it accords presence to meaning. Heidegger attempts to correct this inflection by criticizing traditional ("phonetic, acoustic, and physiological") representations, but he cannot show how sonority can gain access to a place other than that of its subordinate role in its own "autological" conception. He would need, in fact, to postulate sonority or the phonetic as having a *showing* role that is at least as essential as meaning, which would drag him into a dangerous Cratylism.

3. "... we must recognize that from the beginning *aletheia* in the sense of the non-withdrawal of presence has been experienced exclusively as the exactitude of representations and the accuracy of statements. From that point on, even the thesis of a mutation of the essence of truth that would have led from the non-withdrawal at the heart of the Open to the accuracy of the enunciation cannot be maintained" (*Questions IV* 135 [retranslated from the French—Trans.]). In a few sentences, Heidegger destroys his own deconstruction of the history of metaphysics. At its origin, the origin already escaped itself—because it has *never appeared* and can never appear but *in this way*.

4. Heidegger later takes up the question of the fetish as the "primitive" sign in which the difference between the "signifier" and the "signified" is still entirely covered up.

5. Fédier 109. Luckily, he did not give the erection of the phallus as an example of the "direct" sign.

6. The word commonly designates a "cross-section"—of a building, for example. It is not a simple sketch, since it represents the *entire* building from its foundation to its top, but it gives a sense of volume in only two dimensions.

Chapter 4

1. Or when Heidegger attributes the shoes "by" van Gogh to "the peasant" ... (cf. Derrida, "Restitutions," *The Truth in Painting*, 259).

2. Heidegger to Kommerell, trans. M. Crépon, in *Philosophie* 16 (Autumn 1987). [Retranslated from the French.—Trans.]

3. "Where is the Lesser? We must look for it in the place from which Hölderlin calls, looking outside through the philosophical window" (GA4 171). This expression refers to a passage from the letter to Böhlendorff (cf. pp. 157–58). But there it is a question of "*all* the sacred places on earth" and not only of the Greek places. Or must we assume that, for Hölderlin, Greece was the only sacred place? But then how could one sing the "angels" of the native country, how could one "begin anew" in liberating oneself from the shadows of the past?

4. Karl Reinhardt, "Hölderlin et Sophocle," trans. P. David, *Poésie* 42 (1982): 22. [Retranslated from the French.—Trans.]

5. *Innigkeit* is not first of all an interiority, since it does not open itself up as the law of the *infinite* exhibition to the other. It is from the other and the other alone that the proper comes. And yet this other is precisely not exterior. It is *the same* turned differently. The mortal likewise becomes *im*-mortal in dying, that is to say, in its life *as* mortal.

6. At one point, Heidegger says that Hölderlin is not only "also" and occasionally a philosopher, whom we could place beside Hegel or Schelling in German Idealism, but that he is a more profound philosopher than all the other philosophers precisely because his thought is *purely* poetic. Therefore, he can be compared to no one, neither the philosophers who were nevertheless his friends, and with whom he shared the same world, nor to the other poets of his time, since he is the first poet, the founder of a poetry that is still to come. In fact, Hölderlin could be compared only to Heidegger, the *first* person to whom Hölderlin was "destined," and who is therefore himself incomparable.

7. I have already related *Gedicht* and *Gericht* in "Faut-il brûler Trakl?" [Must we burn Trakl?] (retitled "Au nom de l'Autre" [In the name of the Other]); see my *Tombeau de Trakl*. In this sense, the translation of *Gedict* as *Dict* is "founded."

8. von Arnim, *Die Günderode*, 246. Further references are to this edition and will be cited as "von Arnim."

9. It would be somewhat unjust to assert that Heidegger reduces the poem to a chain of names. For example, the *Aber* ["but"] of *Andenken* plays a rhythmic punctuating role not only for the poem but for its commentary. I only want to demonstrate a general tendency here, and in no way am I trying to discuss a possible "exactitude" in the commentary. The "contents" do not interest me—if there are any.

Notes to Pages 102–9   247

Chapter 5

1. "The term 'hermeneutics' was familiar to me from my theological studies" (*Way* 9, 96).

2. Elsewhere, Hölderlin writes that the "highest poetry is that in which the non-poetic element [. . .] also becomes poetic" ("Reflection," in *Sämtliche Werke* 4:1 234–35). Kommerell would see in that the "breath of Empedocles" capable of metamorphosing everything. But this is also the entire aesthetic of German Romanticism with its theory of generalized prose. Heidegger does not want to hear another word of such an aesthetic, because it would lead Hölderlin back into the genre and the age of literature.

3. "Andenken," in GA4 107. (The translation has been nuanced to bring out the secondary role attributed by Heidegger to women, who content themselves with softening and protecting the fire of the heavens by "domesticating" it.) We could of course allege that if History is not the fact of women, it is not that of men either, since only the gods can make History come. But only men have a primary relation to this History. We also do not know whether the name of *Dichter* admits of a feminine.

4. Letter from Suzette Gontard (1 or 8 May 1800) in Hölderlin, *Sämtliche Werke* 7:1 105. Heidegger did not cite any of Gontard's letters, much less mention her existence or her name, or that of Trakl's sister, the "*brown-haired* Greta." To have the right to the city (or to be cited), the right to speech, women must be goddesses like Parmenides' Aletheia, and yet here is a goddess with neither a face nor a body.

5. [See the author's (only) work of "fiction," *La Disparue* (Paris: Gallimard, 1987), where, as in Hölderlin's *Hyperion*, the woman is "put to death."—Trans.]

6. Letter to Suzette Gontard. Undated rough draft (end of October 1799) in *Sämtliche Werke* 6:1 370.

7. Cited by Bertaux, pp. 309–10. According to Bertaux, Sinclair's interest in his poet friend, his obsession with tearing him from the claws of an abusive mother (one of the protective "German women" . . .), had other than purely literary motives; to put it delicately, it bears witness to a very Greek friendship.

8. See the audacious reconstitution of this unfinished poem in the recently undertaken (and interrupted, unfortunately) edition by Sattler, and the translation by B. Badiou and J.-C. Rambach in *Cahier de l'Herne "Hölderlin"* (1986), 64–71. The mere sight of the manuscript makes one

even more dizzy than the knowing, mastered disorder of *Un Coup de Dés*. In the genealogy of the "voyagers," we find very few "poets" in the strict sense: Emperor Henry, Mohammed, the crusaders, the buccaneers, the Knights Templar, and . . . Bougainville. The beauty of the poem, however, is no less stunning: "it is entirely you in your apocalyptic beauty." All languages (French included), all places, all times. . . . All that is lacking is a few Chinese ideograms to prefigure Pound's *Cantos*. There is something diabolical here, as Joyce would say, if it is true that the devil is first of all distance, a throwing into the distance (*diabole*).

9. Quoted in Heidegger, GA52 189. Heidegger notes that these lines are taken from an outline of the elegy, that they were missed by Hellingrath in his edition of Hölderlin's poems, and makes reference to Beissner, p. 147.

10. Cf. Heidegger, GA52 114, note 1: "The extent to which what these lines, which put the law of historicity into this language, are saying poetically can be derived from the principle of the unconditional subjectivity of absolute metaphysics proper to German thought, such as we see it in Schelling and Hegel, according to whom the Being-in-itself of spirit first demands the return to the self, which in turn cannot take place except through Being outside-the-self: the question, then, that we will content ourselves with considering will be the extent to which such a reference to metaphysics, even if it makes 'historically exact' relations appear, obscures the poetic law more than it enlightens it." The predicament, translated by an unusually long and complicated sentence, still does not mask the de-cision performed by the reading except by putting it under cover of a false question that is left open. Heidegger has already decided: we cannot and must not derive poetic historicity from the metaphysics of German Idealism. He is probably right, even though Hölderlin himself, along with his "friends" Hegel and Schelling, was at the source of this Idealism. In another way, however, we must ask whether Heidegger is not once again taking the route of Spirit. We change sites, leaving that of the absolute Subject, but the law (of historicity) is the same: the return to Self becomes the return of the proper, *Ereignis*.

11. de Man, 246–47, 266. Heidegger usually cites the "historical" edition, that by Norbert von Hellingrath, which de Man finds "outdated" and questionable as regards the big Stuttgart edition by Friedrich Beissner, "one of the great achievements of modern philology" (248). But now this edition, which de Man judged irreproachable, has been out-

dated again by that of D. E. Sattler, who presents the different versions, variants, erasures, etcetera, on the same page *without choosing* among them. Between Heidegger's subjective method, which decides upon a text according to the logic of his own commentary, and Beissner's "objective" method there is a fundamental filiation: both believe in the existence of a text, and even a definitive text. With the most recent edition, we are confronted by a dissemination with neither return nor deposit.

12. Cf. *supra*. Heidegger realizes that Hölderlin "was not familiar with the significance of the primary word, *physis*, whose force, today, we can barely measure." But at the same time, he asserts that "in the word *Nature*, Hölderlin poeticizes [*dichtet*] something else that indeed finds itself in a secret relation with what was once named *physis*" (GA4 57). This relation is so secret that Heidegger doesn't say a word about it.

13. [The sentence plays on the difference between the being of love [*l'être d'amour*] and the letter, the writing, of love [*lettre d'amour*]. This difference cannot be heard in French, which is precisely why it is a question of letters and of the disappearance in and of difference here.—Trans.]

Chapter 6

1. The title of Schürmann's book plays on this level. Nothing is less anarchical, even *literally*, than the thought of Being. That it thinks Being as "without foundation" or as an "abyss" (*Abgrund*) does not in any way mean that it purely and simply abandons the demand for a foundation or a *commanding beginning* (it is thus that one could translate *arche*). The thinking of Being climbs back above Being to what sends it, destines it, and what is in no way whatsoever an-archical, but would rather be autarc(h)ic, as I have hazarded to put it in relation to language. The Same (the *Es* of the *Es gibt*: *das Ereignis*) commands, even if the Same is an Other (from what followed—philosophical thought decreeing its "principles"). The political translation of this thought always threatens being a fundamentalism, an arche-fascism, to the extent that heterogeneity is, if not reduced, then at least led back to a single and *same* Origin. But must we and can we translate this thought politically? That Heidegger took such a risk at least shows the path not to be taken.

2. Can we ignore just as royally Hölderlin's sympathies for the French Revolution (itself thoroughly marked by Greek models since Rousseau), then his implicit reference to (or reverence for) Bonaparte (in *Friedens-*

feier, as Jean-Pierre Lefebvre has shown)? We cannot decide upon this question immediately, all the less so since it would be necessary to investigate the source of the very concept of revolution.

3. [*Retrait* would need to be translated as both "retreat" and "withdrawal." I have in general left the word untranslated here in order to evoke both of these meanings, but also to mark the repetition of the "trait" or characteristic, the *re*-trait, that is also signified in the word.—Trans.]

4. Karl Reinhardt, *Sophocles*, 64. [Translations are often modified.—Trans.]

Chapter 7

1. [The translation has been radically reworked in reference to the French translation cited by the author (*Chemins qui mènent nulle part*, trans. W. Brokmeier [Paris: Gallimard, 1962], 98), which comes very close to saying the opposite of the standard English translation. Throughout this chapter, translations from Heidegger will be similarly revised to correspond more closely to the text cited by the author.—Trans.]

2. Faced with the ruins of the temple of Olympia, Heidegger will write, "All that had absolutely nothing to do with a simple pile of blocks of an enormous size" (*Sojourns* 8).

3. ["*parce que c'est là son destin*": the possessive pronoun *son* can be read here as identifying either Oedipus' destiny or that of tragic being.—Trans.]

4. ["Departure," "bias," and "taking . . . side" translate *départ*, *parti pris*, and *prendre parti*. This group of words, all echoing the *part*, therefore suggests that departure is always already a certain bias or taking of sides.—Trans.]

5. [The author is citing an early version of the essay, translated into French by E. Martineau (Paris: Authentica, 1987), 49, 51, 53.—Trans.]

6. See "L'art moderne et la technique," in *Cahier de l'Herne "Heidegger"* (Paris: L'Herne, 1983).

7. Does this having-been simply designate another present, a present "gathered back" upon its essence in the Hegelian manner? This would be to remain enclosed in the meaningful circle of mourning. If it were possible to think this having-been in the manner of Trakl, as in-born, what never achieves presence, the gap that splits the Origin would then be more original than the Origin itself, but at the same time would be unas-

signable as such, as a point of origin. Does the duplicity of the Origin in Heidegger remain ruled by the logic of reappropriation?

8. [The author is playing on the *pli*, or fold, in both sim*pli*city and du*pli*city.—Trans.]

Chapter 8

1. [The word *pas* in French is at once a noun (signifying "step") and the negative particle "not." Thus the word invokes at once a movement and its stopping. The word reverberates throughout the chapter in such words as "pass," "passage," and *passance*.—Trans.]
2. [In English in the original.—Trans.]
3. [In English, the noun "technique" is immediately related to the arts, whereas in French and German (see Heidegger, *Die Frage nach der Technik*) it refers to technology.—Trans.]
4. Paul Valéry, "Louange de l'eau," quoted by Derrida, *Margins of Philosophy*, 277. [Translation modified—Trans.]
5. [In the French system, passing grades are designated "adequate" (*passable*), "fair," "good," and "excellent."—Trans.]
6. [For example, in French "*propreté*" cannot be "properly" translated as "property"; if a good translation were directed only toward meaning, "cleanliness" would be the right word.—Trans.]
7. Here again, I will refer to the problematic developed by Thierry de Duve in *Au nom de l'art*. His approach (to art, but also to the "proper" name) differs essentially from mine if only because he takes as his point of departure modernity as the reign of subjectivity. Since Kant, aesthetics has been a matter of "judgment" and triumphs in the judgment of Duchamp: "It is he who looks who makes the painting." Thus art becomes spectral, opposed to the thingness of the work of art's remaining in itself in Heidegger.
8. [In English in the original.—Trans.]
9. [The word *apparêtre* combines the verb "to appear" (*apparaître*) with "Being" (*l'être*) or the verb "to be" (*être*).—Trans.]

Chapter 9

1. Pontalis, p. 25.
2. ZSD 63. Even if Heidegger relies upon "our" language (German)

here, this linguistic "particularity" repeats a scheme from Greek philosophy (that of the *logos*)—the definition of place as *limit*.

3. These two versions are taken from Hamacher.

4. ["Supplementary turn" here translates *le trop(e) de l'origine*, which is at once a supplement (the origin is constructed after the fact to fill up a gap *it* has caused) and a turn in the sense of a trope, a rhetorical figure. The origin is the product of this re-turn.—Trans.]

5. [*La vérité due ne se rend pas toujours au rendez-vous ou, si elle s'y rend* . . . : the author is playing on the words *rendre, s'y rendre*, and *rendez-vous*, which evoke showing up (as for a meeting or appointment—a *rendez-vous*) but also giving up, turning oneself in (as to the police).—Trans.]

6. *Deception*, in English, is a *false friend*, a traitor that passes for something it is not. This, it seems, is what is proper to translation. In fact, *déception* here signifies "deceit" [*tromperie*] and not "disappointment" [*désappointment*]—but what are we to make of the *appointment* in this word?). To what language should we turn? Is there *one* language that would not be disappointing (as Heidegger thought of the "original" Greek), or isn't language, as languaging, engaging or promising?

7. [See Marc Froment-Meurice, *Solitudes*. It should be noted that *solitude* is how the author translates Heidegger's *Boden-lose* (the groundless, *sol-itude*), *sol* being the French word for "ground."—Trans.]

8. "Being (not beings) is something which 'there is' only in so far as truth is. And truth *is* only in so far as and as long as *Dasein* is" (BT 272, 230). The "there is" of truth has the mode and the meaning of the being of *Dasein* itself: "We must 'make' the presupposition of truth because it *is* one that has been 'made' already with the Being of the 'we'" (BT 271, 228).

9. ZSD 23. The last sentence speaks in quasi-legal language: *Ereignis* does not renounce what is proper to it in the *Enteignis*; on the contrary, this is the only way for it to keep what is proper to it, in withdrawing what is "most proper" to it (*sein Eigenstes*) from the unlimited non-withdrawal. But what is kept is never hidden, is not a secret that could be exposed. It marks the limits, the finitude, of *aletheia*.

10. The only difference between *Unterschied* and *Differenz* is that *Unterschied* is more oriented toward sexual difference.

11. "To depose" could be used to translate *aufheben* to the extent that it unites a double sense that is both positive and negative. First, in the

negative sense, to depose is to relieve someone (a king, a prince, or a principal) of his duties. And it has a positive meaning, since to depose under oath is swearing to say "the truth, the whole truth, and nothing but the truth"; it is to testify. It is just that the deposition is neither a positive nor a negative procedure because it does not aim to occupy or *take* another position. To take position is to take *a* position, to take it from the other, as in a war of "positions" or principles. But what does not change in this "taking" position is the position itself. The same thing takes place as in Nietzschean anti-metaphysics, when we (and we could include Heidegger in this "we") summarily represent it as a "reverse Platonism." The reverse is simply an other place, an other who *pretends* more than the other that he wants to move out of his position to retain the right [*droit*] to be there as head or leader.

Farewell

1. [Heidegger, *Aufenthalte / Séjours*. Page references are to the German text, and citations have been retranslated from the German with reference to the French translations used by the author—Trans.] I could not recommend too highly reading the translator's afterword. It begins as follows: "By its intimate, 'familiar' character . . . , *Sojourns* is a text that surpasses commentary" (89). That is why we have the right to thirty pages of "notes." True enough, the translator himself is "intimate" with the author, is almost part of the "family" . . .

2. "Pure invention" translates *ein bloss Erdachtes* (*Sojourns* 12). *Erdenken* has approximately the same meaning as *erdichten*, "to imagine." Why would "imagination," fiction, or invention belong to thought or poetry *less* than "pure" *Denken* or *Dichten*? And can we conceive of a thought *pure* of all "invention"?

3. Venice becomes "tantalizing imagery for writers short on subjects" (*Sojourns* 3)—more precisely, for disabled (*ratloser*) writers. This characterization is aimed at the author of *Death in Venice*, a certain Thomas Mann, held in contempt for having preferred the United States to the rigor of the *Heimat*.

4. At Ithaca, on the contrary, it is not tourists who are welcomed by the natives but rather "the German guests"—not with open arms, to be sure, but with "a reserved smile." Is it in remembering his stay in Germany, "in bygone days," that the mayor shows himself so benevolent? In

bygone days—should we say in better times, times when "guests" were at home *everywhere*, when Greece was "German"? Then the threat came from "tourists," those Americans Heidegger described in 1942 as being like nihilists ready to destroy the *Heimat*. But where does he come from, this most "disquieting of all guests" (*dieser unheimlichste aller Gäste*), whom Nietzsche described as being already at our door, deceitfully, perhaps having already *entered* into the most holy of holy places—our *home* or *Heim*?

5. Another voyage, toward another Greek island, could leave us hanging: Baudelaire's "Voyage to Cythera": "What is this sad, black island?—It is Cythera, . . . Look, after all it is a poor earth." It is true that Heidegger did not see his image *hanged* upon a "symbolic gallows," and that he could not have seen (not even in a painting or poem) that "ridiculous hanged man" whose "eyes were two holes," not to mention his "collapsed chest" or guts "absolutely mutilated by a bird's pecking."

6. *Aufenthalte* could have been translated as "Stays" or "Stops" (*Halt*!). We find *Aufenthaltsnahme* in Courtine, who translates the word successively as "situation" [*situation*], "stop" [*arrêt*], and "suspension" [*suspension*].

Works Cited

Allemann, Beda. *Heidegger und Hölderlin*. Zurich: Atlantis, 1954.
Beissner, Friedrich. *Hölderlins Übersetzungen aus dem Griechischen*. 2d ed. Stuttgart: J. B. Metzler, 1961.
Berman, Antoine. *L'épreuve de l'étranger*. Paris: Gallimard, 1984.
Bertaux, Pierre. *Hölderlin ou le temps d'un poète*. Paris: Gallimard, 1983.
Char, René. *Œuvres complètes*. Paris: Gallimard / Pléïade, 1983.
Courtine, Jean-François. *Interprétations phénoménologiques d'Aristote*. Paris: TER, 1992.
de Duve, Thierry. *Au nom de l'art*. Paris: Minuit, 1989.
de Man, Paul. *Blindness and Insight: Essays in the Rhetoric of Contemporary Criticism*. 2nd ed. Minneapolis: University of Minnesota Press, 1983.
Derrida, Jacques. "Des tours de Babel." *Difference in Translation*. Ed. and trans. Joseph F. Graham. Ithaca, N.Y.: Cornell University Press, 1985.
———. *Glas*. Trans. John P. Leavey, Jr., and Richard Rand. Lincoln: University of Nebraska Press, 1986.
———. *Mal d'archive*. Paris: Galilée, 1995.
———. *Margins of Philosophy*. Trans. Alan Bass. Chicago: University of Chicago Press, 1982.
———. *Of Grammatology*. Trans. Gayatri Chakravorty Spivak. Baltimore: Johns Hopkins University Press, 1976.
———. *Points . . . : Interviews, 1974–1994*. Ed. Elisabeth Weber. Trans. Peggy Kamuf et al. Stanford, Calif.: Stanford University Press, 1995.
———. *Politiques de l'amitié*. Paris: Galilée, 1994.

———. *Positions*. Trans. Alan Bass. Chicago: University of Chicago Press, 1981.
———. *The Truth in Painting*. Trans. Geoff Bennington and Ian McLeod. Chicago: University of Chicago Press, 1987.
———. *Writing and Difference*. Trans. Alan Bass. Chicago: University of Chicago Press, 1978.
Fédier, François. *Interprétations*. Paris: Presses Universitaires de France, 1985.
Froment-Meurice, Marc. *La chose même*. Paris: Galilée, 1992.
———. *La Disparue*. Paris: Gallimard, 1987.
———. *Solitudes: From Rimbaud to Heidegger*. Trans. Peter Walsh. Albany: State University of New York Press, 1995.
———. *Tombeau de Trakl*. Paris: Belin, 1992.
Fynsk, Christopher. *Heidegger, Thought, and Historicity*. Ithaca: Cornell University Press, 1986.
Gasché, Rodolphe. *Inventions of Difference: On Jacques Derrida*. Cambridge, Mass.: Harvard University Press, 1994.
Hamacher, Werner. *pleroma—Reading in Hegel*. Trans. Nicholas Walker and Simon Jarvis. Stanford, Calif.: Stanford University Press, 1998.
Hegel, G.W.F. *Hegel's Phenomenology of Spirit*. Trans. A. V. Miller. Oxford, Eng.: Oxford University Press, 1977.
Hölderlin, Friedrich. *Sämtliche Werke*. Ed. Friedrich Beissner. Stuttgart, Germany: Kohlhammer, 1941– .
Kommerell, Max. *Le chemin poétique de Hölderlin*. Trans. D. Le Buhun and E. de Rubercy. Paris: Aubier, 1989.
Lacoue-Labarthe, Philippe. *La poésie comme expérience*. Paris: Christian Bourgois, 1986.
Mallarmé, Stéphane. *Œuvres complètes*. Ed. H. Mondor. Paris: Gallimard / Pléiade, 1945.
Merleau-Ponty, Maurice. *L'Œil et l'Esprit*. Paris: Gallimard, 1964.
Meschonnic, Henri. *Le Langage Heidegger*. Paris: Gallimard, 1990.
Nancy, Jean-Luc. *Le Partage des voix*. Paris: Galilée, 1990.
———. *Les Muses*. Paris: Galilée, 1994.
Otto, Walter. *Les Dieux de la Grèce*. Trans. C. N. Grimbett and A. Morgant. Paris: Payot, 1981.
Ponge, Francis. *Le Parti pri des choses*. Paris: Gallimard, 1972.
———. *Méthodes*. Paris: Gallimard, 1961.
Pontalis, J.-B. "Le Souffle de la vie." *Nouvelle Revue de Psychanalyse* 50 (Autumn 1994): 25.

Reinhardt, Karl. "Hölderlin et Sophocle." Trans. P. David. *Poësie* 42 (1982): 22.

———. *Sophocles*. Trans. Hazel Harvey. Oxford, Eng.: Oxford University Press, 1979.

Rimbaud, Arthur. *Œuvres complètes*. Paris: Gallimard / Pléïade, 1974.

Schürmann, Reiner. *Heidegger on Acting and Being: From Principles to Anarchy*. Bloomington: Indiana University Press, 1987.

Steiner, George. *Martin Heidegger*. Sussex, Eng.: Harvester, 1978.

von Arnim, Bettina. *Die Günderode*. Leipzig: Insel, 1925.

Zarader, Marlène. *La Dette impensée. Heidegger et l'héritage hébraique*. Paris: Seuil, 1990.

MERIDIAN

Crossing Aesthetics

Deborah Esch, *In the Event: Reading Journalism, Reading Theory*
Winfried Menninghaus, *In Praise of Nonsense: Kant and Bluebeard*
Giorgio Agamben, *The Man Without Content*
Giorgio Agamben, *The End of the Poem: Essays in Poetics*
Theodor W. Adorno, *Sound Figures*
Louis Marin, *Sublime Poussin*
Philippe Lacoue-Labarthe, *Poetry as Experience*
Jacques Derrida, *Resistances of Psychoanalysis*
Marc Froment-Meurice, *That Is to Say: Heidegger's Poetics*
Francis Ponge, *Soap*
Philippe Lacoue-Labarthe, *Typography: Mimesis, Philosophy, Politics*
Giorgio Agamben, *Homo Sacer: Sovereign Power and Bare Life*
Emmanuel Levinas, *Of God Who Comes to Mind*
Bernard Stiegler, *Technics and Time, 1: The Fault of Epimetheus*
Werner Hamacher, *pleroma—Reading in Hegel*
Serge Leclaire, *Psychoanalyzing: On the Order of the Unconscious and the Practice of the Letter*

Serge Leclaire, *A Child Is Being Killed: On Primary Narcissism and the Death Drive*

Sigmund Freud, *Writings on Art and Literature*

Cornelius Castoriadis, *World in Fragments: Writings on Politics, Society, Psychoanalysis, and the Imagination*

Thomas Keenan, *Fables of Responsibility: Aberrations and Predicaments in Ethics and Politics*

Emmanuel Levinas, *Proper Names*

Alexander García Düttmann, *At Odds with AIDS: Thinking and Talking About a Virus*

Maurice Blanchot, *Friendship*

Jean-Luc Nancy, *The Muses*

Massimo Cacciari, *Posthumous People: Vienna at the Turning Point*

David E. Wellbery, *The Specular Moment: Goethe's Early Lyric and the Beginnings of Romanticism*

Edmond Jabès, *The Little Book of Unsuspected Subversion*

Hans-Jost Frey, *Studies in Poetic Discourse: Mallarmé, Baudelaire, Rimbaud, Hölderlin*

Pierre Bourdieu, *The Rules of Art: Genesis and Structure of the Literary Field*

Nicolas Abraham, *Rhythms: On the Work, Translation, and Psychoanalysis*

Jacques Derrida, *On the Name*

David Wills, *Prosthesis*

Maurice Blanchot, *The Work of Fire*

Jacques Derrida, *Points . . . : Interviews, 1974–1994*

J. Hillis Miller, *Topographies*

Philippe Lacoue-Labarthe, *Musica Ficta (Figures of Wagner)*

Jacques Derrida, *Aporias*

Emmanuel Levinas, *Outside the Subject*

Jean-François Lyotard, *Lessons on the Analytic of the Sublime*

Peter Fenves, *"Chatter": Language and History in Kierkegaard*

Jean-Luc Nancy, *The Experience of Freedom*

Jean-Joseph Goux, *Oedipus, Philosopher*

Haun Saussy, *The Problem of a Chinese Aesthetic*

Jean-Luc Nancy, *The Birth to Presence*

Library of Congress Cataloging-in-Publication Data

Froment-Meurice, Marc.
[C'est à dire. English]
That is to say : Heidegger's poetics / Marc Froment-Meurice ;
translated by Jan Plug.
     p. cm. — (Meridian, crossing aesthetics)
Includes bibliographical references.
ISBN (invalid) 033740 (cloth : alk. paper).
ISBN (invalid) 033759 (pbk. : alk. paper)
1. Heidegger, Martin, 1889–1976. 2. Poetics—History—20th century.
I. Title. II. Series: Meridian (Stanford, Calif.)
B3279.H49F7613   1998
111'85'092—dc21   98-16569
                                                                  CIP

⊗ This book is printed on acid-free, recycled paper.

Original printing 1998
Last figure below indicates year of this printing:
07 06 05 04 03 02 01 00 99 98